Praise for Nina Simons and Nature, Culture and the Sacred

The world seems to be divided into two kinds of people — those who divide everything into two, and those who don't. Reading *Nature, Culture and the Sacred* is a step toward melting this false division into "feminine" and "masculine," allowing each of us to become fully human again and at last.

— **Gloria Steinem**, co-founder of *Ms. Magazine*

Nature, Culture & the Sacred: A Woman Listens for Leadership is the perfect book for this historical moment. Nina Simons not only knows the rare gifts of leadership women can offer, she also reveals how challenge and adversity bring these gifts forth more brilliantly and powerfully.

— **Joanna Macy**, author of *World As Lover, World As Self*

In Nature, Culture and the Sacred, Nina Simons has woven a compelling and honest tapestry of hard-earned personal and collective wisdom, honoring the earth and igniting the revolutionary ways of women. It's a book as much about the inside as it is about the outside, exploring where and how they can meet for a sustainable future.

— **V, formerly Eve Ensler**, founder of V-Day
and author of *The Vagina Monologues*

This is the time when the power of women returns to us, as we reaffirm our relationships to each other and to our Mother Earth. Together we will doula the next economy into being, re-birthing ourselves and this world. Nina's writing explores the path forward on this journey that we will make together.

— **Winona LaDuke**, author and Executive Director,
Honor the Earth

Nature, Culture & the Sacred demonstrates what leadership, women's leadership, is and can be. It is a personal story and a mindful inquiry into the nature of leadership... Simons informs and guides, assures and encourages, leading the reader into the vital relationships necessary for all of us to engage the ways of healing ourselves, and these times, together.

— **Deena Metzger**, author of *La Negra y Blanca* (Oakland PEN Award for Literature) and *La Vieja: A Journal of Fire*

With characteristic grace and great insight, Nina Simons shows us another path for leadership, one that grows from intuition, emotional intelligence and above all, connection in every form, including human relationship. This book is a treasure chest of both knowledge and know-how, giving us what we all need, women and men alike: a larger vision with which together we can save the Earth and ourselves. This book is the real thing.

— **Susan Griffin**, author of *Woman and Nature: The Roaring Inside Her*

We live in a time of regeneration and recreation as the structures of the patriarchy are failing the people and the planet. In Nature, Culture & the Sacred Nina Simons paves the way with the deep wisdom of lessons experienced and shared, and the openhearted listening we all need as we cultivate a future of care and connection. She has laid the bread crumbs we can follow for a robust and resilient future.

— **Jodie Evans**, co-founder CODEPINK: Women for Peace

At this critical moment of interlocking crises for humanity, we have been given a brilliant, wayfinding gift by Nina Simons in *Nature, Culture & the Sacred*. She eloquently and skillfully creates an expansive field guide toward the kind of balanced leadership sorely needed for healing our Earth and ourselves, guiding us with love from peril to promise.

— **Osprey Orielle Lake**, Founder and Executive Director, Women's Earth and Climate Action Network (WECAN)

This book will expand your understanding of who you are and why you are here in profound and soulful ways.

— **Amisha Ghadiali**, author of Intuition, and founder/host of the podcast *All That We Are* (formerly *The Future is Beautiful*)

Nature, Culture & the Sacred shares a wealth of insights to assist us in replacing the old worn-out patriarchal, hierarchical paradigm. Simons brilliantly discusses the issues involved, shares moving stories of women around the world joining together to create change, while weaving in teachings from indigenous cultures of how to reconnect people, nature, and the land. An amazing book that will inspire our current population of women and generations to come.

> — **Sandra Ingerman**, author of *Soul Retrieval* and *Walking in Light: The Everyday Empowerment of Shamanic Life*

Nature, Culture & the Sacred underscores the urgent necessity of shifting our awareness away from the stories that have kept us separate, alienated and divided throughout the centuries of modernity. I especially appreciate the foregrounding of Indigenous wisdom, elders and teachers. I can't wait to recommend this book for Leadership courses at the university and to everyone in my circles! The poetic riffs induce a kind of reverie that kindles the fire in my heart and suffuses me with longing for a future worth waiting for. May it be. *Bathala Nawa.*

> — **Leny Mendoza Strobel**, author and associate professor of American Multicultural Studies, Sonoma State University

Nature, Culture & the Sacred invites all of us into a new way of living, loving and leading in the world; one that embraces the quest towards wholeness, honors the commitment to full integrity and celebrates the courage of true alignment.

> — **Rha Goddess**, Founder of Move The Crowd and author of *The Calling*

This is a foundational guidebook for women, yes, but also a blueprint for humanity on how we can navigate and create; how we can embody and inspire inclusive, regenerative and intrinsically healing leadership that nourishes thriving communities and ecosystems. Read the book. Listen to the audiobook. Use this powerful offering as a teaching text and cultural, soul catalyst within your circles and communities.

— **Sarah Drew**, author of *Gaia Codex*

With honor and respect to the generations of women who have walked before us, Nina Simons writes with clarity and power to awaken a memory of leadership that integrates masculine and feminine, recognizing that their encounter is the source of all life. Nature, Culture & the Sacred is a tool for educators, and all those who wish to cultivate authentic expression and inspire young people to listen to their wisdom and birth a new remembering of the ancient understanding of balanced leadership which we all carry.

— **Naomi Katz**, educator and author of *Beautiful, Being an Empowered Young Woman*

This book is generous, loving, inclusive, careful and kind. It knits wisdom together in a way that wraps intelligently around your heart and opens your mind in the ways we need to be open. For those reaching for more of themselves, this book can both hold your hand and provide profound signposts along the way.

— **Clare DuBois**, founder, TreeSisters

Nature, Culture and the Sacred

A WOMAN LISTENS
FOR LEADERSHIP

PO Box 377 Housatonic MA 01236
www.greenfirepress.com
info@greenfirepress.org

Cover art: *Samantabhadra on Bike* by Mayumi Oda

Interior and cover art by CBB Designs

Page design by CBB Designs and Anna Myers Sabatini

Publisher's Cataloging-in-Publication data

Names: Simons, Nina, author. | Campbell, Anneke, editor.
Title: Culture and the sacred : a woman listens for leadership / Nina Simons;
edited by Anneke Campbell.
Description: Includes bibliographical references. | Expanded second edition. |
Housatonic, MA: Green Fire Press, 2022.
Identifiers: Library of Congress Control Number: 2022903899 |
ISBN: 978-1-7347571-7-0 (paperback) | 978-1-7347571-8-7 (ebook) |
978-1-7347571-9-4 (audio)
Subjects: LCSH Leadership. | Leadership in women. | Social reformers. |
Social action. | Community development. | Women environmentalists. |
Indigenous women. | Community leadership. | BISAC BODY, MIND &
SPIRIT / Inspiration & Personal Growth | SELF-HELP / Personal Growth /
General | SOCIAL SCIENCE / Feminism & Feminist Theory

Classification: LCC HQ1236 .S56 2022 | DDC 305.4201—dc23

Nature, Culture and the Sacred

A WOMAN LISTENS FOR LEADERSHIP

Nina Simons

edited by Annelie Campbell

Green Fire Press

TABLE OF CONTENTS

Nature, Culture and the Sacred

A WOMAN LISTENS FOR LEADERSHIP

FOREWORD

In the months just after the initial birth of this book, my mother became suddenly ill, and we entered the season of her end of life. This plunged me into a deep well of learning, as I tended her through her pain, her diminishing capacities, and her eventual death.

While I was able to fulfill my desire to help create the kindest conditions for her passage, I was unable to share news of the publication of this book that I felt so inspired to offer the world.

Despite little promotion or fanfare, the book's messages seemed to land in fertile soil. Standing as it does at the intersection of gender, racial justice, leadership, and the sacred, college professors used it in their curricula. Women's circles reached out to say they were reading and using it together to inform their learning.

Nature, Culture & Spirit: A Woman Listens for Leadership was awarded a gold medal from Nautilus Awards for Books That Make the World Better, in the category Women in the 21st Century, as well as a silver one for Social Change & Racial Justice. When the opportunity emerged to update it, to share some of what I've learned in the time since, and to expand access by recording an audiobook and adding discussion guides into the print and eBook versions, it was a rare and welcome gift.

Since then, so much has changed, both within me and throughout the world. And yet the insights this book offers still radiate vibrantly and relevantly. Now, with the world on the brink and full-spectrum, purposeful, and women's leadership offering some of the greatest promise, it is now an even more timely resource for anyone wanting to explore their own learning more deeply.

We're increasingly recognizing that we all contain feminine and masculine aspects within ourselves, and that bringing a full-spectrum toolkit to our own life and leadership evolution means drawing from all aspects of our humanity. As nature so clearly shows us, any healthy system requires diversity to survive trauma and thrive, and so learning how to relate and collaborate across difference has emerged as a high priority. I've understood even more deeply the need to cultivate the conditions for connective tissue and alliances to form among people, organizations and movements who share a common purpose, but who are still functioning in separate spheres of influence.

For me, this time has been filled with hard lessons, and a deepening sense of the interconnectedness of the challenges we face as a people, as globally-connected human relatives. I've felt a need to look closely at my own implicit biases, and at the ways I must take responsibility for unconsciously colluding with systems that perpetuate violence and run contrary to my values.

Dr. Kamilah Majied, an educator and thought leader at UC Davis, works at the intersection of contemplative practice and racial and social justice. She suggests a model for addressing individual and social healing by cultivating what she calls 'prosociality' — behaviors that benefit others while increasing awareness of our interdependence. She names a triad of skills worth cultivating to contribute to healing in this time. They are: cultural humility, fierce compassion, and discomfort resilience. I'd suggest adding a fourth leg, especially for women, which involves prioritizing exquisite self-care. Of course, we also need to make peace among the varied aspects and voices within ourselves, to show up with the aligned purposefulness required to be effective now.

What hasn't changed for me is a conviction that liberating female-identifying womxn/women and girls to collaborate with youth, BIPOC activists, people in poverty and elders to stand together on behalf of what they most love holds the greatest promise for our collective future and for all our relations. That cooperative and collaborative uprising is what I believe holds the most potential to transform our entrenched and malignant power structures, and co-midwife a healthier culture and world into flourishing.

I share this recent learning humbly, knowing that I have so much more to learn. Please know that this book is offered with love and unerring faith in the power of women, girls, and the sacred feminine in us all to change the world.

Nina Simons

INTRODUCTION

When I turned 40 years old, a magazine honored me for my leadership in an organization that I co-founded called Bioneers, which identifies and provides a platform for people working on innovative solutions to make visible a world that's possible now, and that's regenerative, healing, and just. We feature environmental and social innovators who address many of our most challenging problems. Back then, I had a very ambivalent response to being named a leader. I knew I should feel honored, but instead, I felt anxious, uncomfortable, and conflicted.

As I shared my experience with friends and colleagues, most of them women, I discovered that they also felt conflicted about calling themselves leaders. At the same time, I knew that our world was experiencing increasing social and ecological crises. I understood that we were in serious need of leadership of all ages and from all walks of life. I wondered how leadership might have to be redefined to meet my own needs and those of this time that we're living in.

From that point forward, I embarked on a twenty-year exploration into the nature of leadership and explored its necessary reinvention. That inquiry has shaped my life ever since.

First, I began by unpacking my own internal definition of leadership. I wondered whether unconscious stories, cultural biases, or the role models I'd seen might be contributing to my discomfort.

In my mind, my previously unexamined assumption was that leaders tended to be characterized as solitary, self-assured, highly accomplished, and experienced people. I saw them as sometimes arrogant or pompous individuals. In any situation, they held final power and had ultimate authority. I realized I believed that leaders exist only within a hierarchical or dominator framework. I'd observed a quality of hubris, aggression, or self-inflation among some leaders. Leaders often seemed to be inclined toward self-sacrifice, or proving how much they could accomplish, often working to the point of sickness or exhaustion.

I started seeing that my culturally-inherited definition of leadership was predicated upon social assumptions of competition, hierarchy, and scarcity. Goal orientation or winning seemed to be a common priority, without much concern or awareness about process, or how a team came to a solution.

As I scanned the leadership landscape, I saw how much of what I deeply aspired to for my own evolution didn't match up with what was conventionally being modeled. I noticed that appearances, stature, scale, and outer achievement were much more highly honored in conventionally-defined leaders than inner awareness, mindfulness, integrity, or deep listening. I saw how certitude was a prevalent attitude among conventional leaders, with little room for uncertainty or questioning. I observed how analytical and procedural thinking were more frequently appreciated than creative, relational and innovative thinking. I saw an imbalance in how conventional leadership was being practiced.

Then, I began to see the same imbalance in myself as I'd been observing in conventional leaders, including men and women. I also saw it reflected in institutions and social structures. I realized how useful it could be to awaken people to that internalized and largely invisible bias — to help all of us to be able to perceive, shed and change it.

Indigenous Peoples of the Amazon believe that the bird of humanity has flown on only one wing for far too long. They say that these times require the feminine to thoroughly join with the masculine so that the bird of humanity can gain full wing, so that we can fly to soar with our whole capacity.

The psychologist Carl Jung attributed the archetypal feminine to our inner worlds, and the masculine to our outer or exterior ones. Of course, I knew that we all contain a full spectrum of human aspects within ourselves, regardless of our sex, orientation or gender. You might wonder, then: what did the concepts "masculine" and "feminine" mean to me?

In my earlier professional career, I usually showed up first from my masculine side. I wanted to appear capable, stable, focused, and self-assured. I was quick, rational, and decisive. I prided myself on how much I could accomplish each day. When I didn't know the answer to a question or how to do something, I masked it with bravado, making up a response while inwardly hoping it would turn out okay. I rarely admitted to being uncertain or needing more time or counsel to consider how to proceed.

Inwardly, of course, there were lots of times I was unsure or nervous, but I never let it show. I devalued many of the other qualities that could have served me as a leader: my ability to listen deeply, to empathize and connect, my compassion, and my skillfulness at collaboration.

I also discounted my way of encouraging and inspiring leadership in others. I set aside my awareness of context, nuance, and the downstream ripples that might affect decisions.

As I realized all this, I promised myself that moving forward in my life, I would more explicitly integrate and strengthen my feminine side. In cultivating myself, it was important to me that my toolkit encompass all of my human capacities. I wanted to be able to draw from anywhere on that falsely gendered spectrum at any given time, as needed. This full spectrum approach allowed me to show up in the world in a much more authentic and effective way. It encouraged me to bring more aspects of myself into presence in my daily life, in all my relationships and interactions.

I discovered that it also gave me a greater capacity for renewal and regeneration after periods of intense productivity. Integrating even brief times for rest into my daily routine nourished and revitalized me. The feminine within me needs periods of rest and reflection, spacious time to re-balance my body, heart, mind, and spirit.

In considering full-spectrum leadership in all its dimensions, I also saw how our Western culture encourages us to avoid what's difficult, vulnerable, or painful. And while I knew that addressing inner turmoil can lead to real learning and personal growth, many of us chronically avoid facing into the tough stuff.

Carl Jung defined what he calls "the Shadow" as unconscious aspects of ourselves or our personalities — the parts that our egos don't acknowledge. When we avoid bringing those shadow aspects into our awareness, they exert undue and often unconscious influence on our actions. I believe that our collective aversion to what we call the 'negative' emotions — to experiencing grief, anger, fear, or depression — tends to have us act out in ways that undermine our conscious intentions, and therefore undermine our leadership.

All of our emotions have a purpose, in awakening us to important understandings, and none are actually 'good' or 'bad.' If we don't face into and integrate our personal and collective shadows, I fear we may be doomed to recycle our wounds. If we do that, we'll perpetuate cultures of immaturity, false narratives, and violence.

I yearned to identify and reclaim new forms of leadership that acknowledged these urgent realities. Seeking models, I looked to leaders we had featured from Bioneers networks from different disciplines, backgrounds and walks of life, all at different stages in their visions, work or life journeys.

These leaders, some of whom you'll meet in the stories that follow, are creative and collaborative, curious and courageous, humble and passionate. They each have diverse, and yet authentic responses to the challenges that their work addresses.

They use both sides of their brains, and all their gendered parts. They marry apparent contradictions. They merge the rational with the intuitive, at once. They weave the relational, the strategic, and the collaborative. They're able to balance deep listening, open-mindedness, and humility with asserting their own perspectives or what they know to be true when they need to.

Some may not even consider or call themselves leaders. But those who most inspire me are the ones who don't necessarily have a title, graduate degree, or any other external markers of authority. What they do have is a passionate commitment to some aspect of the living world, and their dedication or love is so profound that it causes them to act with a quality of dignified authority. To me, it's as if they receive their assignment from their intuition, their hearts, or their spirits. As if their inner voice said, "I have to do something to protect, defend or reinvent what I love."

Reflecting on these new models of leadership led me to co-create a book called *Moonrise: The Power of Women Leading from the Heart* with my colleague Anneke Campbell. It's an anthology of more than 30 essays by diverse trailblazers, including mostly women and some men. We organized the book to illustrate leadership's reinvention. It's being used in university and graduate courses about leadership, women and diversity, equity and inclusion.

I was also inspired to co-create Cultivating Women's Leadership intensives in 2006 with Toby Herzlich and Akaya Windwood. They are two longtime facilitators and transformative process designers with deep experience, both with women and leadership trainings. These six-day residential intensives, housed within Bioneers for eight years, were designed to do several things: to clarify each woman's sense of calling or purpose; to explore the shadow side of women's leadership; to share intentional practices for ongoing self-cultivation; and to experience beloved community among a very diverse group. They also offered an embodied experience of how exponentially women can accelerate and strengthen each other's learning and leadership.

Co-facilitating Cultivating Women's Leadership intensives inspired me to appreciate a wide array of perspectives and people in all forms. I don't mean just ethnic or racial diversity, but the real value of working in community among a diverse range of ages, orientations, classes, abilities, faiths, disciplines, and sectors. It has led me to a deeper understanding of the complementary values of extroversion and introversion, and how we all process information differently, applying visual, auditory, and kinesthetic capacities and ways of learning in varied ways.

None of the women's leadership we've featured at Bioneers has ever been about reinforcing binaries. It has always oriented toward inclusivity, beloved community, and wholeness. Some call it blended leadership, informed by a healthy integration of all of our feminine and masculine qualities.

Many of the people described or quoted in this book are leaders I've learned about through coproducing Bioneers. If you'd like to learn more about any of them, you can search for them on the Bioneers.org site, or on YouTube, to see their talks or hear podcasts featuring their voices.

It's important to note, also, that leadership's definition itself really needs expanding. For me, parenting and raising children are among the most challenging, and most rewarding forms of leadership there are. Being an artist of any kind who reveals future possibilities is clearly a form of leadership. As is caregiving or being a teacher. I could go on and on, as my emergent definition is an inside job, and one that's applicable in almost any field of endeavor.

After many years of working with women who lead change, I now believe that at its heart, leadership is about the nexus or connective tissue that brings together three core elements. I see it as finding the place where each of our unique gifts or talents connect with serving what we love the most, and also with a real need for reinvention or renewal in the world. When we find that connection point, that nexus, and act from that, we become unstoppable. The joy that comes from doing that work creates a self-reinforcing loop.

Once you find it, it's powerful and revitalizing. Because it's so fulfilling and regenerative, it defies that tendency toward burn-out and self-sacrifice that I'd had such an aversion to earlier. It amazes me to feel how much energy, joy and creativity has been unleashed within myself as I reclaim and learn to love aspects of my own inner wholeness — my council of Ninas, I call them.

Integrating all our internal or personal parts must also, I believe, be mirrored by acting externally — ecologically, socially, or politically.

Learning from nature reveals that diversity is not about political correctness. It's about resilience and survival. In natural systems, diversity means having an abundance of options for adaptation. Options that ensure survival and mitigate against extinction. Ecosystems that are rich in species diversity rebound much faster after trauma, while systems with monocultures are far slower to recover and heal. Human systems are a subset of nature's systems, so if diversity serves nature's well-being, it will serve ours as well.

I now believe that there's nothing that will serve our future better than bringing the aligned capacity of each of us — our own full spectrum diversity — to our leadership in all its forms. It seems to me the most potent and useful response to this moment when the world is asking so much of us.

This book is organized into three sections, and it can be read or listened to from front to back, or in any sequence that calls you.

The first section shares stories of my own inner discovery and healing from internalized biases.

The second addresses some of the external, behavioral, and political aspects of women's leadership. It also speaks to the imbalance of the archetypal feminine in us all, and it includes stories about some of the leaders that inspire me most.

And the third section speaks to my own growing awareness of racial equity, what Kimberlé Crenshaw named as the 'intersectionality' of racial and gender biases. It describes my ongoing awakening to the places where systems of White supremacy, misogyny, colonialism and capitalism converge, and the impacts they're having on people and places that I love. It also shares best practices for gathering in diverse groups.

As you read these pages, I invite you to notice any parts of yourself that may have been previously hidden, silenced, or kept small. Perhaps ideas or stories within this book might enter your dreamtime, or motivate you to grow into or reclaim previously undervalued or banished qualities.

I hope you find this book inspiring, expansive and heart-nourishing. If you're interested in using it to help facilitate your own or others' learning, there are questions for reflection that you can find after each essay or poem, with embodied practices after each section.

I'm honored, humbled, and thankful to invite you to join me in this journey of exploration.

To do so, I suggest that you first give yourself permission to fall in love. Fall in love with a place, a people, with children, a cause, an organization, a creature, a species — anything that really lights you up. Then give yourself to it in some form of purposeful action.

You don't have to know what that means, exactly, or have it strategically mapped out in advance. You just have to commit to being its ally, its relative, to acting to defending or protecting or improving its life. Then see who else is committed to it. Who else is in this river you've opted to swim in, on behalf of our collective future?

I suggest bringing yourself to it with all the wisdom of your magnificent body, the knowing of your heart, your mind, and your intuition. Call on all your aspects, from your discipline and rigor to your compassion and empathy; from your strategic thinking and analysis to your body wisdom and instinctive feelings, from your masculine to your feminine, and everything in between. Bring all of yourself.

Lastly, I suggest that you trust that exactly who you are is what is needed at this moment in the world. Know that you are already enough in every way to meet this assignment. And here's the best part: I'd suggest you do this not because it's right (though it is), not because it's needed (though it surely is), but because it's the most joyful, purposeful, and fulfilling way to live your life.

INTRODUCTION TO THE GUIDE FOR DEEPENING LEARNING

Following each piece in the book, you will find a set of reflection, writing, or discussion prompts & embodied practices. I invite you to use these as your own intuition and inspiration may guide you. We often learn best what we discover for ourselves, through our own styles of perception and discovery. Towards that end, these questions, writing or discussion prompts and practices are offered to help create conditions conducive to self-reflection and deepening discovery.

So, please feel free to adapt questions or prompts for your best application in personal, classroom, or circle practice. My hope is that they'll be fruitful to deepen your learning in any context — and perhaps in multiple contexts. Use this guide in whatever ways most resonate with your intentions and help to illuminate your learning edges.

I hope you'll be curious, brave, and experimental. I encourage you to explore the prompts and engage with the practices, choosing the edgiest and most challenging responses that arise within you, to discover more of your own essence, and what lights you up, not only to identify your own particular path, but to activate the lived experience of your body, heart, and spirit.

When applied in groups, this guide invites you to take the risk of sharing your truths with each other. Exposing vulnerabilities can build personal strength, trust, and communal connection, which in turn can help accelerate everyone's learning.

May the book and this guide serve your highest purpose, deepest longings, and fondest dreams for yourself, as an instrument of loving service toward transforming and helping to heal our relations. If it does, then it will serve my own highest aim and longing as well.

PROMPTS FOR DEEPENING LEARNING
THROUGH REFLECTION, WRITING OR DISCUSSION

Introduction

THEMES
- Reimagining leadership as full-spectrum, holistically, and through a culture-informed, gendered lens.
- Strengthening and cultivating oneself as a leader through self-awareness and expanded definitions.

PROMPTS
WRITE OR TALK ABOUT YOUR EARLIEST MEMORY OF EXPERIENCING YOURSELF AS A LEADER.
- Before you started this book, did you identify as a leader?
- If you don't, do you know why not?
- Do others consider you a leader?
- If so, what do you think they see in you?

For me the idea of leadership was closely linked to the influence of patriarchy, and later to White supremacist, capitalist, and colonial cultures, as well.
- List any connotations, positive or negative, that leadership holds for you.
- Where do you sense that those associations arise from, in yourself, those around you, and the culture at large?

For me, the phrase "full-spectrum leadership" encompasses all of my human capacities.

- Do you experience 'masculine' and 'feminine' aspects within yourself?
- If so, can you name them? How do you relate to each of them?
- What of non-binary capacities, such as courage or competence or other qualities of character?
- How useful are gendered concepts to you, given gender fluidity?

Make a list of how you see your unique gifts or talents. As you reflect on them, notice whether you appreciate yourself when you apply them well.

Inventory and list your 'learning edges,' or the places you know you want to grow yourself. How might you cultivate yourself or your skill sets in those areas?

PART I

Cultivating Inner Balance

MARRYING THE MOON AND SUN WITHIN

SHIFTING GUIDANCE FROM HEAD TO HEART

All the brilliant, innovative, and effective solutions and strategies won't
be enough to shift our collective course
   without an accompanying — and radical — change of heart.

For me, what's central to alleviating humanity's strife
   and addressing the devastation we are wreaking upon
   our mother Earth
   is tending to an imbalance of the masculine and
   feminine.

Reclaiming the value of the feminine within each of us
   is essential to bringing our human wholeness
   to this time of revolutionary reinvention.

We have to practice loving, re-awakening, and strengthening
   the feeling parts of ourselves:
   our intuition, our body wisdom,
   our dreams, and our deep listening.

As we re-enliven the inner knowing of our hearts
   (understanding that relationships are far more important
than accomplishments, goals, or tasks),

We'll become better partners to ourselves,
      each other and the Earth.

If we practice our capacity to be comfortable
      with vulnerability, with uncertainty,
      and with attending caringly
      to the cues and clues that surround us,
      it will help us to re-synchronize with the world and become
      more resilient, flexible,
      and adaptive to change.

This is not about devaluing the masculine side of ourselves;
      it's about re-evaluating what a healthy masculine means.
It's about reclaiming the whole of our dimensional humanity.

For me, I find I must begin with my inner self,
      since what I see out there likely reflects what's within me.
      If I don't, it's far too easy (and not ultimately effective)
      to blame others without cleaning, updating,
         and reorienting my own operating system, first.

I am practicing re-sequencing my inner
      voices so that my heart's instruction can lead,
      and be supported by the plans, analysis,
         structures, and strategies my mind creates.

      When I listen with my heart,
I am pierced with an empathic awareness
      that calls me into action beyond what any amount
of learning, reading, or mental understanding can prompt.

I am stunned by the power of women, and our capacity to heal.
Wise elders, friends, and mutual mentors
      among the women I am honored to work with
remind me to listen deeply to all my sources of guidance —
      to seek assistance from nature,
      from my dreams and intuition, to inquire of my ancestors,
      and listen for responses, before determining a course of action.

This requires me to peel away layers of patterning,
      of rushing to respond to prove my value through productivity.
It requires me to question old and deeply ingrained habits.

As I practice composting layers of acculturated learning
      that I absorbed unknowingly through the
          invisible water of culture we swim in,
I wonder whether I will ever be free of it.
I realize I need to decolonize my mind,
      and practice reclaiming and remembering
          other ways of knowing.

Along the way, I've discovered something about the feminine.
I'm learning that listening is not a passive act.
Life is teaching me that it doesn't just require my ears.
I'm learning to listen with my belly, my dreams, and my intuition.

Not only does it require actively attending to receiving guidance,
I've discovered I also have to ask, in order to receive,
      and then wait — patiently if possible — for a response to come.

As I practice this —
with my inner self, with nature, with my body,
          with ancestors, and dreamtime and intuition —
I find I have many more sources of insight or guidance
          than I'd previously imagined or remembered.

May we remember how to bring the wholeness of our humanity —
          our deep listening; our patient observation;
our loving, powerful, tender hearts; our humble hands; and our prayers —
          to co-creating the conditions for thriving life.

PROMPTS FOR DEEPENING LEARNING
THROUGH REFLECTION, WRITING OR DISCUSSION

Shifting Guidance from Head to Heart

THEMES

- Decentering mind as primary navigational system.
- Shifting inner compass from head to heart through deep listening, and attending to guidance from other ways of knowing — body, heart, intuition.
- Seeking to balance 'masculine' and 'feminine' within oneself.

PROMPTS

Sometimes I write in prose poems because I like how that form allows me the freedom of being less linear, more evocative and creative. It seems to offer me greater flow, and less internalized judgment.

I encourage you to respond to these pieces in whatever way offers you the same freedom, liberating any kind of expression that opens a flow for you.

- How do you relate to the form of your own response?
- What does "listening with your heart" mean for you?
- How else might you listen, besides with your ears?

How would you define "deep listening" and why is it so important to leadership?

"Reclaiming the feminine" is a theme throughout the book.

- How would you define "the feminine" in your own life, experience, and psyche?

Pay particular attention to any somatic or body responses that might arise, or any emotions or judgments that may come up in relation to 'the feminine.'

A RIVER OF PURPOSE

A Human-Nature Landscape

If anyone had suggested to me as a youth that I might spend my thirties, forties, and fifties co-creating an annual environmental conference serving a vision of restoration, I'd have said, "No way!" In college, I always found biology and chemistry classes to be utterly boring and lacking any potential relevance for my life.

As a child growing up in New York City, however, nature provided comfort and sanctuary. When I was a girl of six or seven, I had a large and varied collection of stuffed animals that lived on my bed. One day, after my parents had read us *Charlotte's Web*, I piled them into shopping bags and took them to Central Park, at the edge of Spanish Harlem, where we lived. There, I set each of them carefully into their own nook within a huge tree, returning them to nature, to be free among their own kind. I came home to an empty bed, happy with what I'd done.

Since that day, a strong sense of purpose has continued to grow and morph as new experiences and learning have shaped me. It's manifested as an evolving call, or assignment, and not something that remains static. In significant moments along the way, I have fallen in love, my heart and mind converging in newfound commitment to a people, a creature, a place, or a challenge.

I have come to understand purpose as being what happens when one's own particular loves, commitments, and talents converge with a need for change in the world. Those moments have shifted the course of my leadership, creating a long and windy river of expression, and not the direct and linear pathway I'd anticipated. As more of myself has become consciously engaged, bringing a full spectrum of my capacities into play, that has also informed how I've come to understand my purpose.

A daughter of artists, I assumed that it was through producing radical art that I'd make my contribution to the world. After college, I worked for a theater company, as I'd hoped to contribute to creating what I called transformational theater, theater that was capable of transforming peoples' hearts and minds. Discovering how hard it might be to earn a living that way, I managed restaurants and studied extensively with a school for consciousness called Arica.

In my late 20s, I moved to Santa Fe, New Mexico, and a few years later, I met Kenny Ausubel, who later became my husband and partner. It was early 1987, and he was completing a documentary film, *Hoxsey: How Healing Becomes a Crime*, which told the story of the politics of medicine and the history of alternative cancer therapies in this country. As I learned about the growing number of cancer patients and their lack of access to good information or options, I became passionate about addressing that gap, and helped him to complete, market, and distribute the film.

Kenny said that we came together like peanut butter and jelly, and it's true — our collaboration happened organically and seamlessly. We were so complementary that we finished each other's sentences and manifested each other's ideas, effortlessly. Working on distributing *Hoxsey* was a breakthrough experience for me in many ways. I learned that I loved helping get stories that are important for healing widely told. I found myself enthused and tireless in that pursuit, and strengthened by the synchronicity of my emerging partnership with Kenny.

A couple of years later, Kenny was asked to film footage of an unusual garden at San Juan Pueblo near Santa Fe, New Mexico. He went to visit the garden and became fascinated by the garden's diversity, uniqueness, and fertility. The pueblo had hired master gardener Gabriel Howearth to design and plant the garden. Previously, Gabriel had traveled all over Central and Latin America learning about indigenous agriculture, expanding his repertoire of diverse plant families. As people began to trust him, they shared with him what for them was the most precious of gifts — the gift of seeds.

At that time, I was working with the Santa Fe Chamber Music Festival, but walking through Gabriel's garden in Gila, New Mexico, changed the course of my life. Strolling through it, I encountered whole societies of tomatoes and peppers, of every shape, size, and color, and the smells were beyond anything I'd ever experienced — totally intoxicating. There were tall stalks of glowing red amaranth, golden braids of quinoa, and other things that I had never seen before. As we walked, I was encouraged to taste, so I picked leaves and munched my way through, feeling the utter vitality of the whole environment coursing through my senses. There was chocolate basil and lemon licorice mint. The richness and the fertility of the garden resonated deeply within me, and I felt as though my senses were dancing.

Then, Gabriel told us of the impending crisis in the food system. He shared how dozens of small seed companies were being gobbled up by multinational corporations, diminishing the number of varieties being grown and thereby threatening the diversity of life itself. As we left the garden, I felt the spirit of the natural world tap me on the shoulder and say, "You're working for me, now."

Kenny and Gabriel entered into partnership to begin a biodiversity seed company. I knew nothing about gardening, farming or plant diversity and very little about the crisis in biodiversity. But I did know that the life force I'd encountered in that garden had what I saw as a thrilling capacity to renew and heal our world, and I threw myself into the work fully. I quit my job and began working as Director of Marketing for Seeds of Change. While it was daunting to realize how little I knew, it was exhilarating to work for something I believed in so deeply. I found myself feeling more alive than with any work I'd previously done.

In 1990, after Kenny bemoaned in a hot tub about all the amazing innovators working to heal nature with nature that his research was revealing, (but that no one knew about,) he was offered a grant by Josh Mailman to start a conference. Kenny had never been to a conference, and wondered about it as a strategy, imagining conferences as inherently boring.

Knowing of my theater background, he approached me to partner with him to produce a conference, and Bioneers was born. Since neither of us had ever experienced a conventional conference, we were able to co-design something with beginner's mind, and we created a form that could simultaneously integrate a sense of the sacred with ceremony, that could speak to the heart and imagination with arts and culture, and bring brilliant and largely unknown ideas, projects, and people to light.

I embarked on three steep and deep learning curves — one about food and farming, another about being a social entrepreneur, and the third about leadership. Those inquiries led me into a lifelong exploration of indigenous wisdom, and how to interact, design, invent, educate and organize on behalf of the sacred web of life on Earth.

When I first heard the speakers that Kenny invited at that initial Bioneers conference in 1990, my jaw dropped. Science came alive for me through nature for the first time, and I felt my childlike sense of wonder return.

Here were courageous and curious explorers whose experiments with natural systems were revealing the complexity and brilliance of 4 billion years of evolution. Contrary to the arrogant and mechanistic way I'd previously experienced science, here were people quivering with the delight of discovery, humbly studying at the feet of a real master — nature herself.

It was at Bioneers, too, through Kenny's commitment to indigenous voices and values, that I first heard First Nations people speak about healing from a Native perspective — one that included greater relatedness to place, to each other, to the Earth and all its creatures. Hearing them, I understood that their knowledge and experience were essential to our survival as a species. Having already adapted to thousands of years of change, Indigenous Peoples have information about how we are meant to live that I believe must be reintegrated in order to reinvent our entire culture.

At the 1992 Bioneers Conference, to commemorate Columbus' tragic landing on Turtle Island, we assembled a group of indigenous leaders to discuss what could be learned from considering this 500th anniversary. A governor from Acoma Pueblo, Petuuche Gilbert, said, "Five hundred years ago you came, and we welcomed you with open arms. If you came again today, we would do exactly the same." I was humbled, awed and shaken by his words. I sensed how much wisdom his culture carried about forgiveness and generosity, about how to be a good person, as well as about survival. Many Native growers knew about dryland agriculture, about seed breeding for resilience and nutrition, about how to live in reciprocal relationship with nature. Relating to all life as sacred seems just about endemic to Indigeneity.

My days were on fire with learning and producing and convening, but it wasn't until a few years later that my path took another unexpected turn, when I began exploring my identity as a woman. I had always assumed, coming out of college, that I was stepping onto a relatively level playing field thanks to the hard work of the feminists of the 60s and 70s. It wasn't until I was working in my thirties that I began to realize how untrue that assumption had been. I had the repeated experience of sitting in a board room, saying something, and having it fall flat, and then the man next to me would say it with slightly different language and everybody would nod their heads, saying, "What a great idea." I began to understand how bifurcated and unconsciously biased I, like our whole society, still was around issues of gender.

One day, after we'd left Seeds of Change and my father had suddenly died, I went to a favorite video shop seeking a film to rent, hoping for solace, or to fill some of the void I was feeling. Carmen Blue, the woman who ran the store, said, "I've got a film for you. I feel it's so important for everyone to see that I lend it out to people for free." She handed me *The Burning Times*, which is an hour-long, Canadian-made documentary now viewable for free online. Seeing that film altered the course of my life.

When I learned about the period in European history between the 14th and 17th centuries — a time many refer to as *The Burning Times* — my mind and heart's eyes were opened to a root cause of centuries of pervasive gender patterns and biases. Something of that genocide still lived within me, in my cells or bones. I marveled that this immense event in human history wasn't being taught to every child in school.

I discovered that seven generations of children across Europe saw many of their mothers, grandmothers, aunties, cousins, and sisters tortured and burned for the supposed crime of being witches. Men, too, lost loved ones — wives, daughters, local healers. To save their families and themselves, women were often turned against each other.

The culture also sustained deep institutional losses that further cemented structural biases. Traditional systems of healing, spiritual practice, communal land use, and economic relationships were upended, as power was systematically transferred from the collective purview of women in these domains to the primary control, authority, and leadership of men. What some have called "The Hidden Holocaust of Women" lives on in my cellular memory, and I believe still insidiously permeates our society, institutions, and collective psyche.

It was also the first time an irrational fear I'd always had of speaking my truth in public made sense to me. At this point, all of the issues I'd become passionate about through Bioneers began to come into focus *within a single lens*: the imbalance of "masculine" values and a patriarchal relationship to competition, hierarchy, and power over "feminine" values: cooperation, shared authority, and the equity of women. I saw this as evident both externally, in the disproportionate allotment of leadership roles to men in nearly all spheres of life, and internally, as an archetypal inner imbalance that affects the design and functioning of every individual, institution and sector.

I began a deep inquiry about the role of gender in my own life and realized that I carried stories within me that were self-limiting. I observed how long I'd held myself back due to unexplored fears and unconsciously adopted stories. For example, once I was asked to write the story of my relationship to Bioneers, the organization that I co-midwifed and co-shepherded into being. I wrote that my role consisted of supporting my husband's vision, and then I wondered, "Ugh, is that the whole truth?" What I found was that other people around me, including my husband, didn't see this story as true at all. They perceived its evolution as co-created, and they frequently valued my contributions more than I valued my own.

Along with many other self-limiting beliefs that I had unconsciously absorbed, I recognized that I was relying upon these internalized stories to make myself small. And the gift in that, of course, was realizing that if I had let those stories shape my thoughts or constrain my dreams, I could, now that they were exposed to the light, let them go, or at least re-craft them. Much of my work on myself since then has been to do that. As I shared my own discoveries with other women around me, I saw everyone nodding their heads. Then I realized, "This isn't just me; this is a rather pervasive pattern held by many women, a pattern that must be illuminated so it can transform."

As I investigated my inner landscape, I realized that I had lived much of my outer life through my more "masculine" qualities — showing up as competent, self-assured, intelligent, decisive, linear, and rational, while my more "feminine" aspects — my intuition, relational intelligence, embodied awareness, empathy, flexibility, and a tendency toward a chaotic process of creativity — I tended to keep hidden and rarely revealed in a public context. Of course, I knew that we all have feminine and masculine aspects within us, but when I saw this imbalance within myself, I wanted to claim more of my human wholeness. I began to practice valuing my more "feminine" aspects, exploring how I might express them more fully in my work, relationships, and everyday life.

At the 2001 Bioneers conference, a remarkable activist named Diane Wilson closed her speech by adopting a quote from George

Bernard Shaw. She said, "A reasonable woman adapts to the world, and an unreasonable woman makes the world adapt to her. So, I encourage all of you women out there to be unreasonable." After the conference, she called Kenny and me at home and told us how so many women had thanked her, tearfully, for what she'd said, and that she'd had a vision that there would be a movement of unreasonable women.

With Kenny's encouragement, I decided that I would help seed this vision by bringing together a diverse group of women leaders to explore what such a movement might look like. I expanded the title of the gathering — as I knew that resistance wasn't enough, and we had to be *for* something — to "UnReasonable Women for the Earth." I invited 34 remarkable women ranging in age from 23 to 70 years old, from across many disciplines, social classes, gender orientations, and ethnicities. They worked in domains as varied as environmental health, law, poetry, social organizing, performance art, writing, seed diversity, urban farming, spiritual teaching, and science.

When we first arrived at the meeting, each spoke about her own feelings of isolation, and we recognized that we each had a need for a community of peers. By the end of the four days, a solidarity developed among us — a pledge to stand at each other's backs — that nourished us in unexpected ways.

One thing that grew out of that gathering was the emergence of CODEPINK: Women for Peace. Jodie Evans, Medea Benjamin, and Diane Wilson, inspired by the collective energies of the retreat, and prompted by the urgency of that time and their resistance to the U.S. invasion and war in Iraq, founded CODEPINK several months later.

We had been programming diverse women's voices in leadership at the Bioneers Conference for several years, and had also

explored the theme of what I called "Restoring the Feminine." Our
radio/podcast series had long featured shows that explored and helped
promote multicultural women's voices, visions, and perspectives, but I
wanted to go deeper.

I wanted to explore how women can come together and
strengthen each other. We had experienced conventional forms
of leadership, based upon hierarchy and competition rather than
relationship, and power rather than respect, for 6,000 years. It had left
our world in dire shape. The time had come to model the respectful,
relational connectivity that we know as a true pattern of life and stand
up for that option to emerge among women leading change.

And so, in 2006, I reached out first to Toby Herzlich and
then Akaya Windwood, a couple of very skillful facilitators of group
transformative processes, and together we three co-created a six-day,
deep-dive immersion training into leading from the feminine, which
was incubated and housed as a program within Bioneers. We named it
"Cultivating Women's Leadership" (CWL).

During these 6-day residential trainings we prioritized probing
what leadership meant to women. We focused on exploring how
it differed from conventional male models and investigated how
we might more wholeheartedly claim leadership and aspire to it.
Through experiential learning, we encouraged the women who were
participating to identify and overcome internalized limitations and
to face and acknowledge the shadow side of women's leadership.
We developed exercises to help clarify each woman's purpose in
life, and to learn how powerfully women in intentional alignment
can strengthen each other's capacity. Toby and I, as the primary
cofounders, have produced CWL trainings each year since 2006. Each
cohort of twenty women was caringly selected (through an application

process) for their leadership vision and capacity, and we also sought to optimize diversity in all its forms among each group.

This group process included many aspects; it was intentionally highly multi-dimensional, but for me, a highlight has been that's revealed how we as women have the capacity to rapidly and exponentially enhance each other's skillfulness and to stand at each other's backs. Once the women hear and see each other's visions and gifts and power, they become committed to supporting each other. Everyone who comes has an opportunity to do her own deep inquiry and to explore fundamental questions: What is calling me? How can I refine my sense of assignment or purpose? One of our core premises is that each of us has a very distinct, unique purpose/reason for being alive on Earth at this momentous time.

Later in the program's evolution, while continually improving the program with cofounder Toby Herzlich, and with wise contributions from co-facilitators Sarah Crowell, Rachel Bagby and Elsa Menendez, we added skill-building around body movement and dance, freeing women's voices, awakening body awareness and sense of play, and dealing with relational ruptures that occur around power and privilege.

I learned from Linda Tarr Whelan that in order to feel comfortable enough to fully express themselves, members of any minority group need to have at least 30 percent representation, so we established that minimum for women of color in our trainings, and now often attract 35–50 percent. About five hundred women leaders, across a huge span of ages, disciplines, races, backgrounds, and orientations, from the U.S. and around the world, have now been through CWL. A vast majority of them report that they were profoundly changed by the experience.

As my understanding grew, I sought to identify patterns among
the leaders I'd most admired throughout my years with Bioneers. In
2010, Anneke Campbell and I edited an anthology called *Moonrise:
The Power of Women Leading from the Heart*. We collected the stories
by reading scores of transcripts, and in spite of the publisher's protests,
we realized that we wanted to include the stories of some men who also
embodied relationship intelligence and leading from the heart. I think
of the book as an homage to my mentors, as everyone profiled in the
book has inspired me deeply with the way they've modeled innovative
and effective forms of leadership. The book is being used in colleges
as part of the curriculum for Women's Studies, Leadership & Social
Change, and Multiculturalism classes, in addition to, of course, being
read by individuals and shared in book clubs and other organizations.

Seeing the need for some larger organizing principle to build
power among diverse factions of women's movements, in 2014, I began
convening diverse women leaders of networks and organizations to
explore their interest and availability in creating such a connective tissue.
These gatherings were called "Co-Madres," borrowing from the Chicana
term for women who've pledged to have each other's backs, for life.

Although they have been relatively small and intimate, they
have been effective at seeding key relationships. Through that work, and
CWL and Bioneers, I've formed some deep friendships with women
from many different cultures. The more I got to know and heard people
of all colors and classes speak, the more I understood the degree to
which our culture operates in a hierarchical paradigm that systemically
devalues people of color, people of lower income, and ultimately
women as well.

I must have been naïve, or culturally conditioned by racial
blinders, but what I learned about our racialized culture and the ways

it impacts people I love shocked me and woke me up. Experiencing it personally through friends I'd come to know helped me to understand that if I had felt limited, oppressed or constrained because of my gender identity as a woman, it was minimal compared to the experiences of the Indigenous women and women of color I was coming to know. They typically had many of the internalized oppression and self-limiting beliefs that come with gender in our culture, but they also had had to face the intense constraints a racist social order and colonization places on people of color, double whammy.

I began to learn more directly about the physical impacts of living among some of those African American, Indigenous, and Latino communities that suffer the worst toxic health threats as well as the toxic psychic and psychological impacts of current and intergenerational trauma. This began radicalizing me, awakening within me a far more visceral understanding of the depth of the injustices racism has wrought.

What shocked me most was coming to see my own prior ignorance, denial, and complicity. Over time I began to challenge myself to compare the experiences all women have had of gender bias with that of racial bias. I have to admit that exploring these charged topics has been unsettling and has stirred up a lot of deep fears I'd not previously known I carried within me.

As painful as it is, facing these fears is something we all have to do in order to realize the dream of building sustainable multicultural and cross-class alliances. I've tried to continue learning from women of color, and as they shared their stories, I began to feel in my gut the insidious, pervasive costs of White privilege we all ultimately pay for, and how those deep wounds are compounded by how we are all programmed around gender. I'm still working to shed my own blinders, ignorance, guilt and shame, something I'll have to continue to do for the rest of my days, but I'm slowly learning, and I'm now able to recover sooner when I make mistakes or find I've made false assumptions.

I am also finding it helpful to explore my own Jewish heritage, to relate to my own lineage with dignity and respect and gratitude for what it can offer me. In this way, I can bring my own culture with me into relationship, and not just behave as if I don't have roots, though, of course, Jewish culture has been uprooted repeatedly throughout its long history as well. Perhaps we are a people who've learned over thousands of years of displacement how to carry culture on our backs, like turtles carry their shells.

If you had told me ten years before that my interest in the arts, healing, and leadership would lead to this, I would have been shocked. It was never in my game plan or vision for myself but following the path of what I most cared about led me there, organically, and I am deeply thankful for it. My life continues to be an unpredictable and winding road, and I'm finally making peace with that aspect of my true nature.

A theme that has come up frequently at Bioneers over the decades is that in nature the systems with the greatest biodiversity are the ones that are most resilient and most capable of rebounding after trauma. Our human systems are exactly the same. Therefore, well beyond tolerating diversity and valuing it, I am committed to a future where we celebrate and recognize how essential our human diversity is toward regenerating our relationship with ourselves, each other, and the Earth. We've inherited deep relational imbalances in those three fundamental relationships. They are interdependent and interrelated, and all need to be healed for the system to be transformed.

The issue of climate justice has also emerged as a central focus for me. I have found that the movement emerging to address it encompasses so many of the things I have cared most deeply about in my life: art, healing, biodiversity, environmental justice, indigenous wisdom, women's leadership and racial justice. My heart is now calling me to find new ways to engage with some aspects of that movement's framing and organizing, and supporting frontline leaders in the struggle, especially the indigenous ones, in defense of our mother Earth.

Through this twenty-year, multifaceted engagement with women's leadership and the feminine, I have come to see how these fractal, yet mutually dependent issues are essential to us all — individually and collectively — in order to unearth, explore, and reframe our narratives as we navigate this immense systemic transition we face. If we're humble, persevering, and honoring of the wisdom that's all around us, respecting the true value of the feminine to bring new life, and guided by our hearts, intuitions, dreams, ancestors, and bodies, as well as our minds, we may just find our way through.

May it be so.

PROMPTS FOR DEEPENING LEARNING
THROUGH REFLECTION, WRITING OR DISCUSSION

A River of Purpose:
A Human-Nature Landscape

THEMES

- An intimate relationship with nature can be a source of calling, or purpose. So can any issue, place, or social environment you feel drawn to protect, defend, or change.

- A sense of 'calling' is not static, or a goal, but can be continually evolving. It can seem disparate and non-linear, yet still be informed with pattern.

PROMPTS

My winding path led me eventually into exploring my relationship to leadership, and to cultivating myself toward who I wished to become.

- What strikes you most about your own journey?
- Do you have negative judgments you could release about the shape of your own exploration or path?
- Do you perceive any patterns or clarity when you look at it from a bird's eye view?

My early connection to nature offered me comfort and sanctuary, and returned as a devotional throughline later in my life.

- Where or to whom did you turn to for comfort, in your youth?
- What in your life affects or nourishes you now?

This same connection led to my first sense of a calling.

- Can you recall any early experiences that affected you in this way?

In relation to your own sense of calling or purpose:

- Who, where, or what do you love, and might you feel called to serve? (Not necessarily forever, but for now, for your next step…).

To help you clarify, try this either orally in a circle or in writing:

- List the people, places, creatures, or experiences you love most passionately.
- What breaks your heart? What evokes sorrow in you? Depression? Outrage or anger?

Do any of these answers surprise you? They might provide clues to what calls you, for now.

LISTENING FOR GUIDANCE
Mystery, Intuition and Dreamtime

I learned in an embodied way about the power of dreams and of listening for guidance from the mystery to inform leadership through a lived experience of indigenous wisdom. Called the Four Societies process (when translated into English), it is an ancient way of bringing a group of diverse people into alignment — what I sometimes refer to as a transformative practice, or what some call a "social technology." Here is a story of what happened that describes both the unanticipated, intuitive, and sacred way that guidance was received among a group, and that also provides a model of servant leadership that I've found useful and inspiring.

Years ago, Bioneers hosted a retreat led in a traditional way by Jeannette Armstrong and Marlowe Sam, educators from the Okanagan people, some of the First Peoples of what is now called British Columbia and Washington State. One of the things that we learned during this retreat was to listen for the mystery — the sacred information that comes, unbidden. Each night they gave us a topic to explore in a dream and asked us to report back to the group the next day.

On the last morning of a six-day immersion, we'd been asked to dream about the future of Bioneers. In my dream, I'd seen a turtle and a long furry creature I'd never seen before frolicking together, in and out of underwater caves. The tone of the dream was playful and celebratory, and I awoke feeling happy and refreshed.

Having no idea what it meant, I brought it to Jeannette over breakfast, knowing her to be a skilled dream interpreter. After listening intently, she assured me that I'd understand later, when the group gathered. In the circle, we shared our dreams, and several others had dreamt about turtles, too.

Then, Marlowe described his dream. A large shed-like building was on a beach, with a long line of people going in one end and coming out the other. In the center of the shed was a mound of sand, with a hole at its center. Out of it poured a steady stream of newly hatched baby sea turtles. As each person approached the mound, they'd pick up a baby turtle and carry it tenderly away to care for its survival. Now our circle was very still, all of us utterly silent, as we were held in the conjoined mystical web of our dreams.

Next, Jeannette told us an origin story that's been told to children as a teaching story among the Okanagan people for generations. This was also approved by their Elders to be told as an educational story for all people. She said:

One day, the Creator gathered all the creatures together for a meeting. Once assembled, Creator told them, *"Soon, there will come among you new beings who will not be as intelligent as you are. Once they come, they will need to be shown how to institute stability. You will need to determine which way would work best for them."*

There was much discussion among the animals, as they were uncertain what might work best. Then, Eagle stepped forward, saying, *"I propose that I decide for all of you, since I am strong and fast, and can see a long, long way. I should decide everything, unless any of you are stronger or faster than me. The only way to find out if anyone else is faster is if you can beat me in a race. If you can't beat me, then you have to do everything I say."*

Since nobody else had any ideas, this seemed reasonable, and so they all agreed. One by one, the animals challenged Eagle to a race. But Eagle was very fast, and each time, he won. Finally, there seemed to be nobody left to race, and Eagle became the leader of all the creatures. But as soon as he did, he began changing how all the animals spent their days. He ordered them to build nests for his children, to hunt for them and feed them.

In order to do all that Eagle asked of them, they had to ignore the needs of their own families and their own children. They became thin and hungry. The animals became more and more dejected as they became enslaved to Eagle. Their children were suffering. The land was neglected. With each new race that was lost to Eagle, their spirits sank lower and lower. They didn't see how they could ever reclaim their freedom and restore their community.

About that time, Turtle emerged out of the river and learned what was going on. He was deeply concerned for all the others. He saw their suffering, and he felt compelled to act. He had no idea how he could help free them and restore peace and balance to the land, but he knew he must do his best.

He challenged Eagle to a race. When Eagle learned of Turtle's challenge, he laughed scornfully. Turtle was known to be the slowest animal of all. Eagle said to everyone listening, *"I'll let Turtle pick the time, the place and set the length of the race. If Turtle wins, he can decide for everyone, even the people-to-be."*

Turtle said *"We will race in the morning, after I rest. We will meet here at this big tree where everything began, and then I will let you know where and how long the race will be."*

Turtle went down into the river and prayed for help. He didn't know how he could possibly remedy the situation, but he desperately hoped he'd be able to find a way.

During that night Turtle was given a dream. In the morning the animals all gathered around the base of the big tree to witness the race. Though they were despondent, tired, and discouraged, a few still had a tiny gleam of hope in their eyes.

Turtle walked up, and Eagle condescendingly inquired where Turtle would like the race to begin. Turtle replied that he would like to race from the top of that same tree, and asked Eagle to give him a ride on his back, and when they reached the top, to deposit him there. Eagle agreed, and flew Turtle to the top of the tree.

When the race started — a race to the ground — Turtle pulled in his arms, legs, head and tail, and dropped like a stone. Eagle tried his best, folding his wings in and diving down head first, but he was no match for Turtle. Turtle was fearless, plummeting straight down and hit the ground first, beating Eagle!

The animals were overjoyed and let out a tremendous cheer for Turtle. Turtle had landed with a thwack on his hard back, jarring him badly, and he lay there, stunned and seeing stars.

His friend Muskrat came to tend him, saying *"Are you alright? You've won, and released all the animals from the tyranny of Eagle! Now, what will you decide for all of us?"*

Turtle arose and happily told all the animals that all living beings would now be free to live their own lives, building nests for their young, finding food for their families, caring for their own places, and keeping balance in the world.

In the future, he said, the people-to-be were to learn to do the same. All the animals rejoiced (except for Eagle), and Turtle and Muskrat returned to the river that was their home.

I was stunned by my dream's relationship to the story, so vividly reflecting the end of the tale. Turtle knew why he had to act, though he didn't know how. His rational mind offered no clues. His determination, caring, and perseverance were undaunted. He sought counsel, and listened — until his way became clear.

This is the inquiry: What is the particular talent within each of us, as unique and unlikely as Turtle's, that might be the unforeseen gift that could help free the world?

May we too learn to embrace all our ways of knowing — listening for the wisdom of body, heart, intuition, and mind. May we tend fully to our relational intelligence, so that we might re-nourish the soil and regrow our roots to form an underground web of connection with each other, like aspen trees do — to help anchor us for the coming storms.

PROMPTS FOR DEEPENING LEARNING
THROUGH REFLECTION, WRITING OR DISCUSSION

Listening for Guidance:
Mystery, Intuition and Dreamtime

THEMES
- Indigenous Ways of Knowing
- Learning through Creativity
- Reclaiming Intuition and Dreamtime

PROMPTS

Has an encounter with another's culture ever evoked learning for you, beyond your rational mind, and if so, can you describe what you felt, sensed, learned?

Recall a time when you discovered something about yourself through creativity. It could be something you or another made, wrote, sang, or danced.
- How was it to learn from that artist part of yourself, rather than through thinking?

How do you experience your own intuition? Recall a specific time in your life when you've felt it.
- Where in your body do you sense it? Is it mostly auditory, kinesthetic, or visual?
- Are there any times of day or year when it seems strongest?
- Has your moon time or that of another near you corresponded to any heightened sensitivities? If so, please describe them.

Think of a time or situation when a dream or an intuition guided you and may have affected the outcome.

Now consider a time when you didn't follow your intuition or instincts. What happened?

Share a story based on an experience with intuition, dreamtime, instincts, or synchronicity.

CULTIVATING RELATIONAL INTELLIGENCE

What lies at the heart of many of the toughest issues that we face, both as a culture and as a species? Innovative environmental solutions and strategic social models are crucial for us to illuminate a future landscape of hope, but they alone won't be enough to alter our collective course. What's ultimately required is a change of heart, a shift in how we relate to each other and to the whole of the living Earth. For me, the root source of our gravest challenges — both socially and environmentally — is a crisis of *relationship*.

The tear in our relational fabric is apparent in every area of our lives. The evidence is all around us — from the corporate invasion of our schools to the profusion of divorce and domestic violence; from toxic factory farming to the loss of civil liberties; and from deforestation and global warming to people making war on each other all over the world. We've got a lot to learn about how to be in relationship in a way that is not only enduring, but can help us to heal our personal and societal wounds.

In times of drastic change, like the one we're living through now, the social philosopher Eric Hoffer said: "It is the learners who inherit the future. The learned usually find themselves equipped to live in a world that no longer exists." How, then, can we enhance and accelerate our learning about cultivating conscious kinship?

First, we might stop idolizing rational intelligence to the exclusion of our other capacities to relate to the living world. As the biologist Candace Pert noted: "We have bodies for other reasons than to transport our heads around." A wealth of additional information might be available to us, if we also valued the abundant physical, emotional, and intuitive cues we receive. Western culture has long over-emphasized the importance of rational intelligence or IQ.

Unfortunately for most of us, re-orienting ourselves toward a broader focus that integrates emotional or relational intelligence means swimming against the tide. For many centuries throughout our history the value of emotional feeling, sensing, and other relationship skills have been vastly underrated, derided, or even scorned. Most often they have been relegated to the disrespected world of "intuition" or sentimentality, and ascribed mostly to the women, children, and the elderly. Our other ways of knowing, through our hearts, hands, and spirits, have become weakened from disuse and are often internally discounted, especially by ourselves.

How, then, can we reorient ourselves to reclaim those gifts, or ways of listening and learning? How can we bring a full spectrum of our capacities into play to become more adept at navigating and sustaining respectful relationships? How might we bring them into how we live, not only with each other, but also with ourselves and with the sacred and diverse community of life upon which we all depend?

"The real voyage of discovery," Marcel Proust wrote, "lies not in seeking new landscapes, but in having new eyes." To have "new eyes" to seek a deeper understanding of what it means to become more fully human, let us look to the biology of love. Ultimately, I believe, there is nothing with as big a capacity as love to turn our collective path towards one that is life-affirming, and to reweave wholeness into our tattered social fabric.

What do we really know about the current state of relationship and how it manifests among our families, organizations, and institutions? We live in a culture that cultivates despair instead of joy, numbness in lieu of feeling, and separation in place of intimacy; a culture that seems to believe that the domination of mind over feeling is our civilization's crowning glory and that material gain is more important than emotional fulfillment. While romance novels and bridal magazines flourish, divorce rates remain staggeringly high. In our educational system, children are taught to memorize facts, equations, and theorems but not how to cultivate and retain friendships, respect each other's perspectives, or navigate the demands and challenges of intimacy. In business and governance, historically the brightest, most powerful debaters or strategists have held sway, though that's beginning to change.

However, this is not a contest between head and heart — that peace treaty is long overdue. The most encouraging news is that our capacity to love is something we can learn.

A collaboration among three San Francisco Bay Area professors — Thomas Lewis, Fari Amini and Richard Lannon — resulted in a remarkable book, *A General Theory of Love*. This team combed the neuro-scientific literature, seeking to learn how to map human relationships, hoping to learn about the biology of love. As science has begun, only recently, to explore the brain's mysteries, some surprising insights are emerging.

Their research suggests that it is the supremely complex activity of the one hundred billion neurons of the human brain and the pathways they form — all working together in a collaborative way — that determine the nature of love. The brain is actually comprised of three distinct sub-brains, each with a very different function and chemistry. The oldest brain, sometimes popularly called the "reptilian" brain, is the innermost brain — a bulbous extension of the spinal cord.

It is the one most directly responsible, physiologically, for our survival. It regulates our breathing, swallowing, and heartbeat, and also prompts our swift reaction to an abrupt movement or loud noise. It is the only brain that reptiles are known to have, and emotionality was not believed to be in its repertoire. (Though biologists and anthropologists have since learned that reptiles have emotions, too. We're not as different as we may imagine.)

The brain that's wrapped around it, that is unique to mammals like us, developed about a hundred million years ago. It is called the limbic brain. In addition to having different ways than reptiles of bearing our young, we relate to our young differently by integrating nurturing communication that plays into the relationship, while reptiles often exhibit disinterest or even sometimes cannibalism in interacting with their young.

The most recently developed brain, the neocortex, provides us with our capacity for problem-solving. Speaking, writing, planning, and reasoning all stem from the neocortex, as do the experience of our senses and our conscious motor control, what we sense as our capacity to reason and our "will."

Problem-solving is a wonderful thing and is part of what we at Bioneers celebrate, but we seem to have gone a bit overboard on the neocortex express. We now undervalue emotions, since our culture, in the authors' words, "promotes analysis over intuition, logic above feeling. And, as it exalts reason, this nation buries its emotions ..." — a practice that currently results in, among other things, the largest use of mood- altering drugs in the history of humankind. Our elevated reverence for the intellect — the reason of the neocortex — has led us to a state of relational illiteracy, of impoverished heart-centered passion and compassion.

As Albert Einstein noted: "We should take care not to make the intellect our god: it has, of course, powerful muscles, but no personality. It cannot lead; it can only serve." Our limbic system, which houses our physical repertoire for emotional relationship, develops in a reciprocal loop with our parents, and later with others. As parents are attentive, providing mirroring, feedback, and responsiveness, the physical architecture of relatedness is built structurally into a child's neural system. As a child matures, its limbic resonance becomes more autonomous, but it is still developed, strengthened like a muscle, from emotional exchanges with others — peers, friends, and lovers.

All healthy people, regardless of age, require shared intimacy to be whole and healthy. Essential in defining who we are, our neural architecture places loving relationships at the very center of our lives, where — alive, generative, and warm, they have the power to stabilize our very nature. Not having an attuned mother is an utter nonevent — perhaps even a blessing — for a reptile, but for a mammal, it is a shattering injury to the fragile and complex limbic brain. For people, neural patterning happens early in life, and then tends to reinforce itself. For those of us who have had a traumatic early childhood, without a course correction, we are wired to repeat the same emotional experiences we've grown up to expect.

Many of those who grew up with neglect or abuse, whose lives have been punctuated with loss, abandonment, and rage, have one thing in common: a profound, lifelong familiarity with the pain of separation.

The sense of prolonged separation or relationship rupture is a huge physical strain for any mammal to endure, as it causes us to produce dramatically higher rates of cortisol, the body's major stress hormone.

The stability that intimate relationships provide also impacts both our individual and societal capacity for discernment. As the authors note: "When a society loses touch with limbic bedrock, spin wins."

The great good news is this: limbic connections can still be grown, even after a childhood of abuse and neglect. The capacity for love cannot be grown through any amount of reasoning or will, but warm human contact can trigger the release of pleasure-inducing neuro-hormonal secretions in the brain, a feel-good sensation that is potent magic indeed. Developing a living relationship is a form of therapy that takes time; it's not adapted to the "quick fix" orientation of our culture. Rebuilding neural pathways requires that the formerly traumatized person find enduring care, appreciation, and love in others.

Sustaining a relationship demands care, attention, and sensory inputs that are visceral, vivid, recurring, and frequent. In a relationship, we can change each other, depending upon the strength of our limbic connection. The encouraging revelation of our mammalian legacy is this capacity for limbic revision: the ability to change and expand the people we love, emotionally. In this way who we are and who we become is dependent — in large part — on whom we love. And, as Dr. Martin Luther King, Jr. put it: "Along the way of life, someone must have sense enough and morality enough to cut off the chain of hate. This can only be done by projecting the ethic of love to the center of our lives, since love is mankind's most potent weapon for personal and social transformation."

In witnessing the lifeways, cultures, and practices of most Indigenous Peoples, we are reminded that they strengthen their relationships to the Earth and all the elements of life through dances, ceremonies, and rituals that reinforce those connections regularly. In the evolution of lifelong couples or friends, they often testify to the ways they have healed each other's prior wounds, and grown each other. Children raised in Waldorf schools have stronger relationships to their own creativity and inner lives, and in turn to others, as a result of that system's emphasis on growing the whole person. Youth who experience trainings in nature and school gardens are often more sensitized to their relational skills than those who've only experienced urban realities. The rapid growth of mindfulness and other meditation practices that cultivate the mind's stillness and value deep listening are improving peoples' capacity to accept what is, and to receive guidance. These alternative ways of living and relating, emerging and proliferating throughout the world, are among the most hopeful realities we've got to build on.

A more relational orientation is peeking over the horizon in a wide range of domains and disciplines. Increasingly, research is revealing the value of whole-body learning, proving that our entire neural networks and our emotions are profoundly involved in all thought and in how we relate to the world and create meaning.

New communications disciplines can offer a helpful framework through which to revisit and develop our "relational musculature." The emerging field of nonviolent communication, for example, suggests that in situations of conflict we track the emotions that lie beneath the content of the words. By responding receptively to the emotional message — and not the verbal or mental one — embattled moments can become swiftly defused, creating a real opening for people to question their previous positions and reach resolution.

Promising relational social technologies are emerging in many fields. Thanks in large part to the late Candace Pert's work on the "molecules of emotion," the study of emotional intelligence, or EQ, is expanding rapidly. People who have a higher "EQ" tend to have happier, more productive and fulfilling lives. EQ is defined as "the ability to perceive emotions, to access and generate emotions to assist thought, to understand emotions, and to reflectively regulate emotions so as to promote emotional and intellectual growth."

Cultivating our capacity to step outside of our emotional reactions and noting them more dispassionately might offer the time and space needed to assess a number of possible responses, in order to select the one that's most relationally attuned. With a history of relations that have reinforced hierarchy, domination, and disrespect as the norm, we have a lot of unlearning to do. To alter our orientation to one of partnership, collaboration, and reciprocity will require real commitment, practice, and patience.

As products of a culture that has prized individualism and separation, this is far easier said than done. Ask anyone who's been in a long-term relationship. Based on my own relationship, which is blessed with both co-creativity and shared vision, I can honestly say it's the hardest spiritual work I know…and the most rewarding. When we seem to hit an impasse, or a place where we vehemently disagree, if I can step back from my reactive response, drop into my heart, and focus on my willingness to alter my perspective instead of my need to be right, the story changes and we may again find common ground.

But I believe that our biological orientation toward relationship, and what biologist E.O. Wilson calls *biophilia* — that innate affinity that life has for life — strengthens our likelihood of success. As human beings, we're built for relationship. Our young remain dependent far longer than most other creatures, and our neural systems and limbic brains are hardwired for empathy, compassion, and connection. We're a highly adaptable species, and one of our finest adaptive strategies is as mimics.

Fortunately, we have an abundance of relational intelligence to learn from, if only we can humbly accept its tutelage. The natural world is resplendent with symbiotic, long-term, reciprocal relationships: between blossom and pollinator, moisture and mycelium, plants and herbivores. In nature, no one lives in isolation, and the sense of balanced interdependence is palpable in any thriving ecosystem. If we can quiet ourselves long enough to listen, smell, feel, and learn from nature, our survival as well as our joy may depend on our making this shift to bringing a practice of relational learning to the center of our attention.

In the Cherokee language there's no word for the love of an inanimate thing; love is only possible between two sentient beings. Anyone who loves a thing is considered insane, and, both personally and politically, we've paid a very high price for the commodification of nearly everything in our culture; for, as Jeremy Rifkin says, "valuing belongings more than belonging." Fortunately, there are some encouraging signs of change on levels ranging from the personal to the societal.

We have inherited a false separation between our minds and hearts, which are in fact utterly and interdependently linked. As the renowned Chilean biologist and neuroscientist Humberto Maturana wrote: "Love, allowing the other to be a legitimate other, is the only emotion that expands intelligence."

This is my prayer for us in this pivotal time. May we all attend to reuniting our heads, hearts, and hands, taking some time to be receptive, suspend judgment, and wait patiently for the information that arrives, unbidden. May we practice being still and really listening — to ourselves, to each other, and to the gentle whispers of the living intelligences of the natural world.

To navigate the wild changes ahead to decrease the violence of this tumultuous time and shift our civilization's direction, we will need to invest the same authority and value in our relational intelligence and learning as we've previously given to our intellectual development. If we can do that, we will build a contagious energy that will ultimately lead to real healing and restoration — the restoration of our wholeness as a global community. That evolution may lead to the celebration and flourishing of our deep and fundamental interdependence with each other, other species and the whole interwoven web of creation.

As the Lakota people say, in ending every prayer: *Omatakeosin* — to All Our Relations.

PROMPTS FOR DEEPENING LEARNING
THROUGH REFLECTION, WRITING OR DISCUSSION

Cultivating Relational Intelligence

THEMES

- All our crises are rooted in a crisis of relationship.
- Relational skills are essential to good leadership, and can be learned.
- Expanding intelligence to include wisdom of relatedness, both inside of ourselves and externally with others.
- Relational smarts include body knowing and intuition, and learning from attending to reciprocity in all nature's systems.
-

PROMPTS

In your own experience, have feelings and sensing and other ways of knowing been discounted or undervalued?

- Share a story of when or how you received that message.

What is relational intelligence, how would you describe it? How is it different from "rational" or "linear" intelligence?

- Share or write a specific example of how your relational intelligence serves you in your life or leadership.

Do you tend to prioritize your agenda or "to do" list over tending to your relationships? What effect does this have in your life?

Who taught you to love, and how did they teach you?

- Who teaches you about love now?
- What excites you about the power of love, and what scares you about it?

Do you value your emotions, or only some of them?

- Which emotions seem scary to you, or confusing?
- Which may be your "default" emotions?
- Do you notice any emotions that seem to hide behind others?
- Which emotions would you like to relate to and express more skillfully?

THROUGH DARKNESS, AND INTO VISION

In the darkest, quietest time of year, I was fortunate to experience a retreat called a Winter Dreaming Ceremony. When I learned of the chance to be in the redwoods in the depth of winter, to journey deep inside my own experience in a gentle, skillful, and loving way, all the cells of my body said, "Yes."

There, in sync with the Earth's cycle of hibernation and dreaming, I discovered — or perhaps I remembered — the dimensional creativity and fullness of darkness.

We lay on mats, covered in blankets, deep inside a darkened, womb-like space. In silence, in pitch blackness, eyes open, we practiced "receiving" for several hours, doing nothing but listening and observing with our bodies, our inner sight, and our intuition.

To my surprise, I learned that my notion that darkness might be devoid of substance was utterly unfounded. I discovered that darkness is profoundly peaceful, abundant, and creative, and that turning inward to vision in the depths of winter is exactly what this animal yearns for and is designed to do.

I found that vision can be what you see in the dark.

In working with women leaders, I've seen how powerfully and swiftly we can see, hear, and reflect each other into flourishing, that often the act of seeing another's full magnificence and reflecting it to her honestly can help her more fully see herself.

As a facilitator, I have learned the value of active listening, and I have discovered that more of me can be useful in inviting others to realize their own greatness. I have realized that we call each other into fullness — into healing and strength and greater leadership with our eyes, with our dreams and intuition, and with the insight of our inner vision.

One spring a few years ago, I began to notice that my eyesight was getting worse. An MRI revealed a tumor behind my right eye that was rapidly diminishing my sight, as it was wrapped around my optic nerve.

Tests revealed a startling truth — that my right eye wasn't able to perceive color. A young doctor interpreted my situation and frightened me to the core. He said I'd need surgery very soon, and that there was a danger that I might lose my right eye's vision completely. The most common approach (and what was available in my home state of New Mexico) involved drilling a hole in my skull for the surgeons to be able to biopsy the tumor.

I drove home, deeply shaken, and shared my news with Kenny. We spent the night worrying, tossing and turning, and I awoke pre-dawn, in darkness. The first thing I heard was a soft rain spattering on our roof, which is rare at night and always evokes joy and gratitude in the desert. Next, I realized that Kenny was sitting on the edge of our bed, his head in his hands, weeping.

I reached for him, and we held each other, riding a pure wave of emotion in our love, shock, and dread. I was thankful for how we were together and for the mutual expression of our love, after weathering the twists and turns that come with any long marriage.

Then, the sun broke over the horizon. As I watched, a huge rainbow spread brilliantly across the sky. The moment was crystalline, magic, and filled with a sacredness I have come to know as Gaia, or Mother Life. I knew that I would somehow make it through this journey.

Some weeks later, I had the least-invasive, most successful surgery I could possibly have wished for. Mysterious grace, relationship, and synchronicity led me to find the optimal doctors for my treatment, who used endoscopic technologies guided by a camera. With exquisite skill and care, they were able to successfully remove the tumor through my nose, in outpatient surgery, without any external cutting or wounding.

Though my optic nerve had been damaged, which meant that my right eye's vision might not fully recover, they assured me that over time it would largely return.

Returning home, I embarked upon a journey of healing, learning to become an expert on my body's own needs. Since this strange science fiction surgery I'd received left me with no visible scars, this became a very intimate, interior endeavor. It asked me to focus all my vision inwardly, to listen intently to address the invisible internal bruising, aching, and inflammation.

My color vision returned, gradually but incrementally, subtly and slowly. Time has become essential to my healing and the reclaiming of my vision. I surrendered to my body's own pacing and needs.

There was no amount of ego, will, or clock-time that could serve me in this process, any more than we can hasten a fruit to ripen or rush a flower to bloom. It seems that healing invariably takes more time than anyone imagines, and so I am being reshaped by patience, watching and listening.

Like water nourishing a landscape, if I slow down, I can go deeper. This shift in my inner pacing, staying attuned to my body's needs, is helping me come home to my self.

Another of the gifts of this underworld journey is discovering that healing my vision requires rest, and that rest is more than the absence of activity. In a similar way that darkness involves far more than only the absence of light, I had to learn how to surrender and commit myself — fully and consciously — to the benefits and gifts of resting.

As the famous mystic, theologian and Trappist monk Thomas Merton wrote in *Conjectures of a Guilty Bystander*: "The rush and pressure of modern life are a form, perhaps the most common form, of innate violence. To allow oneself to be carried away by a multitude of conflicting concerns, to surrender to too many demands, to commit oneself to too many projects, to want to help everyone in everything is to succumb to violence. More than that, it is cooperation with violence. The frenzy of the activist neutralizes his work for peace. It destroys her own inner capacity for peace. It destroys the fruitfulness of our own work, because it kills the root of inner wisdom which makes work fruitful."

I've learned that rest comes in many flavors and textures. For repair and for inviting vision, it likes solitude and stillness, and sometimes communing with an animal, a tree, or a cup of tea. It savors emptiness, stillness, and the invitation to welcome whatever comes. There are no instructions for rest's fulfillment; I could learn its needs only by tracking, observing, and listening inwardly.

May we practice surrendering to Mother Life's own rhythms and pacing for healing ourselves and our cultures. May we practice humbly listening, sensing, and watching for what our bodies and the Earth's know, want, and need. May we practice actively seeing each other with our inner eyes, and in so doing invite each other toward fullness, fruition, and flourishing.

May we give ourselves wholeheartedly to loving, tending, and celebrating *all* of our Earth relatives, so that our children's children might still know whales, elephants, bears, giraffes, tigers, lions, orangutans, bonobos, and old-growth forests, pristine grasslands, clean flowing rivers, and bountiful, life-enhancing oceans.

Awomen, Amen, Aho.

PROMPTS FOR DEEPENING LEARNING
THROUGH REFLECTION, WRITING OR DISCUSSION

Through Darkness Into Vision

THEMES

- The gifts in not knowing, faith, darkness, and vulnerability.
- Turning toward (instead of away from) Shadow wounds and uncertainty.
- The value of receiving loving care when you need it, and letting it in.
- The importance of rest and taking time for healing.

PROMPTS

Have you faced a health or other life or loss challenge that took you to a dark, disorienting, or frightening place?

- What did you learn from the experience? Share or write about it.

What arises in you when you don't know what to do?

- Do you ask for help, and if so, are you able to receive it?
- What helps you to center yourself when there's chaos around you?

Reflect on a time when you may have prayed, asked for help, or felt lost. Perhaps you sang or danced your prayer, or just said it internally. Notice what you turned to for comfort, to anchor you in a storm. These reference points can help stabilize us, whenever we need grounding.

Do you become impatient when your body or psyche needs time to heal?

- What could help you to change that pattern in yourself?
- How does uncertainty or mistrust in the natural process manifest in you?

Our need for rest, self-care, and renewal is a theme throughout this book. Take a moment to think about when you last took a break, slowed down, rested, took a nap, did nothing at all.

- Might you be able to take 10 minutes today to relax and rest?
- What comes up for you? What gets in the way?

FROM MOURNING INTO DAYBREAK

How will we ever see daybreak without mourning?

If we don't feel what hurts, surrender to its demands,
      speak the wound,
how can we really begin to heal?

When my father died,
I felt the rock I stood on
      suddenly gone, my identity lost, in free fall.

A friend warned it might take a year for me to heal.
It took longer, and
I was grateful for the crystalline time.

Long, elastic months of feeling transparent,
      of squinting at the striking brightness
      of colors, lines, and light,
of oscillating between emptiness and attunement,
      the tenderness of tears always a breath away.

I was appalled to discover our illiteracy toward death,
   and envied a Japanese tradition I'd heard about,
of wearing a black armband for a year
    following the loss of a loved one,
so that everyone knows not to treat you in the usual way.

Walking in the shimmering New Mexico light,
    a huge crow swoops to meet me.
His large beak stuttering open,
    he croaks his hello, frog-like,
      focused on me, inciting a conversation.

When I respond, he flies closer, perches to stare at me,
    black eyes reflect red against shiny indigo feathers.

He caws in clusters of three,
    his wings inflating with each inhale,
Cccaaaawwwww, cccaaawww, ccccaaawwww.

My responding calls intrigue him, and we converse,
    an arc of connection cutting through
      the apple-crisp autumn air.

He pauses, turning his head to an improbable angle
    to suck water through his long thin beak
      from the shallow pool puddled in the cement birdbath.

I wonder if he is a bird of sorrow,

      or a creature of connection,

           and immediately I know he is both.

I learned this duality from my father,

      a man whose lion heart was far too big

           for the losses his love suffered in its youth.

But his affection was a tender bath of papa-love,

      the sun I basked in when I was small,

           arms I knew I could count on.

Isn't it strange,

      how unspeakably beautiful life becomes

           when death draws near?

It hovers close now, all the time,

      with extinctions everywhere,

1800 species disappearing every day —

      my mind reels at it, staggering.

The tundra melting,

      trees tilting drunkenly as they lose their ground,

entire cultures losing their lifeways,

      the terrain too erratic for hunting anymore.

Who mourns these losses?

How can we not go mad with grief?

Afraid I'll start wailing, I rock inwardly, and don't stop.
Yearning to speak out, I feel fearful.
The voices within me are at once so young, agitated,
       and also ancient, sitting stone-still and calm.

They know the words that must be spoken, but
       giving them voice raises quaking fear within me.
I ask that the elder hold the young one,
       to lend her stillness, solidity, to offer her strength.

How will we grieve
   for the vividly colored corals bleached white,
         for the animals brutally hunted,
            for all those whose habitats have been logged
    to make mail-order catalogs, phonebooks,
      toilet paper, and newspapers?

    The crone wants to shake us all awake, screeching
    Don't you get it?
    This is no time for small talk.
    This is a time for mythmaking.
    This is a time for epic poetry.
    This is a time to tell the tales
       that will become our compass
         for the days ahead.

A time to remember the grace
      and celebrate the magic
            that infuses and informs this world.

We live on the only planet we know of
      where the sun and moon appear the same size,
the only planet where an eclipse is possible.

      Doesn't that seem like instructions to you?

To awaken from this self-induced slumber,
      to emerge from this contracted isolation,
we've got to drink down the darkness
      and dive to our deepest fathoms,
peel off our fancy garments
      of presumed protection
to land at the bottom, naked, cold, and bruised,
      with nowhere to go but up.

Time to shed the venom that got us here,
      the red rage of blame and shame,
and choose instead to embrace the outrage that
      rises, pure and clean, up through our feet,
that draws us to our full height,
      knowing what must be done,
igniting us to stand for what we love.

How else can we begin the healing?

Indra's web is dangling
        and can't be repaired with Band-Aids.
Only our tears can begin to mend its shattered strands,
        tears and giving ourselves to keening, pining, grieving
mourning how much is dying,
        mourning so that the light can return.

The revolution must have dancing, women know this.
The music will light our hearts on fire,
The stories will bathe our dreams in honey
        and fill our bellies with stars.
The interlacing of our souls enlarging our humanity,
        our rhythms will merge with the heartbeat of the Earth.

What breaks the mourning open for me?
It shines through my connections, my friends, my kin
        some who are human, and some who are not.

I soar in the sea,
glide stealthily among sea turtles and
        swoop over snowpack like an eagle.

I am lifted by the courageous uprisings
        of women and girls,
and of the emerging voice of the feminine within us all.

And I am strengthened
        by my kinship with the land,
with the high desert hills of New Mexico.

At dusk, I wander down the arroyo by our house.
Further up the same canyon,
      flanked by crisscrossing dogs chasing scents,
            a crow swoops low over my left shoulder, cawing.

At the bottom I stop, standing still on a sandy spit
      savoring the dry, clean air of the ponderosa forest.
Glancing down, a perfect white shell catches my eye,
      spiraling pristinely,
speaking to me in sacred whispers of a life long before my own.

As my friend Akaya Windwood reminds me,
      the world shifts every time a woman speaks her truth.

May it be so.

PROMPTS FOR DEEPENING LEARNING
THROUGH REFLECTION, WRITING OR DISCUSSION

From Mourning Into Daybreak

THEMES
- How we find healing: the necessity of grieving what we have lost and are losing.
- The power of losing our moorings, when we lose someone close, to be reborn in a new or different way.
- Identifying and listening for the council of voices within ourselves.

PROMPTS

Reflect on how you think about, relate to, and talk about death. Then consider how you feel about the big losses we face collectively: Creatures. Family. Climate. Oceans. Violence. Forests. Refugees.
- Are your ways of relating to these losses and death connected?

Our culture doesn't offer many opportunities to feel, yet we're living through times when waves of emotion are frequent and intense.
- How do you give yourself space, permission, or practices to feel the emotions that arise in you?
- How might you tamp them down, or avoid or deny them?

Reflect on or write about how you disconnect from, or relate to these emotions. If needed, how might you shift the pattern?

Do you ever sense a circle of characters within you, and if so, can you listen for their voices, or intuit their characters? Perhaps they are different ages, or from different genders or species or traditions.

- How might you deepen your relationship to the varied facets of yourself, to help liberate greater expression?

The theme of healing runs through these last two pieces.

- How does personal healing relate to leadership?
- How do you resource yourself so you can stay present to grieving, either personally or societally, and keep going?
- And if you feel anger or outrage, how do you express and allow for that in a healthy way?

REINVENTING LEADERSHIP
Reclaiming the Feminine

Interview with Lauren Schiller,
Host of "Inflection Point"
a podcast about how women rise up.

The following is edited excerpts of a longer interview from May, 2017.

Lauren Schiller: As you made your way through your career and discovered what your skills and talents were, did you think of yourself as a leader? Did you have a certain style that you were trying to create or emulate?

Nina Simons: I don't think I ever thought of myself as a leader, or not until very recently. Now that I can reflect back on it, I think that in some ways my tendency to be extroverted and my love of connecting with people was a tremendous skill and asset for me, and it encouraged a kind of natural leadership in me. I followed what I did well and what I enjoyed, and that meant building teams of people and helping groups orient toward a common vision and a common goal.

With Seeds of Change, I remember discovering that I had a knack for business although I had never been to business school. Learning that I was good at managing budgets and writing business plans was a total surprise to me, and what I realized was that as long as I was really honest about saying what I didn't know and that the people who I was working with were OK with that, then I could stumble my

way along and learn as I went. Those natural pragmatic talents that
I had around business and people served me well, and I didn't think
much about it until my late thirties, when I was acknowledged by a
magazine, *The Utne Reader*, for being an up-and-coming leader. And
I remember being simultaneously honored and horrified. I felt so
uncomfortable about it.

I wasn't even sure why I was so uncomfortable. I realized
afterwards I felt like it painted a target on my chest and it felt egotistical
to me in a way that made me squirm. It felt like a label that I had never
aspired to. And yet I knew from my work with Bioneers that what the
world needed was for us all to become leaders.

I wondered whether, if I had this reaction to being called a leader,
then maybe other people do, too. The more women I talked to, the
more I learned that most of us have a really negative reaction to calling
ourselves leaders. As I began to unpack that, I realized that I had all kinds
of belief systems, images, and ideas (that I had never consciously adopted,
but that were in me nonetheless) about what leadership was and what it
looked like. And I didn't want to be any of those things.

*LS: It's so interesting — especially nowadays when everyone is trying to
get 15 minutes of fame through a personal brand on social media. People
are putting as many photos of themselves and selfies out there as they
possibly can. I mean, talk about putting a target on your chest, and then
being featured in a magazine as an up-and-coming leader under 40. I
would imagine many people probably aspire to that as a career goal, right?
And yet your reaction to it was so negative.*

NS: I think part of that was because I grew up with a model in my
head that said service to others is good and selfishness is not. As a

result, my sense of identity was really built around being of service to the greater good. And also, I'd had the gift of producing Bioneers for many years, and witnessing and meeting hundreds of leaders from all backgrounds and walks of life. I certainly didn't want to be a leader if that meant being aggressive and dominating, charismatic, hierarchical, and putting other people down. Those were my previous associations with leadership, but many of the figures who spoke at Bioneers weren't like that, so I thought, 'Well, who are the leaders who really inspire me? If I can get clear about that and understand what they are doing, I can begin to see models I can emulate and perhaps grow into.'

What I found when I looked for themes and patterns was that the leaders I respected and admired most were humble. They were leading change because of something that they really loved and felt passionate about, and most often they didn't have formal training to do it. No one gave them a degree or a job or a crown, but they served something they really believed in. Through that devotion and focus and passion, they attracted other people to get involved, and in many cases they led collaboratively. They led by raising up other leaders. They were not really interested in being in the spotlight. Their goal — contrary to the current Instagram and Facebook world — was to save a redwood forest or sea turtles and the ocean or to create peace in the world. And if I was going to be leader, that was the kind of leader I aspired to be.

As a result of that inquiry, I co-edited with Anneke Campbell an anthology book called *Moonrise the Power of Women Leading from the Heart*, which is an homage to my mentors.

LS: And when you were exploring all these leaders, were these all women, or did you start with both men and women?

NS: I have to admit to having had a certain bias for women at that point. I had an epiphany moment earlier in my life when I was turned on to a film called *The Burning Times* that tells the story of the 300-year period in European history where millions of women were systematically persecuted and tortured, and many were burned at the stake for the supposed crime of being witches.

The film changed my worldview because for the first time I saw that all of the problems that I had learned about from Bioneers could be seen as a function of the imbalance between the masculine and the feminine in our culture.

Investigating further, I learned that women had owned more wealth in Europe than men before that period, but not after. That centuries-long war that the church sustained against women created a huge transfer of resources from women to men. Also, a number of social systems and institutions that had largely been under the purview of women (folk healers, herbalists, midwives, etc.) were radically upended and reinvented by men. By the end of the "Burning Times" only men could practice medicine, for example.

Of course, these events occurred in Europe, but this patriarchal legacy has affected women everywhere. For instance, in Central and South America, and throughout Africa, colonialism brought systematic persecution of women folk healers, as well.

With the emergence of Christianity, European culture shifted away from a largely earth-based, polytheistic culture to a patriarchy where religion was practiced in a church and led by a priest who intermediated between people and the divine. From what had been a direct, widely shared, community-wide connection with nature and the sacred, most forms of spiritual practice became mediated by male authority figures, and women lost much of their previous authority and autonomy. The period of the "Burning Times" was the final brutal, violent nail in the coffin of that process.

It's a huge story, and one that I believe explains a lot. I did have a bias toward women when I began seeking models of new leadership styles. I saw that embedded gender bias or lopsidedness as being equally true in men as it is in women. In my view, regardless of our gender, we all have that internal bias that needs to be healed and rebalanced, if we are to live healthy and fully effective lives.

That said, I found that there were some wonderful men who were also personifying leading from the heart, and it became important to me to include them in the book. My publisher was very uncertain and said: 'Are you sure? This is a women's book. Why are we putting men in it?' I said: 'Because this is a model of leadership that anyone can practice, so we must lift these men up as models for others to see.'

LS: That just solidifies the idea that none of us is one thing or the other, that we can carry both "gendered" traits with us, and we don't always have to behave in the future the way we've behaved in the past.

NS: Well, that's for sure. One of the gifts of being human is our capacity for change. What I am advocating is what I would call "blended" or "full-spectrum" leadership, in that I want to be able to draw from a full spectrum of all my human capacities, which of course includes everything within our humanity, from yin to yang. It includes a full array of ways of being. Thankfully, I see younger generations as being already much more fluid in that spectrum than people my age, but it's clear to me that for us to meet this moment of life on earth that's asking so much from us in leadership, we need all of ourselves present, and that means addressing the shadow of women's leadership, which I think is part of that root story.

LS: Let me ask you this: What would you say that the things people value in a leader are, and what percentage of them would you say are considered masculine traits?

NS: I think that the traits people valued in leaders of yesteryear were rationality, decisiveness, aggression, and strength, as well as endurance, stoicism, and perseverance. Not that any of those things are bad — they're all great. There's a great book called *The Athena Doctrine* which describes how of the huge data pool of people that they polled in 13 nations around the world, 67 percent said the world would be a better place if more people led like women. What they are referring to is that the leaders that are being prized now are being appreciated for their capacity to listen, their open-mindedness, for their ability to stay calm in stressful and challenging situations, for their emotional and relational intelligence, and for their ability to evaluate context and the big picture and consider complex dynamics.

I think that what *The Athena Doctrine* is pointing to is that there's evidence from all sectors that the more women there are in leadership in corporations and on boards, the better the bottom lines of those enterprises are and the more ethical their governance. In governance and diplomacy, the more women are involved, the more peaceful things tend to be. The evidence is consistent and pretty astounding, coming from every sector and direction. It's important to note that this is not about putting down men. It's about saying we're all in a giant shift in relation to those gendered definitions that we've all absorbed without questioning them previously. One of my favorite metaphors comes from some indigenous groups who say that the bird of humanity has been trying to fly with only one wing for far too long and needs now to be balanced for all of us to survive and thrive.

LS: That's just such a great visual. I can see the bird flying in circles but not getting anywhere. And I would say that pretty much sums up the state of affairs at this particular moment.

NS: Although my other favorite metaphor is that we're living through a time when the dying dinosaur of the patriarchy is flailing its tail and doing as much damage as it knows how to do on its way out, and it's scary and unsettling and is asking a lot of all of us.

LS: It's so true. And one of the ways that it's manifesting itself — at least from what I've observed and what I've heard — is that women who try and lead "like men" are experiencing a backlash against that; they're actually not rewarded for working in that way. And that's now a bind, like 'What am I supposed to do it if that's the way we're supposed to lead, but I'm going to get penalized for being like a man?' If we can start to embrace some of these other ways of approaching leadership and having that be valued it certainly seems like a step in the right direction.

NS: I completely agree. It takes a lot of personal courage to do that, because it's risky. And the truth is there's a lot of implicit bias in all of us. I had an interesting experience recently: a young woman who had taken one of our women's leadership trainings and who is a consultant in the Bay Area contacted me about a company that she was consulting to and she said, 'They've asked me to give them a proposal to shift so that in five years they're going to be known as one of the best places for women to work. Will you help me?' And I said, 'Yes, but do they have any idea what they're taking on?' The more we talked, what became apparent was that it's not just about adopting women-friendly and family-friendly policies, although those are really important. What about educating the men? I mean you really have to shift the whole system to truly address gender bias, and that's deep work that requires time and commitment.

LS: Will there ever be an end to that? I mean what will it take for that shift to happen, so that we're no longer fighting the system but we've created a system in which both the masculine and feminine are valued?

NS: I think we'll get there, but I'm optimistic by nature. There's evidence of it when I look at couples in their 20s and 30s raising children right now. There's an awful lot more sharing of housework and parenting. I see how beautifully their parents just pass the ball, sharing the workload, and there's no expectation about what's mom's role and what's dad's role. They're just co-parenting. So, I think there's a lot of evidence of change. I think it's a generational shift that we're experiencing. I also think this is related to how we heal from systems of privilege and bias because White privilege and racial bias obviously intersect with gender biases.

Just being a White woman in this country confers privilege, and that privilege creates blinders. It took me a long time to understand that I had privilege compared to women of color and to move beyond guilt or shame about it, so that I could start to try to make a difference and transform that biased system at its roots.

It's very hard to get out of patterns that seem so pervasive, entrenched and 'normal' in our culture. Women all know the experience of being in a mostly-male meeting and initiating an idea or suggestion and having it fall flat and then the guy next to you says the same thing with slightly different language and everybody jumps on it. Every woman around nods her head when someone complains about that because it's something we've all experienced countless times. Men, however, don't notice it when it happens, and it's not anyone's fault as an individual. The challenge is to become aware of the blinders that privilege creates for us.

LS: Tell me about some of the work you've been doing with women's leadership training.

NS: For the last 12 years, we have been developing a program that we called Cultivating Women's Leadership within Bioneers. It's a six-day immersion experience that we invite women to apply for and then select each cohort of 20 women very carefully. We've selected women using a number of criteria. One criterion, for example, was how passionate they are about making change in the world because those are the women we most want to work with. Another is what evidence we can find of this woman being able to influence change in her community. Yet another criterion (which is perhaps the most interesting) is that we've selected each group to optimize for diversity in every way. What that means is that each cohort typically has women ranging in age from their 20s to their 70s or 80s. We've intentionally selected for the most diverse group, across ethnic diversity and class, and across sexual orientation and issue area, sector or discipline.

So, we get a group of women who, in normal life in our country, would never get to encounter each other in a deep way and give them six days to do a lot of deep work both on an individual level and with each other. By the end of the six days, what's been remarkable is that very often those women have bonded really deeply with each other, and they've formed connections that are lasting years later, which is part of our intention. So that's been a journey, and we always knew that it was important to us to have a lot of age and racial diversity in the room.

In the early days of the program, it was harder to attract the mix we wished for, partly because at that time I was doing most of the facilitating with my co-founder Toby Herzlich, who is another White woman. When women of color saw our fliers and saw the program being led by two White women, they likely figured it wasn't for them.

Then I read a book by Linda Tarr Whelan called *Women Lead the Way*. What I learned was that there is social science research that shows that for any members of a minority to fully show up in a group, they need to comprise at least 30 percent of the room. Until they're at 30 percent, they just don't feel flanked enough to take the risks to relax, be outspoken, and really be themselves.

I reflected on that in relation to the percentage of women in our U.S. House and Senate, which is not even remotely close, still well under 20 percent. We decided that from that point forward we would always have a minimum of 30 percent women of color in our groups, and we invited facilitators who are women of color to join us, so that there was always a third facilitator so that one third of us in facilitation was a woman of color. As soon as we did that, we started getting 35 to 40 percent women of color in our trainings. And that's been an incredible teaching for me and really interesting in terms of all the things we're talking about from the boardroom to classrooms to, in this case, learning environments and gathering groups together well.

LS: *Could we apply that 30 percent rule to other situations? You just brought up the House and Senate.*

NS: Yes, I believe so. In fact, our political and economic institutions don't remotely reflect the demographics of our nation, not only in gender but in color and class and in just about every other way. So, yes, reaching at least 30 percent would make a big difference. There's evidence and data that proves it, and quite a few countries are far ahead of us. Some Scandinavian political parties have actual quotas in the 40 to 50 percent range for women candidates, and Sweden's parliament was, last time I checked, around 45 percent women.

There's another piece to this, too. Through the work I've been doing, I've come to believe that mothering is one of the greatest acts of leadership that any woman can do in her life. And we're all trying to recover from a culture that has so systematically devalued mothering and degraded it. Often, I find that mothers who are also leaders who do this work with us are so grateful to have motherhood appreciated as the act of leadership that it is. I'm in awe of mothers, as a woman who is childless by choice. In many ways, I get to mother a lot of women, but in other ways I just look at what women who are mothers do, many of them also juggling leadership roles in the world, and I am just gobsmacked. It's amazing.

LS: How exciting to imagine the generation of kids that are growing up now with really strong models of fathers who can cook and love them and read to them and snuggle with them and who don't chew them out for crying or feeling. It's exciting...As we try and imagine our future, putting a higher value on motherhood is a good thing for many reasons. I think not many people would argue with that, but right now, according to very credible research, if you are a woman and you have a child, your lifetime income is almost certain to be 20 to 30 percent less than a man of same age in the same position.

NS: There was a *New York Times* article recently about Janet Yellen (the former chair of the Federal Reserve Bank) speaking at Brown University. She said that the best thing we could do to grow the economy and develop jobs is to adopt the family-friendly maternity practices and reproductive rights practices that nearly all of Europe has adopted, because it would allow us to support so many more women to be in the workplace. So, in terms of job creation and our nation's economic bottom line, we absolutely need more family-friendly policies and practices.

LS: *I'd love to talk more about how you ultimately embraced your role as a leader after The Utne Reader honored you, why you felt so conflicted about it, and how you came to terms with yourself?*

NS: I had this big turning point moment 20 years ago when I turned 40. I made myself several promises, and one was that I would seek to understand and unpack this leadership conundrum that I'd gotten into. Another was that I decided that I needed to learn to live more from my feminine side, to better balance myself inwardly. All my friends said, 'Are you kidding, you're so feminine.' I said, 'Well it may look that way to you, but on the inside, I can tell you the way I've navigated my adult life has been through what I have experienced as my more masculine qualities.'

I had relied heavily on my intellect, my capacity for strategic thinking and my strong body to power through situations and to persevere at all costs. Many parts of me felt underutilized and under-acknowledged, so I began exploring what they were, and every cell in my body said, "Yes." When I started attending to those under-used parts of me, something deep inside me was feeling affirmed. I began to pay more attention to my dreams and my intuition. Basically, I'd been ignoring my body's wisdom. Part of the inheritance of a biased culture has been that we value the intellect over all of our other ways of knowing.

I went through a conscious process of trying to turn up the volume on all of my other ways of knowing and practice valuing them. Part of how I did that was through gathering and facilitating groups of women.

The first time I gathered women was in 2002. I convened women leaders for a gathering called Unreasonable Women for the Earth. I invited 35 accomplished and very diverse women, letting my intuition guide me. I had no idea what I was doing. I sensed into it and made it all up as I went along. We spent four or five days together in a very beautiful place. Among other outcomes, the very dynamic direct nonviolent-action group, CODEPINK:Women for Peace, emerged from some of the women present during that retreat. I learned that the name you organize under deeply affects the outcome.

LS: So, for you, what came out of it in terms of how you approached the work that you had set out to do?

NS: As I reclaimed all these parts of myself, I saw how women who could embrace and stand with their own vulnerability and their own intuition and their own body wisdom and their dreams and playfulness and humor could mobilize to act. I saw how powerful that could be.

Since I aspired to it, I think I cultivated myself to become more and more like that. In many ways, the Cultivating Women's Leadership retreats of the last 12 years have cultivated me and my colleagues as well as all the women who have been through it. When I started doing those retreats, I had a lot of ideas about what women should do and what kind of leadership was needed. I very quickly disabused myself of those ideas as I realized that women were showing up in more shapes and forms, styles and assignments than I could ever have imagined.

I saw that my job, my purpose, became not to tell anyone what they should do (because it's hard enough for me to know what I should do) but rather to create the conditions for them to discover for themselves how their best expression in the world could manifest (or *womanifest* as we like to say it).

That's given me a lot of hope because I've realized that this great uprising, which we're all part of and which is so urgently needed to save humanity from ourselves, will include many more facets and modalities than I can even dream of. I long ago stopped saying 'to save the Earth,' because the Earth will survive — it may take her two or three million years to get over us — but she'll survive. It's really we who are in danger here, and so leadership is needed, I believe, in as many forms now as there are humans on the planet. There is leadership that we need to learn from all the other-than-human life in the biosphere as well, from the trees and the fungi and the insects and animals and creatures of all kinds.

LS: Would you say that leading from the feminine and leading from the heart are interchangeable expressions or would you define them slightly differently?

NS: I think we're in a time where language can be a trap. Leading from the heart is much more accessible to most people. However, for me, it's not the same because leading from the feminine is bigger than leading from the heart. It includes leading from your connection to the divine or sacred as well, and also from intuition and your body's senses and awareness. I think they're all intelligences that have been chronically undervalued. For me, leading from the feminine includes all those realms, and not just the heart.

LS: It's so refreshing. I just feel like we're living in this world that is being led by fear and that all of the decisions being made at the governmental, corporate, and even sometimes family levels are based on fear. What you're talking about feels like the complete opposite.

NS: Yes, we are living through a time when pretty much anyone alive and paying attention is dealing with some post-traumatic stress. Among young people growing up with climate instability, increasing economic inequality, persistent racial injustice, gun violence, etc., chronic stress is rampant.

What I am interested in is how to develop the capacity for resilience in ourselves as leaders, and some of that means going against the tide. With things speeding up so much, and so much media and information coming at us all the time, it's so important to slow down and go inside for guidance to inform our actions.

There's a very interesting correlation to all this stuff about the feminine that I love and remind myself about often. Carl Jung suggested that the feminine is our interiority and the masculine represents our exterior. When you think about all that fear-based, panic-driven emotion, it's very reactive and externally focused. It's about pursuing some imagined safety or security that probably isn't very real.

The only real security lies inwardly and in our relationships, through a web of connection to the people we love and who love us, and also to the places and creatures we love and whatever it is we love; that's the only real security. We all know that the economy will shed millions of jobs due to technological change and other factors, so the notion that you're going to have a straight up career and then retire with a gold watch is so over. It's not happening anymore.

We need to shift our understanding of what security really means. For me what's also exciting about the path that keeps revealing itself to me is that it involves inviting people into a life of meaning. There's an awful lot of distraction out there. It's part of the work we do in these women's leadership retreats. We do something we call a purpose marathon; it's a very long afternoon during which we engage in a lot of repeated questioning. It's sort of like peeling an onion; you go deeper and deeper inside yourself to notice what really lights you up. What do you really love dearly? What has been a really resonant or important thing for you all your life? What breaks your heart?

I know that when I read stories about whales dying of stomach cancer because of all the plastic inside them, it breaks my heart. When I learn about the rate of extinctions and that a number of large mammal species could go extinct in the coming decades, it really hurts. I don't know or care why that is. I care that it motivates me and that it's a way to help me identify my deepest passion. As I see it, the work of this time is for each of us to find what we're most exactly called to do and then invest ourselves fully there.

I used to be very impatient about finding my path. I asked someone I viewed as a guide how I might become clearer about it. She suggested that I invest in my longing. She said, 'Your longing lives in a chamber behind your heart, and if you invest your attention there, it will attract to you the path that your soul is here to walk.' And I didn't know if I believed in it or not, but I tried it, and I think it works!

LS: Maybe because instead of fighting to figure out what you want, you're embracing figuring out what you want.

NS: Partly yes, but also instead of trying to figure out what I wanted with my head, I invested in my heart's yearning, and it guided me. Einstein said something like: '…we should take care not to make the intellect our god; it has, of course, powerful muscles, but no personality. It cannot lead, it can only serve; and it is not fastidious in its choice of a leader.'

LS: *What's the best advice that you've ever been given about how to slow down?*

NS: A couple of things come to mind. One piece of advice was also about identifying one's purpose, but it's related to how to slow down and how to listen inwardly. I had a wise woman tell me to 'pay exquisite attention inwardly to what makes your flame grow brighter.' She said you have to be very still and pay a lot of attention because sometimes that flame just perks up only for an instant. If you're not paying exquisite attention, you'll miss it. That was great guidance, and it's necessary to slow down to practice it.

The other thing: I'm teaching a workshop on regenerative leadership with a woman who is a wonderful relational mindfulness teacher named Deborah Eden Tull, who lived in a Zen monastery for seven years. I think what she has done is to feminize Buddhist practice, meditation, and Zen by inventing this idea and practice of relational mindfulness, and she's just written a book by that title. She teaches that meditation is the subtlest form of self-love. I can't profess to say that I'm a great meditator because I'm not, but there is a quality of really deep listening inwardly to all the parts of yourself that feels to me like a great way to slow down. The other way that I practice a lot is by being truly present and attentive in nature. I always find that when I'm depressed, stressed, freaked out, or confused, being alone in nature is my solace.

LS: *Thank you so much, Nina.*

PROMPTS FOR DEEPENING LEARNING
THROUGH REFLECTION, WRITING OR DISCUSSION

Reinventing Leadership: Reclaiming The Feminine

THEMES

- Legacy of silencing and diminishing the 'feminine' within ourselves.
- Dissonance between our inner and outer stories, the masks we wear.
- Optimizing engagement among diverse people, perspectives, and orientations.
- How leadership is changing already, globally.

PROMPTS

Who in your life most inspires you to be the kind of leader you want to be, and why?

Learning about the witch burnings in Europe brought me greater understanding of the ongoing, cross-sectoral, and intergenerational influence of patriarchal structures.

- How do you think that legacy may continue to affect our interior stories and collective cultures?
- In what ways are women's voices still shut out, silenced, and/or discounted today?

Regardless of our gender, we all have internal biases that need to be made conscious, so they can be rebalanced. Reflect on your mix of gifts or traits, both in terms of how you treat yourself, and how you show up in the world. What gender biases do you find within yourself? Notice if you judge yourself for lacking or possessing certain traits.

Do you think of mothering as leadership? Why, or why not?

For me, "leading from the feminine" includes feeling sourced from a connection to what I most love, and what's sacred to me.

- How do you experience your connection to the divine?
- What does this have to do with leadership?

PROMPTS FOR DEEPENING LEARNING
THROUGH REFLECTION, WRITING OR DISCUSSION

Embodied and Group Practices for Part I

FULL SPECTRUM TOOLKIT

Create your own image or metaphor -- a toolkit, backpack, treasure chest, nest, carpetbag — in a drawing, painting, or collage. List or draw the particular skills, gifts, and talents you use in your ways of leading, that you keep in your toolkit. You might opt to keep adding to this list as you read this book.

HEALING RELATIONSHIP TO SELF

How might you cultivate greater patience, compassion, and self-love? Create an image or write a phrase or affirmation, or find a quote to remind yourself. Place it where you can see it each day.
Each night, before bed, notice all the things you did that day that you feel good about, including challenges you faced, and appreciate yourself for how you met them. Notice what you want to get better at and give yourself permission and kindness around your learning edges, encouraging yourself to keep stretching, risking, and learning.

DREAMS AND INTUITION

Keep a dream journal. When you have a dream, waking or sleeping, or an intuition, record it in any creative way you prefer, writing or drawing or painting or composing a song. As you do so, what might you discover about yourself, or how you are being guided?

GUIDANCE

Where do you turn to for guidance when you're uncertain, both inwardly and outwardly? Reflect on a person or place you seek out for guidance. Go to that person or place, either in your imagination or actually, and ask for their help. Then be present: wait and listen. Write, dance, or create an artistic expression based in this experience.

CONNECTING WITH NATURE

Go out and experience nature through amplifying your sense of smell, touch, hearing, feeling. Close your eyes: Can you feel the earth under your feet? Notice everything you can hear for one minute, what you smell for another. Notice what you feel on your skin, through your hands or limbs. Feel your breath and appreciate the miracle of your lungs working. Open your eyes and observe something you may not have noticed before. Share or write about what you experienced.

For pairs or groups: Go outside, get into pairs and blindfold one. Remaining silent throughout, lead the blindfolded one to things they might hear, smell, or touch. Then switch roles. Afterwards, share about the experience of leading and being led. How does this relate to leadership?

REST AND RENEWAL

A simple practice to help remember to take it easy: Sit or lie down, and gently focus on your breath. Notice what happens in your body and mind as you slow down. What might help you cultivate greater patience, inner kindness, and self-love? Create an image or write a phrase to remind yourself. Place it where you can see it each day.

EMOTIONAL/RELATIONAL INTELLIGENCE

In a private space, select an emotion that is uncomfortable for you to feel. Reflect on how it played out at home in your family when you were a kid. Notice whether you perceive that same discomfort in others. Now try expressing or acting it out: write it, sing it, dance it, draw it.

PRACTICE GRIEVING

Notice what brings up deep sorrow whenever you think of it and allow yourself permission to fully feel it in your body for a few minutes. Write a grief poem or song or create an image that expresses what you feel in an authentic way.

EXPRESSING YOURSELF OR GIVING VOICE

Remember a time you have been silenced or silenced yourself from fear. What lesson did you draw from this experience? Can you turn it around by expressing your voice in a creative way, through a poem, song, drawing, or dance?

Do you notice yourself adding question marks at the ends of your sentences? If so, you might try experimenting with using periods or exclamation marks instead, to strengthen your ways of expressing what you believe is true and right.

CLARIFYING A SENSE OF PURPOSE

This exercise can help to clarify your path, calling, or purpose.

Sit with a partner and take a moment to get present, centered, and connect. Then ask over and over for three minutes, repeating the question without responding after each answer:

- (Name), what really lights you up? (ask 5-10 times)
- (Name), what do you love most deeply? (ask 5-10 times)
- (Name), what breaks your heart? (ask 5-10 times)

Listen deeply without interruption. When 3 minutes are up, stop and let your partner jot some notes. Reflect back what you heard. Then switch roles. At the end, share with each other what you learned.

PART II

WOMEN'S LEADERSHIP

THE CHALLENGES, THE PATHWAYS, AND THE PROMISE

AT THE FRONT LINES
The Global War on Women

Several years ago, I hosted a panel at the UN Commission on the Status of Women. It was focused on Women, Health, and Extractive Industries, and it featured leaders from around the world.

I already knew that women were frequently on the frontlines, but I had not realized the systematized ways in which corporations globally have targeted women in their efforts to plunder the Earth. I had not fully understood the cascading damages to their communities nor the staggering worldwide extent of the corporate deployment of this gendered tactic.

Whether mining for coal, gems, or metal ores, drilling or fracking for oil, multinationals move into communities that are often rural, and frequently indigenous and low-income. The first thing they do is to establish "man camps" — temporary housing for all the workers they bring from afar. The women in these often-remote regions are the *first* to be impacted. Increasingly rape, sex trafficking, prostitution, and domestic abuse grow to reach epidemic levels.

The local men aren't spared either, as they experience their own inability to protect their women, as well as sharp rises in alcoholism, drug abuse, poverty and joblessness. This not only decimates families while it demolishes landscapes, it destroys entire traditional lifeways, cultures, and languages.

At that UN event, after the panel discussion, women from many nations around the globe rose and spoke. Listening, as I heard these women tell similar stories and speak of their anguish at the destruction of their communities, my stomach roiled in anger. I realized how systemic, entrenched, and brutal the global war on women really is.

When I got calm enough to listen to my heart, however, I was enlivened by their courage, and inspired by the outrage in their voices. I remembered that anger is our body's way of telling us that a boundary has been trespassed. I felt in a deeper way how interconnected their lives, mine and ours, really are.

Indigenous communities worldwide have long been hit especially hard by corporations and governments run amok. They've survived intergenerational histories that have included relocations, broken treaties, boarding schools, forced sterilization, systemic racism, and land theft.

In recent years, many Native Peoples have also been showing the world that they are incredibly resilient, persevering, strategic, and strong-willed. They've been organizing, building power, and fighting back, which is extraordinary after 500 years of brutal oppression, expropriation, and forced attempts to annihilate their cultures, knowledge systems, and ecosystems.

When I fully take this in, integrating what Ta-Nehisi Coates calls the "bloody heirloom" of systemic racial injustice, White supremacy and genocide that pervades the history of this country, I am stunned.

It's not only the rot in the foundations of this nation, but my own prior ignorance of the extent of it. It's the unacknowledged legacy that stuns me — the legacy of theft, deceit, and violence that the U.S. was built upon.

A woman leader of huge heart and spirit that I know, a single mother of three, told me of leaving her home in Oakland one morning. As she left for work, there was yellow police tape across her neighbor's door — a woman she knew had been shot while trying to protect her kids. When she arrived at her workplace in Bayview Hunter's Point, she was stunned to find yellow tape there as well.

Many of our fellow citizens are living in war zones, right here at home. Extreme poverty, environmental degradation, and violence don't just exist in other, distant lands.

At one of our Cultivating Women's Leadership intensives, a majority of the women there had been raped or abused at least once. I wondered about the effects of so much violation, but as our days unfolded, I was struck by their strength, and humbled by their commitments, and their visions and resolve.

Their dignity, their pride in their own recovery and their purposeful ways of transforming themselves and society were so solid, so strong, and so creative that I was awed and inspired by their character.

Violence against women is a global pandemic of immense proportions, and one that's diminishing in some nations, but not in others. Relatively few among us have recognized until recently just how prevalent and widespread it really is.

Nearly thirty years after the UN General Assembly declared a framework for ending global violence against women, little has improved.

Try wrapping your mind around these statistics, (which have barely changed in the past several years), from the United Nations, Catalyst, and the World Health Organization:

- Around the world, at least one third of women — that's a BILLION women — have been beaten, raped, or otherwise physically abused, most often by an intimate partner.

- About 1 in 5 women have experienced that within the past year.

- And 45 countries still have no laws protecting women against domestic abuse.

- 650 million women around the world today were married before reaching the age of 18.

- About 200 million women alive today — many in Africa and the Middle East — are living as victims of female genital mutilation.

- Women perform two thirds of the world's work, while earning only ten percent of global income and owning only one percent of global financial assets.

- Of the billion or so poorest people on earth living in poverty, seventy percent are women.

- No one knows the exact numbers, but, globally, nearly four million people are estimated to be trafficked annually. 99% of them are women and girls. An estimated one million children, mostly girls, are forced into the sex trade each year.

- In the United States, which ranks as 53rd in gender equality after Cape Verde in Africa, at least one in six women is a victim of domestic or sexual assault.

- Among Indigenous Peoples, that number is closer to four of every five.

- Every fifteen seconds a woman is battered, usually by her intimate partner, and it's suspected that only about half of the incidents are reported.

- Among girls between the ages of twelve and sixteen, when their psyches are especially impressionable, 83 percent report having experienced some form of sexual harassment in school.

Overall, as I review the global reports of progress in reaching true gender parity over the last 5-30 years, here's what I see:

There's been progress in women breaking some glass ceilings in politics, and a few in business. Overall, there have been some significant shifts in public awareness, in women speaking up, and in the leadership of women working to end violence and towards equality.

But the advances are far too slow, and sometimes there's backward motion.

Gender parity overall declined between 2020 and 2021. The COVID-19 pandemic was harder on women. A majority of healthcare workers, those losing their jobs, and taking on far more of the unpaid labor involved in parenting and home-making are female.

The activist and playwright Eve Ensler, now known as "V," has dubbed what's happening to women in this time as "Disaster Patriarchy."

According to the World Economic Forum, at the current rate of progress, reaching gender parity will take somewhere between 135 and 267 years from now. We simply cannot afford to wait that long.

Within our female psyches, far too often insidious, self-limiting, culturally reinforced beliefs, fears, and stories keep women from leaving abusive relationships. The promise of a women-led revolution will not happen if we continue to sabotage ourselves and see ourselves as competing with our sisters.

Many of us have been conditioned to *give away* our power — to end our sentences with question marks, or to apologize by habit, when we don't really mean to.

We do these things to please others, because it seems 'safe,' or to avoid conflict. Sometimes we do them simply by habit, without being aware of how they undermine our own sense of self, strength, and agency.

We agree to things we don't really want and then blame and shame ourselves for doing so. Many of us have a hard time asking for what we need, or accepting help when it's offered. We tend to deflect compliments and are often far more comfortable giving than receiving.

It's an arduous and lengthy journey to build the conscious muscle of acceptance, self-respect, and self-love through self-awareness. When we do, we can resist those patterns, and cultivate new ones.

I promise you, though it may seem hard, it is doable. I've found that the payoff is larger and more enduring than any other challenge you might take on.

It's not really our power we're reclaiming, anyway; it's actually the power of life's energy coming through us. It's the power of spirit, the power of Gaia, Of Mother Life, of mystery, and the power of ancestors. It's the power of something far greater than any of us.

Meeting women from Serbia in Taos, New Mexico, I saw light shining from their eyes. While I heard about the horrors of wartime sexual ravages that they had experienced, I could feel the power of their eager and buoyant hearts.

I learned their ancient Kolo dance, a restorative ritual that's been practiced by women since Mesolithic times. The women, encircled tightly, clasp hands over the fronts and backs of each other's wombs and then, very close-knit together, dance for hours. Their ways of dancing and singing together have helped to heal thousands who've been raped and traumatized in their wars.

When women are truly aligned and agree to stand for and with each other — when we agree to have each other's backs and become practice partners — magic becomes possible.

In some Mexican communities, women may enter a lifelong pact to become *comadres*, which includes a promise to care for each other's children, if either of them cannot.

Despite the insidious and deeply encoded beliefs that assign women to the home and child-raising, and away from the risk-taking challenges of leadership, many of us are ready to pull the ripcord that may unleash us all.

To support each other and trust ourselves in ways that give us the confidence of knowing that exactly who and what we already are is enough to risk accomplishing what we care most about.

I've learned that motherhood is among the greatest and most courageous learning curves in life that anyone has ever attempted — whoever imagines that parenting isn't leadership clearly hasn't tried it!

Here's what I found in Cultivating Women's Leadership intensives over the years, among women leaders selected for their diversity in all ways — across age, race, orientation, faith and discipline.

Once the women experience each other in all their dimensional beauty and power, once they hear each other's visions for changing the world, and witness the depth of caring, and the skillfulness and commitment that each brings to her work, the sisterhood they experience emboldens each one to step out and shine more fully.

Intergenerational friendships formed between women in their eighties and others in their twenties, who agreed to be mutual mentors for each other. With reciprocity and respect, those relationships ignite my heart with admiration, hope, and delight.

Witnessing varying versions of this phenomenon over the past many years has served to strengthen my vision, and my investment in connecting bold and committed women across the differences that *far too often* divide us.

Shannon Thunderbird, a Coast Tsimshian Native elder, says: "We are Mother Earth's heartbeat, the life-givers; it is our responsibility to bring peace, harmony, and balance back to the world." Her words reinforce what life has shown me repeatedly — that women have extraordinary capacities when we are in authentic and deep alignment.

Together we can heal, transform, and *radically grow* each other's capacity to lead our communities and our cultures toward a world that is healthy, loving, peaceful, and regenerative. We are being called to connect across our identity divides, to come together in true solidarity to defend and protect the sanctity of all life.

We will find the greatest creative opportunities for collaboration and learning in the places where edges meet, to constellate together a web of co-creativity and mutuality on behalf of mother Earth and the entire web of life.

All around us, the old structures of dominance are both overreaching and crumbling. Though at times the forces we're up against may seem impossible to overcome, I have faith in women's and women-identifying peoples' amazing capacity to heal, grow, and strengthen each other. For me, it's the single greatest underutilized resource we have, as a species, for transforming and healing our world.

PROMPTS FOR DEEPENING LEARNING
THROUGH REFLECTION, WRITING OR DISCUSSION

At the Frontlines:
The Global War on Women

THEMES

- Statistics detailing the oppression of women reveal brutal realities.

- Extractive industries enabled by governments have targeted women, to destroy and uproot Indigenous communities all over the planet.

- When women band together, we can strengthen each other to confront harm, heal, increase each other's leadership, and co-create solutions.

PROMPTS

Reflect on how you respond when you are confronted with the ongoing reality of women's oppression: numbness, a sigh, anger, grief, resignation? Can you name and honor what you feel?

Some historians believe that patriarchy was reified by the expansion of systems of supremacy, colonialism and capitalism. Extractive industries treat Indigenous communities as expendable, destroying families, landscapes, lifeways, cultures.

- What combination of forces is driving this destruction? As Indigenous communities fight back, where do you think their resilience and strength comes from?

Few women escape some form of harassment, assault, or oppression, whether in family, at work or on the street.

- Do you have experiences you are willing to write about, or share in your discussion circle?
- Might you share your own strategies for self-protection and healing?

The promise of women-led change won't happen if we sabotage ourselves and compete and undermine each other.

- Have you been able to recognize such behaviors inside yourself?
- Are there ways you have worked to change the general tendency towards competing?

Reflect on how women have helped you claim the confidence to lead.

- How and when have you experienced being strengthened by other women? Share or write about one such time or mentor.

GRASSROOTS WOMEN
Restoring Relations Around the World

One of the most promising phenomena in recent years has been the emergence around the world of grassroots women-led movements. They are creating solutions to social and environmental problems by reconnecting relationships. Not only between people, but also between people and the land, creating cascading positive effects, restoring economic stability, peace, and ecological health.

These women leaders are making visible previously invisible connections among seemingly disparate issues or constituencies, creating connective tissue to align people in common cause. They are creating conditions for solidarity in ways that sometimes involve unusual alliances of strange bedfellows. Coming out of a culture that tends to separate and divide us, I believe this is one of the most crucial strategies we need to adopt in this pivotal time.

A recent, striking example of that is the remarkable mobilization (with only ten weeks for planning!) of coordinated marches to resist the misogynist, xenophobic, and racist attitudes and actions of incoming President Donald Trump. Planned rapidly by four grassroots women organizers of very diverse backgrounds and ethnicities (one of whom had a baby during the planning phase), and then organized in a decentralized fashion in over 600 cities throughout the U.S. and the world, the Women's March of January 20, 2017, broke records for the largest turnouts of demonstrators in U.S. history. Globally, another sixty marches occurred around the world.

Many have estimated the turnout as collectively in the several millions, sending a clear message to the president on his first day in office. Referring to it as the "Inclusion Revolution," the march, while predominantly female, included men, a spectrum of LGBTQ people, immigrant families, Black and Latina and Indigenous speakers and performers, and many mothers and daughters, and the rallying cries were for solidarity, bold love, standing together, and continuing to resist. Stunningly, there was no violence and there were no arrests.

It's also true that the weeks and months that followed revealed ruptures in the movement. Examples abounded of groups that had felt snubbed or disrespected, revealing just how much social healing and repair is yet to be done. Still, the embodiment of solidarity across divides that the events globally represented was profoundly historically significant and provided a beacon of hope in dark times.

Many other current examples of women's leadership also exemplify approaches to problems that the agrarian philosopher, poet and activist Wendell Berry characterized as "solving for pattern." There are, he notes, many well-meaning solutions that create new problems or make the existing ones worse. Creating a dam across a river to build a reservoir, for example, might help regulate water flows and help irrigate crops and generate power, but dams often displace whole communities and can drastically degrade large ecosystems and all the species living in them.

An ideal, elegant solution looks at a problem in relationship to the larger patterns within which it is embedded. This kind of solution, Berry asserts, solves more than the problem it is meant to address. It has a positive influence on a whole web of relationships, increasing the vitality of an entire system. It can result in what he calls "cascading benefits," generating positive outcomes affecting many dimensions of a landscape or a community.

Around the world women are cooking up systemic solutions to problems that are based on respect for the people, land, and cultures involved, and often they are forging coalitions and catalyzing collaboration among thousands of people to effect change.

In the Niger Delta some years ago, for example, hundreds of women blocked the gates of Chevron/Texaco in protests demanding that the company provide jobs, schools, and hospitals, as well as clean up the toxic chemicals in their water. Within 36 hours of beginning this action, as word spread throughout the countryside, they were spontaneously joined by thousands more women in their nonviolent occupation. A turning point was reached in the negotiations when the women threatened to take off their clothes — a powerful traditional shaming gesture — to humiliate the company.

These peaceful, all-woman protests were a major departure from past attempts at pressuring oil multinationals to change, which have frequently involved armed men using kidnapping and sabotage to get the corporations to address social and environmental damage. The sieges paralyzed Chevron/Texaco's operations, costing them millions of dollars before a settlement was reached.

Although this particular effort had only temporary impacts, it did contribute to shifting the dynamics and the narrative in the region, and the women remembered the power they collectively had been able to wield. A spokeswoman for the protesters said "History has been made. Our culture is a patriarchal society. For women to come out like this and achieve what we have is out of the ordinary."

In Liberia in 2003, it was women's groups that led the Liberian Mass Action for Peace, finally stopping an incredibly brutal war that had decimated their nation for years. This historic coalition of Muslim and Christian women sat in public protest, confronted their nation's

ruthless president and rebel warlords, and even, *Lysistrata*-like, held
a sex strike to stop the violence. Subsequently, they elected a woman
president from among their ranks. When women enter government in
large enough numbers, studies show, in many cases the economy, the
ecology, and the general welfare in a country benefit, and a country
tends to become less aggressive in its foreign policy. Much of this work
begins with community organizing and brokering collaboration across
differences at the grassroots, just as it did in Liberia.

More familiar to many is the example of the Green Belt
Movement in Kenya, led by the late Wangari Maathai, who received
a Nobel Peace Prize for her work. Not only did her organization
plant over 51 million trees, but under her leadership, the movement
recognized and addressed the profound interconnectedness of
environmental restoration to sustainability, democracy, and the
empowerment of women and girls.

In India, grassroots women's movements are breaking out
all over. With help from a group called the Deccan Development
Society, village women in Andhra Pradesh set up community grain
and seed banks to gain control over their land, their food, and their
lives. By growing mainly food crops and managing the collection
and disbursement of seeds, women have been achieving 'intellectual
leadership' in their villages. Working together through local village-level
groups, the women form markets of their own, establishing prices that
reflect their own needs and priorities. Through a government program
that aims to rejuvenate marginalized lands, the women brought 2,500
acres of fallow land under cultivation. The sorghum they produced in
the first year of the project provided 3 million meals for 30 villages, or
1,000 extra meals per family. In each of 30 villages, the fodder from
their fields fed 6,000 cattle and produced wages for 2,500 people.

Since the program emphasizes reintroducing biodiversity and the restoration of traditional crop varieties, lands that used to produce crops worth 250-300 rupees per acre are now producing food crops worth 4,000 rupees per acre. In two years, 500 women have recovered 50 traditional crop varieties and set up banks for traditional seeds in 30 villages.

Renowned seed activist Vandana Shiva launched the Navdanya movement for farmers to retain control of their local food supply and resist the co-opting of their native seeds and agriculture by multinational agribusiness corporations. She has rallied millions to take a stand.

From India also, the legendary activist Medha Patkar and writer and activist Arundhati Roy, among many others, helped mobilize popular resistance against the dam-building policies of the Indian government and the World Bank that displace millions of traditional villagers while despoiling riparian ecosystems. These movements don't always succeed, but even when they don't, they too leave seeds for the next generations of women leaders to build upon.

These women-led movements often seek to solve several interrelated problems simultaneously with a relational approach.

They seek to enhance local food security, resist corporate control and pollution, increase local economic development, and improve the overall health of their communities. Another hallmark of woman-led movements is the centrality of coalition-building in their strategies. They often bring together uncommon allies who can be made to see they share a common goal.

An interesting example of that approach can be found here in the U.S. A growing collaboration between reproductive rights activists and environmentalists around the issue of the proliferation of endocrine- disrupting chemicals in our environment and bodies. Linked to sterility and deformed genitalia in the offspring of fish and birds, ecologists had been sounding the alarm about the potential risks of these compounds for years, but once reproductive health activists understood the magnitude of the threat to human fertility and women's reproductive health, they began to understand the inexorable connection between the health of the environment and human health.

After struggling for over 30 years to preserve women's right to choose, reproductive rights organizations had become known for their fierce independence and narrow focus, rarely aligning with other issues or movements. Yet both communities recognized that peoples' ability to have healthy babies, the increasingly early onset of puberty in girls, and reproductive cancers in women were all at least partially linked to environmental factors, and both groups understood that this is something a powerful movement could be built upon. Surveys reflect that one of the greatest environmental concerns in opinion polling is chemical toxins, and anxiety is heightened when the worries are linked to reproductive impacts like decreased fertility or birth defects. A serious collaboration between these two groups of unlikely partners could succeed in bringing this issue far greater public attention — and in putting a human face on this huge environmental health concern.

In the last few decades, it has become crystal-clear that what is good for women is good for the Earth. When women's equality, literacy, and socio-economic power increase, women consistently choose to have fewer children (the difference between a woman with no schooling and 12 years of schooling is almost 4 to 5 children per woman). A study by the WorldWatch Institute finds that the only proven, sure-fire way to reduce fertility rates and slow burgeoning population growth in the global south is to give girls access to education, end the rampant violence against women, and empower women in every sphere of society.

Family planning has huge ripple effects in decreasing greenhouse gas emissions. According to Project Drawdown, a research compilation of one hundred ways to fight climate change by lowering atmospheric CO^2, the total reduction of 119.2 gigatons that could result from empowering and educating women and girls makes this an unexpected top tier solution to reversing global warming!

Climate change action at the grassroots is thus another huge potential arena for coalition-building among previously separate organizations. I am very excited about two such recent coalitions between indigenous networks and climate activism: Indigenous Climate Action and It Takes Roots.

Indigenous Climate Action was founded in 2015 in Alberta by five indigenous women leaders. Their organization strives to fill the gaps between the lived experiences of Indigenous Peoples and the policies and strategies being developed to address climate change. They support increasing climate change literacy and the creation of a network for Indigenous Climate Action that supports indigenous water protectors, land defenders, and knowledge holders. Its first director is Eriel Deranger, a passionately fierce organizer, wife and mother, who is a member of the Athabasca Chipewyan First Nation. Her peoples' land was at the site of the Alberta Tar Sands, so she's experienced firsthand the devastation that has been brought upon her peoples' lifeways, health, and culture, as well as on their land and water.

It Takes Roots is a multiracial effort led by women and gender-oppressed people of color and Indigenous People on the frontlines of racial, housing, and climate justice across the country. It is the result of years of relationship building across the Climate Justice Alliance, the Grassroots Global Justice Alliance, the Indigenous Environmental Network and the Right to the City Alliance alongside the Center for Story-based Strategy and the Ruckus Society.

Together these national alliances represent 150 organizations in 30 states nationwide and in Canada. Each of these alliances is led by grassroots organizations, and each brings unique contributions to their collective work: strategies for a just transition to a regenerative economy; connections with global movements and grassroots feminist and gender justice organizations; a strong framework of environmental justice, indigenous sovereignty, and treaty rights; and deep experience in housing and land rights. This extraordinary coalition beautifully illustrates what the ecologically literate have long known: Just as all our problems are interrelated, so our solutions need to be interwoven as well.

The late, great pioneer of eco-psychology Theodore Roszak noted that as women's perspectives and voices are increasingly represented in leadership throughout all sectors, not only will gender equity become the norm, but the qualities that we have long associated as stereotypically "feminine" will grow to be more widely appreciated in everyone and in all organizations. The human capacities for caring, empathy, listening, and compassion — which have so long been associated with mothers, nurses, care-givers, and wives — will become fully embedded in our social values. Those social institutions that have previously been predicated upon competitive and aggressive market values will give increasing priority to cooperation, relational intelligence, and caring.

In the time ahead, we can anticipate that our social and cultural styles will be steadily reinvented and reshaped by the 51% of the world that's female. As proclaimed on placards at the immense

Women's March in Washington DC, following the 2017 presidential inauguration: *The Future is Female.*

In these, and many other emerging grassroots women-led movements here in the U.S. and around the world, we are seeing the seeds of Roszak's prediction, outlines of the coalitions we will need to cultivate, and the creative models we can begin to draw upon to develop an Earth-honoring, life-affirming, just, and liberatory culture.

PROMPTS FOR DEEPENING LEARNING
THROUGH REFLECTION, WRITING OR DISCUSSION

Grassroots Women:
Restoring Relations Around the World

THEMES
- "Solving for pattern" means applying solutions that create cascading benefits to the whole system, beyond the initial problem it sought to solve.
- Grassroots, women-led movements create solutions by reconnecting relationships, and forging and cultivating relationships among disparate issues or constituencies.
- Women-lead grassroots approaches are based on collaboration and cooperative leadership, and respect for people, land, and culture.

PROMPTS

The January 2017 Women's March was an example of fast action emerging from creating connective tissue between disparate groups aligned in common cause.
- If you participated, what was your experience?
- Did you find yourself aligned with more than one group?

This chapter describes several examples of grassroots, women-led movements for rights, sovereignty, and the Earth.
- Which were already known to you? Which not?
- What does that tell you about "grassroots movements?"
- Which of these would you like to know more about, and why?

You might research one of these further to see how it might serve as a model for your own activism. Share whatever you learn to inspire others.

It is clear to me that "What is good for women is good for the Earth." Discuss why that might be.

Project Drawdown shows that "empowering and educating girls" is a vital solution to lowering carbon, and is an example of "solving for pattern." Reflect on a main concern/problem/issue you are devoted to.
- How might it intersect with other problems/issues?
- How might you come up with solutions or collaborations that affect a broader range of issues?

Coalition building is central to women-led movements.
- In your own life and work, how do you practice forging connections?
- How might you be able to enhance cooperation with other kindred change agents to leverage power?

RECLAIMING ACTIVISM

Indigeneity, Leadership, and Collaboration

(Interview with Ayana Young, *For the Wild*)

Ayana Young is in service to the redwoods, to the salmon, to the whole wild Pacific Northwest ecosystems that seem to have spawned her and call her kin. She is deeply aligned with indigenous culture-bearers and aware of how Indigeneity can and will affect movements to come. She conducts deep and insightful interviews on her podcast, *For The Wild*, seeking to illuminate the nexus between people and wildlands, between heart, spirit, and action. I found her capacity to light up the connective tissue among seemingly disparate elements inspiring and particularly conducive to the leadership from the heart that's so needed in this pivotal and dangerous time.

Ayana Young: The environmental movements have historically been on separate tracks than human rights or women's movements, but in this time of convergent crises, it's undeniable that these challenges are inseparable, and just as corporate polluters are merging, the resistance must also merge. Bioneers has been instrumental in connecting these movements and showing how the environmental movement really must broaden its aims to remain relevant. Could you speak about how your ideas about activism as a holistic endeavor have evolved through the years at Bioneers, and would you share some of those connections you draw between issues of ecology and race, class and gender disparities?

Nina Simons: When we first started Bioneers, I didn't consider myself an activist. I considered myself a communicator and a producer, but I thought of activism in a very prescribed way, as people who demonstrated and got arrested or did direct actions. And those were not forms of activism that I was readily called toward.

Over the years, my exposure to Bioneers and all the diverse leaders that we have featured there really helped me to broaden my understanding of what activism can be. I've come to understand that there are as many ways to respond to the multiple interdependent crises and challenges we face as there probably are human beings on the planet. I now see communication absolutely as a form of activism, but so is raising children, and being a teacher, or a hospice worker, or a politician, or policy maker. That's how Bioneers has helped me redefine activism as a holistic endeavor.

Drawing some of the connections between ecology, race, class, and gender...I had this sequential awakening about how all those other ways that we divide up human beings relate to our ecological crises. I think one of our first big "ahas" with Bioneers was perceiving the degree of factionalism that existed even within an environmental movement that, as you mentioned, was historically predominately White and mostly middle class, but yet still wildly divided within itself.

At Bioneers, we sometimes refer to Indigenous People as not only the first Bioneers but as the old growth cultures who live among us. That began an awakening for me around history and racial justice. Then, the more that I got to know and hear people of all colors and classes speak, the more I understood the degree to which our culture operates in a hierarchical paradigm that tends to devalue and diminish the voices of people of color, people of lower income, and women, as well.

AY: I'm wondering what you see as the barriers to embracing direct action on a larger scale, or at least supporting that as an individual or as a group?

NS: If I were to hazard a guess, I think the barriers are numerous and probably different for each individual. There's a barrier that has to do with the simple fact of self-preservation and a fear of putting oneself in harm's way.

We also have a lot of conditioning, depending on who we are. As a woman of Jewish lineage, I have identified conditioning in myself that has caused me in the past to try to smooth over ruptures that occur about racial difference and even the discomfort of sitting with another's trauma or pain. That tendency toward avoidance or pacifying has required me to intentionally build some courage and muscle in myself on a psychological level to be able to keep turning towards the discomfort of addressing those systems. I've had to keep asking 'How do I develop my own capacity to stay in that conversation so that I can act on behalf of the world I want?'

We have been societally conditioned to be individualistic, and our solitary orientation gives us little practice at, and few tools for, acting collectively. Even in the formation of our movements we tend toward competition and factionalism, and we're not yet skillful or practiced at collaborating together toward greater impacts.

AY: As North Dakota militarizes its response to the Standing Rock protest, the racial injustices that the tribes have suffered for centuries are being brought again into the spotlight. Even today, poverty, incarceration, and unemployment rates among Native Americans in North Dakota are some of the highest in the country. For the first time in modern history, we see 200 indigenous nations uniting to protect water and their role as Earth guardians. Do you believe the climate movement will continue moving towards uplifting indigenous priorities, perspectives and leadership, and how would that benefit the movement?

NS: I'm not 100 percent sure that the climate movement will ally itself with indigenous justice movements, but I sure am throwing everything I know or have in that direction. So, I hope it will. I pray it will. And I'm doing everything I can to help it align in that way.

I think that there are a number of large-scale movements that are orienting increasingly towards honoring the role of First Nations as leaders of the climate movement. To be honest, we're going to need so many leaders, and leaders of all colors and of all ages. I think that leadership is emergent on many fronts right now.

What's happening at Standing Rock is simultaneously incredibly exciting and deeply tragic, as you say. The militarized response is not dissimilar to what has happened at other Native uprisings that have occurred in the past, but the advent of social media and of some independent media sources like Democracy Now! is making it harder for repression to happen in a way that's invisible to the larger public. I think the visibility of the violent, orchestrated response is a tremendous help to our movements.

In addition to the representatives of more than 200 sovereign indigenous nations there at Standing Rock, there are a great many non-Native people there too, and to me that's part of what's most exciting about what's happening. There is an openness and receptivity, in spite of all the history that tells Native People to be mistrustful of non-Native allies; this continued receptivity and welcoming and true generosity of spirit that's welcoming the non-Native allies who are showing up there is remarkable and could augur well for future coalition building.

I believe that Native Peoples have an essential role in leading the climate revolution that is to come, but of course it's not only a climate revolution, as you point out, it's about water, it's about clean air, it's about the future of our children, and it's about the future of ourselves as a species, to be blunt. It's also about rebelling against the corporate state, which in many ways is what makes Standing Rock different than past Native stands, because in the past it was governments who were quashing Native rebellions. This time it's banks and corporations backed by governments that are behind the violence that's happening there.

My hope and prayer are that the visibility of Indigenous and Aboriginal Peoples leading this movement of movements will help translate into a shift in our worldview. There are ways that I keep learning from indigenous friends and acquaintances the depth of how they relate to every aspect of life around us as a living relation, filled with consciousness and spirit.

At a gathering that I attended to strengthen efforts to protect the Bears Ears as a national monument, there was an eloquent Lakota man named Tiokasin Ghosthorse who broadcasts First Voices Indigenous Radio out of New York's WBAI. We were doing a soil ceremony, and he said, "In my language, the word we use to describe soil means 'Who we used to be.'"

I thought that was such a profound way of invoking the longer timeframe that many Indigenous People live with, the recognition that the soil is who we used to be and that we will go back to being soil after our brief experience in human form on this planet. It's a whole different kind of perspective and respect of relational intelligence than our Western culture has been raised to recognize, so my hope is that Indigenous Peoples' centrality to this movement will help accelerate cultural shifts and a real transformation in worldview that's so needed right now.

AY: As you've alluded to, generosity and mutual aid characterize many indigenous societies around the world, but in capitalist societies where greed is rewarded, sacrifice is almost nonsensical. It's a major hurdle to overcome, this aversion to sacrifice, and it prevents people from making substantial commitments to positive change. You've spent much of your life in service, and I'd love to hear from your point of view, what would be needed for us as a society to shift towards a culture of simplicity and service, to overcome our energy-intense lifestyles, to break that inertia?

NS: Thank you for asking big questions that push me to venture deep inside myself to see how I'm going to respond. One of the things that my own life has brought me to is an inquiry around how we are reinventing leadership in this time, because I realized that what was most needed from everyone was leadership, and that our inherited model of leadership was not one that many people I knew (including myself) could wholeheartedly embrace.

One of the complex parts of our inherited model that I've grappled with is the question of sacrifice. When I first started looking at it, I thought, why does leadership necessarily have to involve sacrifice? Maybe that's part of the old paradigm; maybe it doesn't have to involve sacrifice. Now, when I look back at the "me" who asked that question, I have to chuckle because of her naïveté, because life has taught me that sacrifice is often integral to real leadership. As an example, Kenny and I ran Bioneers for eight years with almost no compensation, basically doing it in our spare time on top of our day jobs. We did it because we loved it. We did it because it felt really important and necessary to us. We certainly didn't do it for personal gain. At the end of those eight years, we were exhausted, so it was kind of a sacrifice right from the beginning, but of course compared to the sacrifices of so many people around the world in far more challenging environments, it was not that traumatic, and we ultimately reaped great rewards for doing it.

Part of what's needed, I think, is new models of leadership, and one of the things that's important to helping shift our culture is to see examples of leaders who have embraced leadership in a wholehearted way and who have made their peace with sacrifice as a part of that, but who still exude joy and who live balanced lives and take care of themselves as well as others. There's an old mental model of a sort of heroic leadership that fetishizes tireless effort. We need a new model of leadership that integrates all of our human capacities and qualities. That means being vulnerable enough to say, 'There's a lot of blood, sweat and tears that went into my work. It has led to some of the most rewarding moments in my life, and I would not retrace my steps and undo those risks or those sacrifices for any amount of money.'

Part of the answer to your question lies also in lifting up role models of all races and backgrounds and ages and genders so that we can all see the plethora of options that are open to us and recognize that there are elements of working for the common good that provide a level of meaning and fulfillment that outweigh any monetary gain.

One guiding principle in my life comes from a quote by the Austrian physicist Fritjof Capra. He said that the shift to an eco-literate society, a society that knows how to live in right relationship to nature, involves a shift from an emphasis on counting and accumulating things to an emphasis on mapping relationships — from quantity to quality, from a goal orientation to one that's much more process-oriented.

Part of how I believe we can shift from this egocentric, greed-motivated culture to one that is more collaboratively, communally-oriented is to focus on relationships as the things that give us the greatest meaning in our lives, and not just relationships within the human world but to the more-than-human world — to the elements, to the ancestors, to the plants and animals and fungi upon which our lives depend.

AY: Thank you, Nina, for sharing those thoughts and some of your personal sacrifices. It's a question I've been thinking about for a while as I moved onto raw land a little over two years ago, living in a tent through very rainy winters, and tried to look deeply into what is actually fulfilling, as we move through this extremely over-consumptive system. What does real purpose feel like, and how can we actually reciprocate and sacrifice for what we love, the more than human world, as you so beautifully put it?

I think back to something you said earlier in the interview: it can sometimes be challenging for people who are interested in the same things to really learn how to work together or even know of each other, and I'm wondering, what are some ways that you're experiencing collaboration really taking off, and what are some of the tools we can all keep in mind as we try to build regenerative projects with others?

NS: Honestly, I feel like I am in a process of trying to identify those tools and really codify them so that they can be more accessible to all of us, but one thing I would say is that intimate relationship is one of the hardest spiritual practices — perhaps the hardest — that I have encountered in my life. Anyone who is in a very long-term relationship, who's paying attention, would likely agree. It's no accident that our divorce rate is as high as it is because we get so little training in how to be in effective, close, long-term relationships.

Some of what I can suggest, Ayana, is that building collaborative capacity takes time. It takes practice, just like anything else. One of the principles that I have found really helpful (and this has come out of our women's leadership work, but it's true for people of any gender), is to prioritize relationship over task; to actually take the time to really build relationship and to choose to share intimate stories. They then help you understand why you may be coming from different perspectives or disagree when you do because one of our greatest challenges as human beings is that we tend to think that people who think like us are smart, and people who don't think like us are not. Because of that we tend to form into groups of like-minded people. That is understandable but not very helpful for movement- building or collaboration.

One of the ideas that I have found as a countervailing force to that tendency is the notion that comes from my friend and mentor Jeannette Armstrong, who's an extraordinary First Nations educator from the Okanagan people in British Columbia. In her tradition, they practice something called the Four Societies or E'Nowkin Weh. In that tradition, what they say is that the most valuable perspective that anyone can bring is one that's 180 degrees opposed from my own, because that requires me to be able to expand my thinking and my vision enough to incorporate their perspective. Wow, how would the world be different if we all practiced that.

So, the clearest offerings I can respond with are to suggest prioritizing relationship ahead of task, to give time and space for that relationship to evolve and mature, to recognize that partnership or collaboration is a practice, and to make some agreements about what happens when you don't agree, and what happens when you might inadvertently trigger an emotional response in someone else, and how are you going to deal with that.

If you talk about those things at the front end and make some agreements about them, that can really help, because those eruptions often happen, and they occur not by intention but because privilege comes with blinders, and we often don't know another's reality enough to be able to avoid offending them, so we inadvertently say or do things that offend, and if we know in advance and we've talked about the likelihood that that might happen, we might make agreements that could include how we name it when something like that happens and how we agree to respond to it. Do we take a break for a time and then re-meet to try to unpack what happened? What is our commitment about how we're going to move through difficult challenges?

Another of the guiding principles that's been really helpful to me comes from a mentor named Dawna Markova. She says that the durability, flexibility, and resilience of relationships are a function of how we navigate rupture and repair. All our relationships, whether they're parent/child or sibling or partner or colleague or friend or life partner, all of our relationships will encounter ruptures. When the rupture happens, it's whether and how we choose to turn back towards repair that confers strength and endurance to our relationships.

AY: Thank you so much. You were expressing at the beginning the value of really being able to commit to sit in the discomfort sometimes and not running away, and I know a lot of that's come up with racial justice issues and White privilege. If we give space and give time and love and dedication and commitment, we can come through these messy growing pains and learn to work together in a new regenerative way.

PROMPTS FOR DEEPENING LEARNING
THROUGH REFLECTION, WRITING OR DISCUSSION

Reclaiming Activism: Indigeneity, Leadership, and Collaboration

THEMES
- Expanding the idea of what activism is defined as and looks like.
- Movements for change suffer from factionalism, hierarchies, discounting voices of women, the poor, and POC: We need to learn coalition-building towards greater impact and leveraging power.
- Indigenous cultures and lifeways can inspire shifts in consciousness to focus on our connectedness to each other and the land.
- Befriending sacrifice as part of leadership, and balancing it with joy and self-care.

PROMPTS
Do you identify as an activist?
- If so, what does that mean to you? If not, why not?
- Do you think a mother can be an activist through mothering, a farmer through farming, a writer through writing? How exactly?

The principle of "prioritizing relationship over agenda" can be a means to rebalance our world and our activism. Think of the balance of those in your work life, in your activism life, and at home.
- How would such prioritizing shift your work? How?
- How might it enhance your effectiveness?

- What skills might you have learned in your intimate relationships that translate to movement-building and influencing change?
- How might you strengthen your partnering with others to leverage power?

Can we embrace a model of leadership that includes sacrifice yet at the same time integrates joy, creativity, and self-care? Or does that seem contradictory?

Generosity and mutual aid characterize many traditional indigenous societies around the world. In our competition-oriented culture, how might we learn from those models without engaging in cultural appropriation?

ILLUMINATING POSSIBILITIES
Leaders Lifting Others Up

I'd like to describe a few of my many sheroes, women leading innovative change whose stories show just how diverse are the paths and options toward emergent, love-inspired leadership. I offer them to give you a sense of what a wide array of methods and approaches women leaders are choosing. And, to be clear, these are only a few of the scores of women leading change who inspire and expand my vision, with more emerging and becoming visible every day.

Their stories illustrate the movement from inner guidance, love, or prompting to outer expression, and their many accomplishments as innovators and cultural or ecological healers are mirrored by their embodiment of values I hold most dear.

Those include: deep listening, embodied connectedness, relational intelligence, a passion for justice held within healing, reverence for nature, joy, creativity, a sense of the sacred, and celebration. Many of them also lead by creating events, forums, and conditions for others to flourish and emerge as leaders. For those, leadership is defined by how many others they can lift up. These women have augmented my learning, and many others are profiled in *Moonrise: The Power of Women Leading from the Heart*, which shares stories of many more of my earlier mentors and role models.

KATSI COOK

There is a saying, about the Iroquois or Haudenosaunnee Six Nations: "If you want something done, get a Mohawk to do it." There is no better living proof of that than Katsi Cook. A member of the Mohawk Nation, one of the Iroquois Six Nations Confederacy, she commits herself unerringly and with great love toward unleashing the potential that exists within the North American Indigenous world.

After decades of connecting people, purpose, and initiatives, she is renowned especially for two immense contributions: she has been the most important visionary leader in the revitalization of traditional Native American midwifery, and is one of the earliest and most influential researchers on environmental health impacts on Indigenous People.

It all starts with Katsi herself. A mother of five and grandmother of 11, she exudes a healing, nurturing aura and a quality of being that's grounded in vibrant family and community, which feeds her seemingly endless energy.

Katsi has profoundly affirmed the value for women of reinhabiting our bodies, listening and learning from our inherent biological wisdom. Katsi's sense of embodiment is informed by her people's Longhouse tradition. "Women are the first environment," she says. "We are an embodiment of our Mother Earth. From the bodies of women flows the relationship of the generations both to society and the natural world. With our bodies we nourish, sustain, and create connected relationships and interdependence. In this way, the Earth is our mother, our ancestors said. In this way, we as women are Earth."

When she began witnessing the profound effects upon women's health of toxins in the water, she shifted her focus to initiate the famous Akwesasne Mother's Milk Project, which launched highly influential studies on PCB and heavy metals contamination in her community. As a community organizer, and natural networker, Katsi's commitment to Indigenous Peoples has led her to be widely known throughout the hundreds of tribal nations and communities that comprise Indian Country. She has sought out and connected with grassroots and community leaders, whether they are known to mainstream culture or not. Thanks to her influence, I now have a greater appreciation for the leaders who often fly under the radar, who are not necessarily represented as leaders of stature in the media but are deeply respected and valued in their own communities.

And as is true for so many women leaders who become drawn toward new or later-in-life callings, her path has evolved into new ways to serve her community, now as the Director of the Spirit Aligned Leadership Program. There, she is convening an Inaugural Circle of eight indigenous elder women who will together inform future circles and approaches "so that what lives deep within our indigenous girls and women and Mother Earth can connect and come forth now in these extremely critical times."

Cultivating sisterhood through the generations is at the core of Spirit Aligned Leadership philosophy. The project recognizes the legacy of knowledge and experience that indigenous women carry. From these beliefs, Spirit Aligned seeks to create a circle of Legacy sisters who will help to create a balanced world.

For me, indigenous women and the traditional cultural values and knowledge ways they carry hold the keys to all women's — and all peoples' — survival. So, this expression of Katsi Cook's work thrills me to the core. It's deeply aligned with my heart's purpose, and I feel that it offers tremendous promise as a strategic investment in our collective future.

LENY MENDOZA STROBEL

I first met Leny when she participated in one of the trainings I was leading, and as sometimes happens, we became fast friends. This elegant, sophisticated, and dignified professor impressed me with her clarity and directness about colonialism's impacts. She wowed me with the beauty of her Filipino indigenous culture, and her profound insights about decolonizing herself, and the value of multiculturalism.

Leny was Chair of the Department of American Multicultural Studies at Sonoma State University. I discovered that, in addition to having written three wonderful books, she was also the Project Director of the Center for Babaylan Studies, which works to help Filipinos around the world reconnect with their indigenous cultures. The Center is now run by Lily Mendoza, who is also an educator and cultural healer.

Leny's endlessly curious and open mind and heart taught me about being receptive to new people and ideas while staying purposefully and with great integrity on path. She invited me to speak at her university to a class on multiculturalism, and I realized that — in addition to living in a California county that's predominantly White, the students that this radically-committed woman worked with on a daily basis came mostly from very privileged, wealthy homes, and had little embodied experience — beyond her teachings — of the true value of multiculturalism. She has deep respect for her students and is dedicated to lifting up other Filipino immigrants — despite challenging odds and a pervasively unsupportive environment.

Perhaps more than anything, Leny embodies the integration of the values of her indigenous roots. She explains her discovery process, illuminating pathways for others to follow her

self-decolonization efforts. She offers an elegant balance of humility
with tremendous dignity. She bridges her indigenous inner world with
the modern Western world in which she lives and works.

Leny (who was born Elenita) has produced cutting-edge
curricula, conferences, books, and webinars all of which create pathways
of healing for people of all cultures, especially those of the Filipino
diaspora. Filipinos suffered enormous hardships in several wars in the
20th century, and many who had to migrate to other countries in order
to survive have had their labor ruthlessly exploited.

They've had few champions, but they can be very proud to have
produced as impeccable and luminous a leader, teacher, and defender as
Leny Mendoza Strobel.

JULIA BUTTERFLY HILL

It may sound like a cliché, but Julia Butterfly Hill really is a force of
nature. She is best known for having lived in a 180-foot tall, roughly
1500-year-old California redwood tree for over two years — for 738 days
— between December 10, 1997 and December 18, 1999. Julia climbed
that tree, which she lovingly named Luna, when she was 23 years old, to
prevent Pacific Lumber Company loggers from cutting it down.

While living in Luna, Julia learned many survival skills, such
as seldom washing the soles of her feet, because the sap helped her
feet stick to the branches better. With ropes, she hoisted up survival
supplies brought by an eight-member support crew and to keep warm,
she wrapped herself tightly into a sleeping bag, leaving only a small hole
for breathing. She used solar-powered cell phones for radio interviews,
became an "in-tree" correspondent for a cable television show, and
hosted TV crews to protest old-growth clear-cutting.

During her ordeal, Julia weathered freezing rains and high winds, helicopter harassment, a ten-day siege by company security guards, and attempted intimidation by angry loggers. A resolution was reached in 1999 when the Pacific Lumber Company agreed to preserve Luna and all trees within a 200-foot buffer zone. In exchange, Julia agreed to vacate the tree.

I first met Julia virtually, by audio only, when she spoke at Bioneers from her perch in Luna. We were able to pipe her into our conference in San Francisco, and as her voice rang out with all the love, anger, pain, devotion, and commitment that coursed through her, chills ran up and down my spine. When she spoke of how sacred the old growth forest is to her, and her reverent relationship to Luna, she moved everyone to tears.

So, it's no wonder that since her tree sit, Hill has become a motivational speaker, a bestselling author, and the cofounder of the Circle of Life Foundation and the Engage Network, a nonprofit that trains small groups of civic leaders to work toward social change. She is the author of the book, *The Legacy of Luna*, and co-author of *One Makes the Difference*. More recently, Julia has also become a proponent of tax redirection, resisting payment of about $150,000 in federal taxes and instead donating that money to afterschool programs, arts and cultural programs, community gardens, alternatives to incarceration, and environmental protection programs.

When, some years after her tree sit, Julia spoke in person at our conference, she noticed how few young people were there. She responded by helping to initiate the Bioneers Youth Program. She turned to me and Kenny backstage and said "There aren't enough young people out there. Do you want me to help?" And, of course, we said, "Yes!" This is another quality I've witnessed about feminine leadership: the ability to respond in the moment without questioning the impulse or doubting one's ability to act. Julia trusts her own inner voice, and she just exudes natural spiritual authority because of it. I reflect now upon her actions with tremendous gratitude, and part of her legacy is that hundreds of young people now attend our youth program each year since.

LILY YEH

Lily Yeh, with immense courage, opted to shift her professional course after becoming well-established in her field, due to a soul calling, or change of heart. An artist who grew up in Taiwan and later moved to the United States, she worked as a professor of painting and art history at the University of the Arts in Philadelphia for thirty years. By all external measures, she had succeeded at all the "normal" things, like family and work, but this outer success had not fulfilled her. It hadn't given her an authentic sense of purpose.

She was to find that purpose when one day she was invited to a traumatized, poverty-stricken part of Philadelphia, a neighborhood she didn't normally visit. She felt a sudden urge to help co-create an art piece in this challenging environment. She invited residents to join her in creating a large mosaic out of the shards of broken glass in an empty lot. Soon the word got out, and Lily's magnetic personality drew people in: local kids and their parents, homeless folks, even street hustlers, all became collaborators in what would become the most important art project of her life. The whole neighborhood became engaged in cleaning up the area, painting murals, and creating an "art park."

Soon, it became The Village of Arts and Humanities, which yearly serves over 10,000 low-income, primarily African American youth and families, covering several neighborhoods within a nearly three-hundred square block area in North Philadelphia. Lily witnessed the power of collaborative art to help create new bonds among members of a hitherto neglected community. As its founder and executive director, Lily had created a national model in creative "place-making" and community-building through the arts, but she did not rest there.

When she heard a man from Rwanda speaking about the devastating genocide that had ripped apart his country, she said: "My heart moved, and I responded." With just $5,000 in her pocket, she went to Rwanda and accompanied him to a village where hundreds of traumatized survivors lived. There she helped create a collaborative mosaic memorial chamber for the bones of the murdered. Not only did this activity help knit the community together, the memorial project helped foster other development, including animal husbandry initiatives, a sewing business run by orphans, a traditional basket weaving cooperative, and the training of solar engineers so that now every home has solar energy. She trusted her heart's and intuition's guidance, and with the village in collaboration, a memorial art piece set in motion a whole cascade of locally empowering projects.

In 2002, Lily founded Barefoot Artists, Inc., and she has since helped launch arts projects in countries all over the world, including Kenya, Ecuador, Syria, China, Haiti, India, Taiwan, and Palestine.

Lily is always scared when she starts a project, but she starts anyway. Her tiny, delicate body contains tremendous courage. Now in her 70s, she is doing what she feels she was born to do, with quiet dignity, following her inner instructions.

This has given her an incredibly luminous aura: people everywhere are drawn to her; they just want to work with her. Her passion is contagious and transformational. She follows her muse and her inner spirit, not letting fear deter her, and as a result she has brought hope and healing to dozens of traumatized communities around the world.

FANIA DAVIS

Fania Davis grew up in Birmingham, Alabama, and experienced firsthand the impacts of the violence that accompanied the movement to end segregation and racism. When she was 15, two of her close friends were killed in the infamous Birmingham Sunday School bombing carried out by White nationalists. Only six years later, her husband was shot and nearly killed by police because of their activism at the time in support of the Black Panthers. In her early twenties, she devoted herself to getting a law degree and organizing an international movement to defend her sister, Angela Davis, from politically-motivated capital murder charges aimed at silencing her calls for racial and social justice. These experiences set her on a quest for social transformation, and for the following several decades, Fania was active in many movements for justice.

As a civil rights trial lawyer, Fania spent much of her professional life protecting people from racial discrimination, but after more than three decades of relentless fighting, she started to feel out of balance. She intuitively knew she needed more healing energies in her life. Like so many women I deeply admire, her path kept evolving as she responded to changing inner and outer realities. She ended up enrolling in a Ph.D. program in Indigenous Studies that allowed her to study indigenous cultures and apprentice with traditional African healers. This opened up a whole new world of deeper knowledge and experience that ignited a new phase of her activism. Fania then went on to become a radical innovator in social healing. Realizing from her work in the trenches how deeply flawed our criminal justice system is, Fania was inspired by South Africa's Truth and Reconciliation Commission and New Zealand's juvenile justice reforms to found Restorative Justice for Oakland Youth, RJOY, in 2005.

RJOY has been getting exceptionally positive results in the Oakland public school system and is becoming a luminous model for the rest of the country. Fania's concerns extend beyond establishing restorative justice in the human realm. She has come to understand that the rights of the natural world need be central in order for human psyches to be healed. She has become one of the key thought leaders in the emerging field of Restorative Justice in law schools and universities.

A grandmother of three, Fania continues to practice law in Oakland, but she is also a dancer and a yoga and qigong practitioner. To be in her presence is to bask in beauty, serenity, and grace. While her journey has changed course many times, she has always stayed true to serving the communities and people she loves. This is a woman who has learned to listen attentively for inner guidance and to adjust her approach. This has enabled her to help not only individual people in their quests for justice but to go deeper to seek to transform the very systems that perpetuate injustice. She has the remarkable capacity to inspire and lift up those she works with and for, cultivating leadership in everyone around her. She is one of the most impeccable and effective change agents I have ever met as well as one of the most balanced and serenely radiant women on the planet.

TAIJ KUMARIE MOTEELALL

Taij integrates her profound skills, passion, and devotion in service to her communities, alongside a balanced dedication to her personal and spiritual practices and learning. I am always struck by her integration of right- and left-brain analysis, her strategic vision, her capacity to bring visions into form, and her sense of sacred calling service to all of life.

An Indo-Caribbean artist and activist, Taij has developed a portfolio of diverse accomplishments. They include philanthropy, women's leadership training, and innovative arts/media and communications. As I've known her over the past decade, and witnessed her flourishing, her many facets have floored me — her entrepreneurship and her vision, combined with her devotion to her family, to nature, ritual, and to beauty.

Taij braids together multiple commitments: to motherhood, to creating pathways for women of color in leadership across multiple disciplines and sectors, to her own health and self-care, and to the arts and spiritual practices that are foundational to her core being. All that combines with her insightful mind, her will that's determined and just won't quit, a creativity that seems boundless, and a stunning ability to womanifest what she sees is needed.

She's launched a great many successful and potentially groundbreaking initiatives — and sustained them in the last several years. They are nimbly raising up BIPOC leaders, while transforming the philanthropic civil society landscape. Taij is the founder of Standing in Our Power, an intergenerational network of women and gender-resistant people of color leaders. Beginning with an initial gathering in 2012, they kicked off a 10-month Transformational Leadership Institute the following year. In 2016, Standing in Our Power began partnering with foundations to offer capacity-building services and leadership development programs to their grantees.

Previously, Taij co-founded Media Sutra, a business she started with her beloved life partner as a vehicle for self-determination and collective liberation. It's a socially-regenerative business led by people of color that provides creative, strategic and transformational services. They've committed to building a solidarity economy that works for all. Through Media Sutra, Taij empowers people to thrive, honor the planet, and reinvest profit for the collective good.

They've raised millions of dollars, launched high-impact organizations and campaigns, created award-winning films, supported organizations and networks to be sustainable, facilitated transformative leadership development, and coached leaders to really be game-changers.

Deeply connected to her roots, Taij also co-founded Jahajee Sisters. It's a movement-building organization that supports the leadership development of Indo-Caribbean women who are organizing against gender-based oppression and violence. Next, Taij started a Women of Color in Philanthropy initiative, then went on to co-design a retreat to center Black women in the aftermath of the Ferguson uprisings.

Previously, she was the Executive Director of Resource Generation, a network where she worked with young people with wealth to help them align their values with their philanthropic giving. She also supported their members to organize and leverage their capacity as change-makers.

And, as if all that wasn't enough, she's also working on a novel about her Indo-Caribbean heritage and immigrant experience that she aspires to later develop into a film.

Taij inspires me with her vision, and her boundless yet balanced energy. I sometimes see her as the embodiment of a beneficent, twirling, many-armed goddess who generates positive outcomes for herself, her family and her people as she dances with grace and fierce dedication throughout the world.

AI-JEN POO

Ai-jen Poo has been organizing immigrant women workers since 1996. The daughter of pro-democracy activists who emigrated from Taiwan, she felt called to work for those who help raise our children and care for the ill and elderly, without whom many families would be unable to function. Until recently, these people who are so essential to our families and communities have labored incredibly long hours under appalling conditions with almost no protections or rights, no overtime, no health insurance, and no safety net. Watching her grandfather deteriorate in a nursing home but finding a good caregiver for her grandmother, she experienced firsthand the impact that a good caregiver had on her entire family's life, but she knew that domestic work is among the most underappreciated forms of labor in our society.

"What," she asks, "could be more important than caring for the people who care for us? It's the kind of job that's not even seen as a real job. Domestic workers and caregivers go to work every day and support the dignity and wellbeing of others. There is something uniquely human about caring and doing for others," she declares.

By mobilizing caregivers to fight to improve the systems that support them, she's taking a stand on behalf of the nurturing and relational part of our humanity, and seeking to transform core aspects of our culture. She has had very large-scale successes and gained a lot of national recognition for her organizing and advocacy work, but she remains consistently humble, caring, and receptive herself, modeling the kind of care she's defending.

She is a remarkably skilled organizer who has been successful in helping large groups of some of the most disenfranchised people in our society achieve dignity and a better life. She has been able to help incorporate new constituencies into the labor movement and to build broad, effective coalitions and alliances. In 2000, she helped start Domestic Workers United (DWU), a New York-based organization that spearheaded the passage of the state's historic Domestic Workers Bill of Rights, which in turn help lead to the creation of the National Domestic Workers Alliance, an alliance of domestic workers in 19 cities and 11 states, working to gain respect, recognition, and legal protections for America's 2.5 million domestic workers.

Ai-jen then helped launch the visionary "Caring Across Generations" campaign that seeks to unite mostly immigrant home-care workers with the increasing number of elders needing care as the baby boom generation ages. If these two very different groups could recognize their common interest in creating a healthy, well-regulated home-care sector that provides decent wages and high-quality care, then, Ai-jen figured, a powerful, mutually beneficial movement that protects the rights of immigrant workers, provides good jobs, and offers excellent healthcare for the young and the elderly could coalesce and help address a number of our most pressing social problems. This is truly a stroke of political genius and "whole systems thinking."

Ai-jen radiates both profound compassion and a burning desire for fairness. The way she sees leadership is that her role is fundamentally to mobilize resources and people to achieve a positive social goal. She does that as effectively and graciously as anyone I've ever seen in action, because it's obvious that all her work is based in genuine love. She exquisitely balances humility, self-respect, and dignity, and as a result she creates communities of respect and right relationship around her. As I've learned how hard it can be to reach that equilibrium and maintain it, my respect and admiration for her has grown exponentially over the years.

Recently, she took a sabbatical and spent four months re-energizing in Hawaii, in "places where mountains and ocean meet," where she spent time alone practicing yoga and sleeping at least eight hours each night, which she had rarely been able to do for years. In this, she modeled what so many women leaders need — an ongoing attention to exquisite self-care. So many of us desperately need to interrupt patterns of nonstop work that inevitably lead to burn-out. We have to learn to care lovingly for our bodies as the vehicles for our leadership, as much as we care for the communities, lands, and places we are seeking to serve. In this aspect of life, too, Ai-jen is offering us an example to emulate, if we want to be around and effective for the long haul.

JUDY WICKS

The most joyful and innovative businessperson I know, Judy Wicks brings unparalleled exuberance and celebration to business. She reinvented her successful restaurant enterprise repeatedly over the course of several decades. She took a restaurant and made it not only an extraordinary eatery but a groundbreaking vehicle for education and consciousness-raising, as well as a catalyst to reknit the very social fabric of her community. Judy founded Philadelphia's White Dog Café, which became an early pioneer in the farm-to-table movement and a truly exemplary model of a sustainable and socially-engaged business. Her other business practices that were far ahead of the curve included: paying a living wage, instituting fair-trade principles in her purchasing, stringently recycling and composting, using solar heating and eco-friendly cleaning products and office supplies, and purchasing 100 percent of her electricity from renewable sources (the very first business in Pennsylvania to do so). She even incorporated the mentoring of inner-city high school students in her business model. Her restaurant may also be the only such establishment to have had a foreign policy: she led a number of tours to developing countries, including Cuba, to study sustainable agro-ecological practices, bolster fair trade relationships, and enhance international and cross-cultural understanding.

When she tried something new that worked, she shared it with her competitors in order to better transform the city. Judy mentored several generations of entrepreneurs in Philadelphia and well beyond. Before starting White Dog, Judy had had two other successful local businesses: Black Cat, which sold locally made and fair-trade crafts, and Free People Store which later became Urban Outfitters.

She is also far more than a successful entrepreneur: she has been a thought leader in reimagining what business is and should be, as well as the types of economies local communities need to develop in order to thrive. She has absolute clarity about an economy's true purpose: maximizing relationships, not profits. She co-founded Fair Food Philly and the Sustainable Business Network of Greater Philadelphia, and then went on to co-found the highly influential nationwide network BALLE, the Business Alliance for Local Living Economies. It started with the simple premise that an environmentally, socially, and financially sustainable global economy needs to be based on a network of sustainable local economies. BALLE's network has grown to over 80 local business networks in the U.S. and Canada that together include over twenty thousand small businesses.

Judy recounted many of her adventures and ideas in her award-winning memoir *Good Morning, Beautiful Business.* Her achievements speak for themselves, but they are not what I admire most about Judy. In service to the well-being of her community, no political win or holiday goes without Judy spearheading a huge block party or some sort of celebration. For her, localization means collective joy at home, dancing in the street, balls and comedy skits and holiday festivities.

Currently, it means three projects that she's dedicated to: The first is All Together Now Pennsylvania, which connects rural and urban communities to create regional resilient economies. Another project is Circle of Aunts & Uncles, which gives low-interest loans and social capital to under-resourced entrepreneurs in the Philadelphia area. And Proud Pennsylvania, which elects and supports state legislators who champion regional economies, reduce the influence of fossil fuels in policy, and are transitioning Pennsylvania to 100% Renewable Energy.

Her strategic focus and commitment to Pennsylvania make me wish there was a Judy Wicks in every state of this nation. She reminds me also that personal fulfillment and pleasure are not only possible, they're essential along any activist path.

ALIXA GARCIA AND NAIMA PENNIMAN, CLIMBING POETREE

Each and every time that I've heard Climbing PoeTree perform, they've enlivened my heart, mind, body, and soul. This spoken word duo has elevated awareness and engagement through their intense open-heartedness, their piercing intelligence, inspired writing, musical talent, impeccable performance skills, and luminous presence.

They've delivered some of the most radically awakening and uplifting socially "conscious" artistic performances anywhere. They are both multifaceted in their creative endeavors: each is an award-winning multimedia artist, committed social justice activist, and professional educator.

Their unshakeable integrity made them insist on maintaining complete control over their artistic production and their appearances.

They're bold cross-cultural experimenters who engage in what they've called 'international, bilingual, pansexual, poly-racial, multi-media, cross-genre, intergalactic collaborations.'

They're true independents — women who would rather perform in a prison or disaster zone than on a reality TV show.

They've performed, for example, at the notorious Rikers Island jail, as well as at such diverse venues as a TED talk, the Brooklyn Academy of Music, the United Nations, Harvard, at conferences and festivals, and to benefit countless community-based organizations.

They independently self-organized over 35 national and international tours, from South Africa to Cuba, from the United Kingdom to Mexico, and throughout the United States. This included 11,000 miles touring with an all-woman crew on a bus that was converted to run on recycled vegetable oil.

In one of their most remarkable initiatives, they collected over *ten thousand* stories on square pieces of fabric and then stitched them together. They formed an ever-growing *tapestry of truth* that they used to lead workshops around the power of storytelling for movement building.

They also developed an arts-based curriculum to inspire the next generation of social change agents, a course that's been piloted in several high schools and universities in five states.

And since doing all this extraordinary collaborative work, they've also each pursued distinct solo professional and creative projects.

Alixa Garcia is an award-winning poet and filmmaker. She's a social justice visual artist, storyteller of the unknown, published science fiction writer and political essayist, musician and music producer, an educator and social movement facilitator. She was an originating member of Truthworker Theater Company and is founder of Alixa Garcia Studio.

For several years, she's been conducting interviews with undocumented to first-generation LGBTQ immigrants. Inspired by each interviewee, she then created large-scale, multidimensional paintings in handcrafted light boxes.

Through the use of multiple media, "Shadow Boxing" weaves a holistic and multi-sensory experience of diverse narratives that deepen the cultural and social conversations about — and within — our marginalized communities.

Her visual art has been featured in museums and galleries nationally and internationally, including on the mega-screens in Times Square in New York City, and at the Contemporary Museum of Art in Los Angeles.

Naima Penniman is a devotee of seeds, a soulful storyteller, a multi-dimensional artist, movement builder, medicine grower, healer, and educator.

She serves as the Program Director at Soul Fire Farm, where she trains a returning generation of Black, Brown and Indigenous farmers.

There, they acquire the skills needed to reclaim leadership in the food system and to chart dignified futures in relationship to land.

She is the Co-Founder of Wildseed, a BIPOC-led, land-based community focused on ecological collaboration, transformative justice, and intergenerational responsibility.

Naima is also an originating member of the Black Healers Collective, Harriet's Apothecary, and founder of the Haitian resilience project, Ayiti Resurrect. She continues to write and perform poetry and music that's illuminating, enlivening, and Life-loving.

For me, it is impossible not to be awed by these two women. Their uniquely powerful poetry, art, and activism can burn with the fire of justice and rage against oppression, but it can also be tender and loving and always shines light on the sacredness of all life.

Their creativity, passion, work ethic, wisdom, soulfulness, integrity, and literary genius blow me away. And their arts and our friendships consistently evoke in me intense joy, gratitude, and inspired glee.

JOANNA MACY

A widely beloved mentor to so many of us in this movement to reconnect ourselves with Mother Earth, Joanna Macy is a wise elder, environmental activist, author, and scholar. In the course of her many decades of service, Joanna has woven six pathways into a powerful, coherent, inspiring philosophical framework — a compass for effective action and meaningful living. The six streams she has braided together are: traditional indigenous wisdom, "whole-systems" thinking, Buddhist wisdom, Deep Ecology, empathic connection, and engaged action.

Through experiential learning and by her example, she teaches that love's power to transform our world must be inextricably woven with our often less appreciated emotions of outrage, grief, despair, and loss. She has understood more fully than anyone that to be able to transform our world, we need to embrace the full gamut of human emotions and rekindle our connections to all of life, including our ancestors and our future descendants.

Joanna became an internationally renowned activist in anti-nuclear, peace, social justice, and environmental movements, and most recently she created an initiative called "The Great Turning," which maps in a profoundly sophisticated way how we can transform our consciousness, so we can transition from our unsustainable, destructive industrial society to a far more just and sane civilization. She also developed an approach called The Work that Reconnects, designed to help people respond creatively to the global crises we face rather than feeling overwhelmed or paralyzed.

Connecting with Joanna, experiencing her teachings and seeing her example, helped me acknowledge the power of my own emotions, especially my grief. She showed me that when we open our hearts to the overwhelming suffering in our world, and we face that pain and let ourselves grieve fully, we not only become more complete human beings, we become far more effective at doing good, because we are then able to place our own pain within a larger context that gives it meaning. Rather than being afraid of our own emotions, they can become the most powerful tools to re-enliven us, and, paradoxically, to help us reconnect to our sense of joy. In this state our capacity to create change dramatically increases.

Now in her nineties, Joanna continues to write, to evolve her work, and give lectures. She reminds me that to be fully integrated, transformative learning must reach our whole selves, including our bodies, hearts, minds, and spirits. She has long embodied the values of practice, lifelong learning, ceaseless commitment, and the regenerative power of love.

In her persevering quest to develop tools for navigating the dire challenges we face as a species, she has brilliantly woven together disparate strands of wisdom to create unique, dynamic new systemic forms of learning. She has shared them generously and tirelessly, and her legacy will live on far, far beyond her lifetime, as the thousands of us she has inspired will carry forward her transmitted teachings and pass them on in turn to generations to come.

While hugely divergent in ethnicity, age, background, education and form of expression, each of the leaders I have sought to describe above embodies moving from inner authority and a sense of purpose or love outward, into the world of action. They all seek to bring the totality of themselves to their engagement with the challenges of our era. They all practice deep listening to others and to their inner light for guidance, know how to balance humility with self-respect and dignity, and have honed the ability to respond spontaneously in the moment. Many are particularly skillful in seeing what the world needs and are joyous in fulfilling their unique purpose in service to it. Each also embodies a celebration of connection and an intimacy with the spiritual realms of life. It is my good fortune that through my work I have encountered so many of these extraordinary women who have taught me more than I could ever repay.

All are healers in their own ways, and also warriors on behalf of Life. Many are artists, creating new visions and possibilities as they innovate; and all are storytellers. It is through changing the story, I believe, that we are changing the world.

PROMPTS FOR DEEPENING LEARNING
THROUGH REFLECTION, WRITING OR DISCUSSION

Illuminating Possibilities:
Leaders Lifting Others Up

THEMES

While extremely diverse in their approaches, paths, and styles for expressing love-inspired leadership, the leaders who inspire me have much in common:

- they move from inner guidance to outer expression;
- they embody deep listening, a passion for justice, ecological and cultural healing, connectedness, humility, reverence, and joy;
- they create conditions for others to flourish as leaders.

PROMPTS

Which of the leaders described in this chapter most inspires you? Why? Pick two that do very different kinds of work: reflect upon and/or discuss what they have in common.

Bring to mind a leader not mentioned here who inspires you, or one you have learned from: what might this person have in common with the two that you picked from this list? What might be different or unique?

Bring to mind a leader you don't like. What might you glean from what you dislike about their way of leading?

How do the leaders featured here work with power?

- From what or where does their power to lead others derive?
- What do you see that draws or repels you about power and different ways to wield power?

Write a list of the values that are most important to you. Then examine your list and see if and how those values underlie your own leadership ways, style, choices, and expression. If your leadership ways don't reflect your deeply held values, reflect on how you might change to embody more of what you most value.

THE POWER OF STORY

...to reclaim our voices, express our truth,
shed negative conditioning, identify what calls
us, become who we yearn to be, awaken our
vision, attract support, connect us with allies,
and mobilize change...

Women's oppression and the degradation of the 'feminine' in all its forms has been enabled, perpetuated, and strengthened by silence, shame, and isolation. When we contemplate the waves of women's liberation and rights movements over time and throughout different parts of the globe, we can see that they are always preceded and combined with women getting together and sharing their stories.

It's only when we stop being silent and start to speak and make our voices heard that real change starts to happen. It is no exaggeration to say that when a woman speaks her truth, the world changes. As Ursula K. LeGuin, the late great poet and novelist, says: "We are volcanoes. When we women offer our experience as truth, as human truth, all the maps change. There are new mountains."

A cognitive linguist focused on political change, George Lakoff studies how we respond to stories and how our behavior is influenced by the narratives and metaphors we use. His research strongly suggests that we humans are hard-wired for story. That means that once we've heard a story and our hearts and minds have wrapped around it, no amount of facts to the contrary will get us to let go of that story. We environmentalists and social justice activists often assume that if we present the facts we can change people's minds, but it's become clear that the facts are not nearly as sticky or convincing as stories are. Only a more compelling story can alter people's prevailing narrative.

The author N. Scott Momaday said: "We live in a house made of stories." Stories are the seed forms of culture we carry around within us. Internalized, they define how expansively or tightly we offer the gift of our lives to the world. We decide how far we can go, how large a stand we're willing to make, or what risks we're willing to take, based upon the stories we tell ourselves.

Sometimes these stories that help define us stem from our family, culture, and social conditioning, and we carry them unwittingly, unaware of how they shape our lives, so it is crucial that we do the work of unpacking and making conscious the stories we tell ourselves.

About 10 years ago, I began unearthing my own hidden stories, and discovered that I thought of myself as *the woman behind the man* (and, as you may have heard: *behind every great man is a woman, rolling her eyes*). It was shocking to realize how self-limiting my inner narrative was. I was horrified to discover that this story or belief had unconsciously embedded itself within me. I asked other colleagues whether any of them — including my husband and partner — saw me that way. They did not. Once I understood that it was only my own story and not reflected by others around me, I understood that I held the keys to my own liberation. This insight expanded my definition of leadership, and an awareness of the centrality of stories has informed and guided my path ever since.

Sometimes stories can help us to reconnect with emotions that have been banished or anesthetized. Given the scope of the losses we face, with species extinctions happening at an unimaginable rate, anger, loss, powerlessness, and grief are totally appropriate responses. Culturally, however, we have no rituals, no safe places to express those anymore.

Stories can reopen us, allowing us to feel our emotions in a healthy way so that we can risk casting aside our numbness to respond to these crises from an awakened and alive place. Those kinds of stories are needed to heal our relations with our selves, each other, and this endangered, sacred Earth that is our home. We tend to be far more adept at resisting what we don't want than articulating a future story of what we yearn for with all our hearts. To paraphrase Yogi Berra: "If we're not careful, we're going to end up where we're heading." I believe the need for a clear vision of where we want to go is essential to help us connect with and inspire a broad range of people, and to help us develop the stamina and persistence we will need in the years ahead. Much of Bioneers' emphasis over the years has been to inspire people to act on behalf of a future they want, to understand how interdependent all the issues confronting us are, and to highlight those stories that can motivate us to help build the sort of movement of movements we now need to save our species from its own worst impulses.

It's vital that we tell stories of a future that's believable, emotionally accessible, sensually connectable, and that we passionately want. I agree with Charles Eisenstein that we're in a time "between stories." There's a story of fear, separation, and scarcity, based upon domination, ranking, and greed. It's got a long and bloody history, and we've all had lots of practice adapting to it.

The emergent story is one of solidarity, of relatedness, of empathy and equity, giving and sharing. It includes meaningful rituals to mark changes and to form new relationships and life passages, respect, and appreciation for diversity and for the sacredness of all life, and operates on principles of inclusion and mutuality. This new culture will simultaneously draw from the best of humanity's ancient wisdom and the most positive emergent new ideas. It's a story of the relationship economy, not one based upon exploitation and transactions. This story has at its foundation the shifting of focus and priority in our societies from counting things to mapping connectedness. It's the story of a security that's based upon love, rather than material acquisition.

We've learned that neither fear nor threat can change people's minds or behavior. It's having a more enticing story — a narrative that speaks to our hearts, that describes a future we would all wish to live in, one that we all want to be invited into. Oh, I want to live in that story. Yes, I want to contribute to that future, that vision that someone just so beautifully evoked in their poetry or song. That's the world I'm motivated to give my time, resources, and love to co-creating.

Stories are also vital to mending the false separations, the pigeonholing that our society is so patterned to reinforce. They can enhance our empathy, our capacity to imagine walking in another's shoes. Most of us yearn for intimacy and deep relationship. Really listening to others' stories and sharing some of our own are among the most effective pathways to transforming our cultures and growing deep connections. They work on us through identification with the storyteller, connecting us with those we might not normally see or hear. They are medicine for our false isolation, a way to forge connection and community and help shift our course.

Jensine Larson's global media project, WorldPulse, connects women from around the world to share their stories and create networks of mutual support. It's an example of just the sort of story-based initiative we need. Fortunately, WorldPulse is not alone. In the last few decades, whole new bodies of story-based practices, some based in ancient indigenous ways, some emerging from newly integrated understandings of neuroscience and psychology, have emerged. The practice of "Council," of which there are many variants, and a slew of hosting and convening approaches and methods that use storytelling as a cornerstone of their methodology, is spreading far and wide.

We're all involved in midwifing a new world into being, as the old world is crumbling around us. How do we engage with the tremendous uncertainty of the current human predicament?

Joanna Macy uses an especially powerful storytelling-based exercise to teach us how to shift our relationship to time. This is an exercise that comes from her *Work that Reconnects*: Imagine that time travel is possible and that you're about to be visited by someone from seven generations in the future. A young person is coming back in time to interview you because you were alive in this pivotal moment. Take a moment to imagine and notice what you anticipate the tone of that interview might be, and let your body feel it. Notice any sensations that come up in your body, your heart, your mind, or your spirit.

Joanna suggests that this young person is coming back from the future because you are a hero, or a *shero,* to them. They are coming back so excited to ask you how you knew what to do. They ask you: "How did you navigate this extraordinary moment when everything about human civilization had to change? What can you teach me about how you gave yourself to this immense and essential transformation?" Again, notice any changes in your body, heart, mind, and spirit, and then, very gently, when you're ready, bring your attention back to the present moment.

Did you assume initially that somebody coming back from the future would be mad, or angry? I sure did. I was pretty convinced that would be their stance. When I heard Joanna frame it that *I was* the hero, *that I was here, that I helped make the change*, I thought, wow, look at that invisible bias that I carry!

It's a story that anticipates and assumes — based in part on experience — that we good guys are losing. We have lots of reasons to have adopted that insidious belief: just turn on the nightly news, it gets reinforced all the time. But this is why it's so radical and so important to monitor and question our inner stories. We can support each other in knowing that the outcome being predicted in the media spin is not the final word. Our attitude towards what happens is key, and if we can show up for a positive outcome in a wholehearted and believable way, we can engage others to join us.

As Gandhi said, "Social change occurs when deeply felt private experiences are given public legitimacy."

PROMPTS FOR DEEPENING LEARNING
THROUGH REFLECTION, WRITING OR DISCUSSION

The Power of Story

THEMES

The power of story to reclaim our voices, express our truth, shed negative conditioning, discern life purpose, become who we yearn to be, awaken our vision, attract support, connect with allies, inspire vision, and mobilize change.

PROMPTS

How has being silenced and silencing ourselves enabled and perpetuated women's oppression?

- "When we make our voices heard, change starts to happen."
- Can you share a personal example of this principle?

The stories we tell ourselves often determine the risks and stands we are willing to take. But some stories we carry unconsciously.

- Do you have a practice to help you become aware of self-limiting stories?
- If not, might you invent a practice or ritual?

Stories enhance our capacity for empathy and connection.

- Can you think of a story that helped or helps you reconnect with your emotions and/or empathy? How did it do that?

Researchers are now finding that fear and threat don't change people for the better, whereas having a more enticing story can. Why do you think that is?

Charles Eisenstein and others suggest we are living in a world between two paradigms or stories: The old story of fear, separation, scarcity, and the new story of relatedness, giving, caring, and sharing.

- Look within. Which story you are feeding internally, both in relation to yourself and to others?

- How does the story of separation live inside you? How are you able to let it go?

THE POWER OF STORY
V (formerly known as EVE ENSLER)

No one illustrates the power of storytelling more profoundly than V. Her lifework has brought home truths about the foundational violence of our society: against women, and against the Earth herself. Her art has revealed the centrality of our archetypally wounded human relationship to matter, to our mother the Earth, and to ourselves. Sharing stories of women's relationships to their bodies, she has inspired and mobilized millions while giving permission to whole generations of women to heal, connect, and bear witness to each other's transformations.

Twenty-something years ago, V did something revolutionary: she began interviewing women of all ages, classes and backgrounds to learn about how women related to their vaginas. Though she initially anticipated writing a play based upon their stories, neither she nor anyone else could have imagined the extraordinary impact that play would have.

She soon discovered that she'd unearthed "the most reviled word in the English language," and set about healing our vagina-phobic culture through theater. Her award-winning play, *The Vagina Monologues*, provided a startling window into the conflicted complexity of women's relationship to their bodies, their sexuality, and their very selves. While performing the play throughout the world, V found lines of women backstage nightly, waiting to tell her their stories of rape, incest, domestic battery, and genital mutilation.

They desperately needed to have their stories heard.

In 1998, a group of women in New York joined V to found V-Day, a movement that has raised over $50 million for grassroots groups around the world working to end violence against women. *The Vagina Monologues* has now been translated into 45 languages and performed in over 120 countries. It has become an unparalleled vehicle to help raise awareness and funds to end violence against women and transform this societal pattern the world over.

When V was diagnosed with cancer and learned it had spread to many organs in her body, she went through an arduous and lengthy healing process. Through her hospital window, she drew strength from a tree she could see from her bed. She realized that growing up in a city, she'd never really related to the healing power and mystery of the natural world. As she healed, she fell in love with nature, which she then wrote about in her cancer memoir, *In the Body of the World*. Through her writing and activism, she never stops transmuting her own trauma and healing into medicine for others as she pursues her dream of a nonviolent world based on cooperation, dialogue, and care.

Art that has demonstrated a real and significant impact on global societies within a short period of time is rare. One could make a case that *The Vagina Monologues* might just be the set of stories that has had the most dramatic, continuing, ongoing positive social impact in history. It has become more of a tidal wave, an unparalleled cultural phenomenon, rather than simply a play. It has captured the imaginations of and given voice to girls and women around the world, and it's been performed in places where women risk their lives to participate. V did not just create an incredibly successful, "viral," self-replicating art form to further women's human rights, already an extraordinary achievement. She has since co-created a movement and

on-the-ground institutions to support women around the world in
healing from violence, with funding and concrete assistance.

In response to a fact-finding mission to the Congo, V-day
launched a campaign in partnership with UNICEF and thousands of
activists on the ground to raise awareness about the epidemic level of
gender violence in that nation. Together, they seeded and helped fund
the creation of the City of Joy in Bukavu, where women survivors of
sexual violence can go to live and be healed.

V takes a lot of heat for being idealistic in aiming to end
violence against women. It takes a particular kind of courage to take
such a powerful stand, regardless of the odds. She has worked tirelessly
to create powerful political and artistic antidotes to brutality against
women and girls, and she is continuously pushing the envelope,
launching new initiatives to further that goal.

Her recent project, One Billion Rising, continues that legacy
but takes it in a new direction, using dance and celebration in events
around the globe. She describes her vision this way: "Every February, we
will rise — in hundreds of countries across the world — to show our
local communities and the world what one billion looks like and shine
a light on the rampant impunity and injustice that survivors most often
face. We rise through dance to express joy and community and celebrate
the fact that we have not been defeated by this violence. We rise to
show we are determined to create a new kind of consciousness — one
where violence will be resisted until it is unthinkable."

A couple of years ago, at a Bioneers conference, V offered a
performance piece that had caught hold of her imagination in the weeks
just before. Though she'd planned to give a different talk, she wrote to
me to ask, "Is it ok if I do this thing that's coming through now, that's
quite radical?" On stage, she performed "Eve's Revolution," a truly

inspired (and extremely funny) re-imagining of what had happened between Adam and Eve. She recast that archetypal, ancient, and deeply rooted narrative, a story that has so heavily contributed to the subjugation of women, and then transformed it into a tale of feminine wisdom and empowerment. It may have been the most brilliant and subversive form of artistic creation I have ever witnessed, one that revealed the awesome power of storytelling to re-imagine and remake the world.

I invite you all to practice storytelling every chance you get. Here are a few practical tips that I've gleaned from V and some of my other mentors:

- Include details that enliven your listeners' senses, that speak to their embodied realities.
- Use the simplest possible language and be specific.
- Encourage your imagination to roam freely, to envision and share far-reaching tales of the future/the changes you want to see.
- Resist telling people what they should think, feel, or do. Instead, model what you're offering through your own transformative experience. This invites peoples' imaginations to engage more deeply.
- Don't be afraid to share your emotional truth and reveal your vulnerability.
- Don't inflate your own importance: humility and humor are critical elements of any good story.
- Speak personally and subjectively; own your own experience. This is the best way to help open pathways for others to honor and respect their own experiences.

I leave you with a metaphor and prayer that I learned from Janine Benyus, the godmother of the emerging field of biomimicry: *May we all learn to carry stories like birds carry seeds in their feathers, to help seed the vision of a new world. Whenever an ecosystem has been traumatized or decimated, it can be brought back to life by the seeds that birds carry on their feathers. In the course of their living, flying and eating, they drop those seeds in seemingly random places, to reignite fertility and diversity, as well as hope, regeneration, and life.*

PROMPTS FOR DEEPENING LEARNING
THROUGH REFLECTION, WRITING OR DISCUSSION

The Power of Story:
V (formerly known as Eve Ensler)

THEMES

- V's play *The Vagina Monologues* brilliantly illustrates the power of story-telling to raise awareness globally about violence against women, and to shift culture towards healing.
- Her life demonstrates her ability to turn her own painful story into inspiration, action, and resources to support others.
- One Billion Rising celebrates women's ability to rise up and express their connection, liberation, and healing.

PROMPTS

How does V use her own story to shift consciousness inside herself and everywhere? How does she uplift the voices of silenced women?

What do you think is central to the amazing success of *The Vagina Monologues?*

How do you relate to V's courage in her stand to actually end violence against women?
How does it feel to you?

- Is your own stand large enough to reflect your heart's true desire?

Here are some story-telling points:

- Don't be afraid of your own vulnerability.

- Don't lecture or tell people what they should think or feel; instead offer your own subjective transformative experience.
- By valuing your own story, you give others permission to trust the value of their own.

How has telling stories enhanced your leadership skills? How might you expand and make more effective your use of storytelling as a leadership tool?

CELEBRATING WOMEN'S WAYS

I find myself appreciating women —
and valuing what we bring to the world —
in this writhing, frightening change-time, more every day.

And I so deeply admire men who are
learning from women's ways,
becoming better listeners, rotating leadership,
and staying connected to others —
even while you stay true to your own purposes.
Remembering the value of beauty, relatedness,
flexibility, pausing, and reflection.

I am oddly reassured by the ancient prophecies
that predicted this would be a time
for the return of the Feminine —
a time for re-balancing the world.

Perhaps I seek reassurance from our ancestors,
for what I already know, deep in my bones,
is true and needed and right.

I'm discovering aspects of myself as a woman
that I'd largely abandoned,

ones that are larger than I've allowed myself to be,
parts that are fierce, fiery, and feisty,
also playful, sure-footed, and wise.

Before, I imagined them too dangerous to reveal.
Now, I feel called to bring all of me to bear —
from the place of my own commitment,
from the place of my deep love for people and nature and culture.
My fear pales in comparison with what's at stake.

I remember that we teach young women
to be good by following the rules,
coloring inside the lines, and not making waves.
We're taught to keep our heads low — to avoid conflict.
To be good at caring for others, and knowing what they need —
   often well ahead of knowing our own needs, ourselves.

But we expect young men to rebel.
To find their own identity,
they're encouraged to defy the norms,
to stand firm in their own convictions,
and to step out on their own.
Boys are applauded for taking risks,
and for bragging, or boasting
about their achievements.

Girls are told to demure and be quiet.
Admonished not to show off,
"not to be so full of yourself."

(Who are we supposed to be full of,

      we might wonder, if not ourselves?)

Many of us are learning, now,

to turn that caring and nurturing inward as well,

and to toss out some of our good-girl conditioning,

to step out and fulfill our purposes

in creative, risky, and authentic ways.

How encouraging to find women emerging everywhere,

stepping out of our safety zones,

mirroring and complementing each other's strength and vulnerability

which is the "power through," not "power over" that is the essence

of power being redefined and reclaimed

      by women all over.

What do I love most about women?

(As reminders for us all

about women's magnificence

in this transitional time.)

When women interact intimately,

there's a lot more going on than an exchange of ideas.

We absorb each other's textures, scents, and colors.

We inhale each other's bearing,

intuiting undercurrents of childhood,

gleaning molecules of emotion —

our bodies trade a hundred unspoken cues.

As women enter deeper relational waters,
our enthusiasms become infectious,
our beginnings and endings blur, seamlessly.
We enjoy the rhythms we form with each other,
concepts coinciding as our passions swirl.

We not only braid our thoughts, ideas, and feelings together,
we let our memories mingle with our intuitions and our dreams.
I love how often women remember how much we don't know —
and that our intuition or silence, dreams or deep listening
often bring whatever is most needed.

At our best, we weave our worlds together,
contrasting combinations of disparate realities.
Creating a multicolored canvas thick with texture and pigment.

Changing our moods and minds as often as the winds —
but rarely our hearts, our truest compasses.

As women, our bodies and the moon instruct us
to recognize the cyclical nature of change.

We understand innately that the destruction and death
all around us
          also mean that a birth is immanent.

Each of us, men and women alike,
are being asked to assist in this labor.
To deliver the profound, fierce, single-focused commitment to life
      that accompanies any successful birth.

The midwives know that
      it's just when the labor is becoming most
          scary, bloody, and intense,
just when the mother feels she cannot
      bear the pain any further —
that is when you know that
      the baby is about to be born.

As women, we attentively attune to our bodies,
relishing the pulses of deep knowing that come
from our bellies.

Together, we knit dimensional patterns of our laughter,
anger, sadness, and the holy water of our tears.

We yearn to mend the tattered fragments,
to turn our anger into compassionate action.
To integrate the painful, frightening,
enraged hot beauty and the flows of
laughter, unity, and celebration into
      dancing a new world into being.

PROMPTS FOR DEEPENING LEARNING
THROUGH REFLECTION, WRITING OR DISCUSSION

Celebrating Women's Ways

THEMES
- Appreciating women stepping out of our safety zones and shedding negative conditioning.
- Celebrating and uplifting women's unique qualities: connectedness to cycles, to each other, to the earth, to intuition, to listening and tending and mending, to color, and movement — while admiring men who support and embody women's ways.

PROMPTS

I find reassurance in the ancient prophecy that predicts the return of the "feminine" as a time for rebalancing the world. I often refer to non-conventional sources such as these.
- Do you find myths and prophecies useful?
- What nonrational sources of wisdom do you learn from?
- How do they contribute to your sense of what is true and your understanding of what is happening now?

In relation to gender roles, what conditioning do you recognize in yourself that you would like to shed?
- What do you love about women?
- What don't you like or trust?

Be real, risk telling the truth of whatever comes up. Go around your circle and appreciate something you've noticed about each woman in the group. Notice how it feels, afterward — in your body, heart, mind, and spirit.

PROMPTS FOR DEEPENING LEARNING
THROUGH REFLECTION, WRITING OR DISCUSSION

Embodied or Group Practices for Part II

EXPRESSING FEELINGS

What happens when you allow the terrible statistics of the "global war on women" into your heart? What feelings arise? Express both the difficult reality and your own feelings in some creative form: writing, chanting, painting, dancing.

CONFRONTING COMPETITION

Do you experience patterns of competition with women friends or co-workers? Identify someone with whom you experience this sense of competition and explore what might lie underneath the pattern: insecurity, jealousy, a wound from the past?

Try thumb-wrestling with another, or racing to reach a goal, or notice if you compete inwardly, comparing clothes, beauty, or sexuality of yourself with another. How does it feel? Notice any positive or negative associations and how they affect how you feel about yourself.

Imagine letting go of that to move towards mutual support, and notice what that feels like, including any resistance you may feel.

TO STRENGTHEN COLLABORATION AND PARTNERSHIPS:

Sit with a person with whom you would like to have a more collaborative, stronger relationship to accomplish a task. First tell each other a story about your lives that's not task-related, one that shares something of your innermost realities. Perhaps introduce yourselves in ways you never have before. Then, identify a common vision or goal.

Next, ask each other: What do you most need to feel supported in this task? Listen with an open heart, and take notes of what your partner is naming. If something isn't working, gently request a different approach.

Appreciate in words something about how you experience the other.

End by asking and responding to the question: How might we hold ourselves and each other accountable? What agreements could support us in that?

OWNING OUR INDIGENEITY

We are all indigenous to some place on planet Earth. How much do you know about your ancestors and where they came from?

Learn about your own lineage and their values, challenges, and customs. Create a way to honor your ancestors and/or forgive them: imagine and write or draw their childhoods, or maybe create an altar, a ritual, an artistic expression, or a family tree.

EMBODY WHAT YOU VALUE

Reflect upon how your leadership behaviors do or don't reflect your deeply-held values. In the places where they may not, first forgive yourself — recognizing that we are all works in progress, and cultivating ourselves toward who we wish to become.

Where they are congruent, appreciate that alignment in yourself. Now imagine a practice or strategy that might help you to align more congruently. Create a reminder to help you engage that practice.

STORY-TELLING PRACTICE #1: Tell a story to another person of a leader you admire or of your own vision or accomplishment, with a goal of inspiring them to join you in something you care deeply about.

Listen non-defensively for their response about what moved them and what didn't, receiving their feedback as an investment in your leadership.

STORY TELLING PRACTICE #2: Write a one-page story about a transformational moment in your life.

Now rewrite or edit it, using these practical tips:

- Be specific and sensory in your imagery;
- Reveal your vulnerability;
- Don't tell people what to think or feel;
- Humor and humility are always welcome.

When you are done, see how those changes may have enlivened the story.

READ/PERFORM LIBERATING STORIES

If you have not attended or participated in a performance of *The Vagina Monologues*, read the play, watch on video, or better yet, get together with a group of women to read it out loud together.

BREAKING TABOOS

In *The Vagina Monologues,* V broke a taboo to ignite a movement. Reflect on what taboos might be stopping you from speaking your truth.

Write a monologue about your discovery of your own sexual nature, or about something else that feels risky to you.

- What fears arise when you think about sharing it?
- Can you go ahead and share with a person you trust anyway?

If you do, reflect on what happened and appreciate yourself for your courage.

EMBODIED MOVEMENT FOR CHANGE

Inspired by One Billion Rising: Move or dance, alone or with others; play some music you love and totally let yourself go.

If emotions arise, let yourself express them with your body.

Afterwards, notice how movement can shift your energy.

LOVING WOMEN WHOLE-HEARTEDLY

Reflect on what you love about women and express it in a creative endeavor: a poem, drawing, collage, song, or dance.

PART III

Toward Wholeness

GENDER EQUITY, FULL-SPECTRUM LEADERSHIP, & RACIAL JUSTICE

VALUING RELATIONSHIP & TRADITION
Towards a Future That Works for All

As seasonal cycles become wobblier, migrations increasingly uncertain, and food harvests ever more unpredictable, wars rage, hurricanes land and millions flee their homes. In the U.S., police violence against African Americans has become so widely visible (thanks to the courage and presence of the young people who videotaped it all) that it reached a tipping point. Political vitriol has been flashing hotter and meaner, reigniting misogyny, fear and hatred in millions. In many places the sweet waters of Mother Earth have become too toxic to drink, and indigenous protectors are gathering from all directions to try and stop the plunder for the sake of future generations and all life on Earth.

I've been listening for guidance. Life has been teaching me to look for patterns to help me understand what's needed to shift our culture, to reorient toward what's sacred and whole.

The first way I learned taught me to balance my body, heart, mind, and spirit. Using those filters helped me to witness myself. It required listening to what my body knew, and heeding my emotions, dreams, and intuition, as well as the reasoning of my mind. Helping knit women together in song and dance, story and ritual — to share our vulnerabilities in webs of relational caring and empathic connection — can fling open the possibilities of healing, collaboration, and aligned sisterhood.

Being in ceremony, practicing ritual and story with open hearts, is what's made those relationships across differences possible. I now believe that these practices could yield the same results toward healing and forging connection among all caring people.

I've seen how recognizing the truths of our shared yet differing wounds can create pathways for our factionalized women's movements to grow into the larger web of resistance, voice, and power that is needed to reclaim our democracy and shift our course.

Recently, I visited friends who live traditionally on the Penticton Indian Reservation in the Okanagan region of British Columbia. I share these learnings humbly and cautiously, as I am aware of my "outsider" or "settler" reality, with no intent of misappropriating Native culture.

My only purposes are towards learning and healing, and honoring the immense value of indigenous knowledge traditions to us all in this precarious time. I visited Penticton during their seasonal Salmon Ceremony, a time when I could experience their practices of nurturing their relationships with the land, their community, the river, the salmon, and their traditions.

The Okanagan culture is designed around teachings called the Four Societies, or Enowkin wixw. It is an ancient social technology that has taught them through generations how to relate in a balanced and respectful way to all the various parts of people, community and Mother Earth.

The idea of the Four Societies reminds us that it's necessary to respect, include, and accommodate them all equally in our decision-making. As Jeannette Armstrong, culture bearer and educator from the Okanagan Syilx Nation, puts it:

Our tradition demands four things from us and they all have equal weight. The Four Societies are: tradition and vision, relationship and action.

The tradition society relates to what's worked before, to the land and the sacred. It corresponds to the elder within us.

The vision society focuses on what's ahead, on the future, on what creatively has yet to come. It is related to the energy of youth.

The relationship society is responsible for caring for any impacts or influences of a decision upon the people, and all beings. It is related to the feminine archetype.

The action society focuses on how to do things, on analysis, implementation, sequencing, tools, and resources. It is related to the masculine part of our psyches.

People are trained by their elders to listen and speak for one of each of the four societies. Any decision the people make must integrate all four perspectives with full equality.

This approach from the Okanagan culture is an ancient, living blueprint for Justice, Equity, and Inclusion. Reflecting on the Four Societies, I see how often we've privileged vision and action over tradition and relationship. I see how our systems and structures have perpetuated a bias, a deeply entrenched valuing of only two of the four. Vision and Action have systematically trumped Tradition and Relationship.

In scanning for patterns among indigenous philosophies, I see how deeply tradition, land, and relationship are valued. In the Okanagan language, for instance, the word they use for their bodies contains the word for land within it. "We're not just part of the land," Jeannette writes, "the land IS us."

From Tiokasin Ghosthorse, I learned that in the Lakota language, the word for soil means "who we used to be." Imagine remembering that relationship to Mother Earth each time we mention soil.

As Jeannette Armstrong writes: "When we include the perspective of the land, and we include the perspective of relationships, people in the community actually change. The desire to secure material wealth and fear of not having 'things' to sustain you disappear. When you start realizing that people and community are there to sustain you, this gives the most secure feeling in the world."

I call that the relationship economy. When the 2008 economic crisis hit, I knew that the only real security lay in the web of relationships each of us has, cultivates, and cares for.

Arriving at the Salmon Ceremony, we drove into a provincial park adjacent to the Okanagan River. The day sparkled with dappled sunlight, and the feast had just begun. While most of the people there were from the traditional tribal community, others included international students and locals who were curious, or friends. Walking in, everyone was welcoming. Each person I met gazed into my eyes with warmth, curiosity and dignity. Everyone was served, a couple hundred of us, and the salmon was sweet and moist.

Afterward, the salmon's bones and entrails were returned ceremonially with blessings to the river. There was a purification ceremony. To traditional drumming and time-honored songs, at the river's edge a woman prayed as she cleansed each person in turn.

At an open mic, Okanagan cousins from Texas had just come from Standing Rock. They spoke with pride of the determination of the Protectors there, noting how many peoples from so many nations were gathering, and praising how their Lakota friends were welcoming everyone, regardless of their background or color.

Next came a give-away, where this community which has so little monetarily and yet are so wealthy culturally, distributed gifts to everyone assembled. Four tarps were mounded high with goodies and one by one, with timeless patience and care, accompanied by traditional songs and the frolicking laughter of children, all were gifted. Generosity and kindness, patience and gratitude filled the air.

When I left, I felt suffused with thankfulness. I had the sense that I'd experienced something of the "preferred state" that Buckminster Fuller spoke about: that state of equilibrium and reciprocity where all is in right relationship.

Well, almost. The contrast between the beauty, richness, and power of their cultural practices and the financial poverty and malnourishment of so many of their people pierced my heart. I wept much of the way home to the U.S., as the contrast was overwhelming, and I was overflowing with gratitude.

May we have the humility to listen for guidance from the land, from our ancestors, and from our bodies and hearts, minds and intuition.

May we then have the wisdom to hear it, and act upon it, even if it comes from the least expected places.

May we face this fractured young nation's history — built upon genocide and slavery, lies, broken promises, and domination — and choose, for the sake of healing, to walk through the fear and traumas, tears and fires needed for healing, together.

May we find the collective vision, courage, and will to decolonize our minds and hearts, reclaiming a balance of feminine & masculine, of tradition and vision, relationship and action in equal measure that will flow through each of us to all.

PROMPTS FOR DEEPENING LEARNING
THROUGH REFLECTION, WRITING OR DISCUSSION

Valuing Relationships & Tradition (Towards a Future that Works for All)

THEMES

- Indigenous life ways and knowledge traditions have much to offer contemporary mainstream society.

- In the Okanagan teachings called The Four Societies (Tradition, Vision, Relationship, and Action), decision-making and community health are designed to integrate all four perspectives equally whereas we in patriarchal culture tend to favor vision and action.

PROMPTS

I describe the Okanagan Salmon Ceremony in detail because it so moved me to be welcomed as a participant and witness to a ritual that expresses the right relations between humans with each other and with the land, creatures, and waters that sustain our lives.

- Have you participated in any kinds of ceremony?

- If so, can you share or write about it, naming what values you recognize as embedded in the ritual?

- What wisdom traditions or lifeways from your own lineage do you love? Reflect, research, and share with others.

How do you balance the modes of action and relationship, tradition and vision in your own life and decision-making?

- Consider an example and notice: which tend to take priority for you?
- How does the Okanagan way of reaching a decision compare to how our Western capitalist societies make decisions?
- How might we learn from this model to improve our own governing practices?

HEALING AT THE INTERSECTIONS
Environment and Social Justice Conjoin at Bioneers

Nina Simons' acceptance speech for the 2017 Goi Peace Award, which she received with her husband/partner, Kenny Ausubel. Based in Tokyo, the Goi Peace Foundation established this annual award in 2000 to recognize individuals and organizations that have contributed to creating a peaceful and harmonious world as well as building a better future.

F irst, I wish to express my deepest gratitude to the Goi Peace Foundation, for honoring Kenny and me, and Bioneers, with this award. We accept this honor with humility, and on behalf of the large and extended community of those visionaries Kenny Ausubel — my partner, husband and co-founder — back in 1990, coined a term to describe: "Bioneers."

What we mean now by Bioneers is: scientific, political, and social innovators, activists, cultural bridge-builders, and leaders from many walks of life and fields of endeavor who are collaboratively contributing to the great global ecological and socio-cultural transformation now underway. It is an enormous validation that you here at the Goi Foundation, who have done so much to promote world peace, and are based halfway around the planet from the U.S., have heard of Bioneers and perceive value in our work. Thank you.

In accepting this honor, I wish to offer some reflections about what I think makes Bioneers a unique enterprise. On the physical plane, it's a relatively small nonprofit organization, but one that has developed into a key nexus for many diverse but intersecting social movements.

It provides a forum annually that highlights some of the most inspiring and practical solutions to humanity's most pressing crises. We sometimes call it a "network of networks." In fact, it's a dynamic, ever-evolving living system whose goal is to help co-create, midwife, and nurture a new world, the birth of a new civilization, one that's far more peaceful, equitable, healthy, and resilient — goals that we, of course, share with you here.

We work toward a future that goes beyond the idea of sustainability as a goal. Merely sustaining ecosystems and communities while much better than destroying them, as we currently so often do — we find to be too timid as an ultimate goal. We aim for not just a sustainable human footprint, but one that is regenerative for all of life.

We seek the restoration of health and vitality to natural systems and to human communities by combining the best of ancient wisdom with the leading edge of contemporary "whole-systems" approaches.

At the heart of this notion is the idea that we humans need to be humble, to become students of nature's extraordinarily sophisticated design genius. We have to reorient our learning by observing how nature operates, and reinvent our civilizations by cooperating with her rather than by seeking to dominate her. This requires us to remember that there is wisdom all around us, including from our old-growth cultures, the Indigenous Peoples of Earth. We see this collaborative vision as helping to strengthen life's capacity for healing and renewal through a respectful and loving partnership with life's mysterious, ancient, and complex nature.

One of the foundations of our worldview is that, just as in the natural world in which the most diverse ecosystems are the most resilient and vital, the human enterprise also thrives best when it is characterized by high degrees of diversity. In our work, therefore, we have always sought to highlight a broad array of innovative approaches to solving problems, presented from diverse perspectives, disciplines, generations, and cultures, including a very strong emphasis on honoring the wisdom of Indigenous First Peoples and of long-lived traditional ecological wisdom.

At a conference in 1994, the physicist, ecologist, and activist Vandana Shiva from India offered some crucial distinctions between a "bioneer" and a pioneer. She warned that rapid scientific innovations intended to improve upon biology posed tremendous risks. Highly aggressive biologists and corporations seeking to profit from poorly conceived genetic manipulation look very much like the European pioneers, who thought that every land they conquered was an empty land. They believed that land had no people, or no people that they respected as full human beings, so they saw no need to respect any pre- existing rights.

Those we have called bioneers, on the other hand, recognize that every step we take is on a full Earth populated by a tremendous variety of species and many other people. The pioneer "empty land" ethic, Shiva noted, "leads to violence against species and to genocide. The colonizing pioneer's mind assumes there are no limits to be respected, no ecological limits, no ethical limits, no limits to greed or accumulation, no limits to inequality. No limits to the violence to be unleashed on other species and people." And no limits to seeking to reshape molecules in complex living systems that we don't understand.

"Whereas authentic bioneers," she said, "know that limits are the first law of nature, encoded in the ecological processes that make life possible. Limits of the nutrient cycle in soil, limits of the water cycle. The limits set by the intrinsic right of diverse species to exist set limits on our actions, if we genuinely respect other beings. Ethical limits are what make us human. To be sustainable, a society must live within those limits."

Shiva spoke of a Hindi term, *vasudhaiva kutumbakam*, which means "we are one-earth family," or the "democracy of life." She explained that "to bioneers, it means not just diverse human cultures, but all beings. The mountains and the rivers are beings, too. We bioneers respect all the beings, large and small, without a hierarchy of superiority and inferiority, because everything has a part to play ecologically in the web of life, even if we do not fully understand how."

And being a bioneer also means recognizing that, just as the web of life is interconnected and interdependent, so too are all the issues we face.

Over time, the large annual conference we have produced for the past 28 years expanded to present a wider spectrum of interrelated issues and solutions. It became increasingly clear to me that there could no longer be any perceived separation between people and the "environment." We are a part of nature, not apart from it. We are not separate from the environment or from nature. Our bodies are made of the same materials, the same DNA as plants, fungi, and animals.

We are all connected, both biologically and spiritually. Since the Earth is a closed loop, the cup of tea you drink today may have once been Cleopatra's bathwater.

What we do to the Earth, we do to ourselves. When we harm ourselves and other people, we wound the Earth. Therefore, being a bioneer must include pursuing social justice and equity for all humans as well as protecting ecosystems.

For the first ten years or so, I used the term "bioneer" to describe the people on stage, the presenters we invited to speak, leading figures who offered brilliant new approaches and practical models of ecological or social restoration. I was unconscious of my own internalized hierarchy, but all that changed when the late J.L. Chestnut spoke in 2001. He was a renowned attorney and legendary Civil Rights activist since the brutal struggles in the U.S. South of the 1950s, and he expanded my definition of a bioneer into something larger.

He was telling the story of winning the largest class action lawsuit in the history of America — against the U.S. Government for institutional racism against Black farmers in the Southeastern U.S. It was a powerful talk, and he did something I'd never heard before. He began to use the word bioneer to address everyone in the room.

He noted that the progress that's being made, slowly but surely, to bring our country toward racial and social justice and true democracy was due in part to the efforts of "You bioneers, dedicated progressive people like you." He went on to say, "I raise these concerns to you because fighting on behalf of women, on behalf of minority people of color, fighting on behalf of the environment and the planet are all one big battle. We bioneers know that violence, greed, racism, unchecked materialism, and abuse of this planet and the nature in and on it is its own form of terrorism, and will eventually destroy us if we don't first put an end to it."

It was a revelatory moment for me. Suddenly, that word didn't just describe the visionary innovators on stage, but applied to us all. Not only the speakers, but every man, woman, and child present, or hearing Bioneers podcasts or radio, or seeing our videos, or anyone working toward healing our relationship with Earth in thousands of different ways.

We each have a role to play. We are all *bioneers*, if we choose to be. All our contributions, all our collective creativity and imagination are needed to help reinvent this world.

As J.L. Chestnut said, the way our cultures have treated women, people of color, Indigenous People, immigrants, and the Earth are all just different octaves of the same legacy. We all, regardless of our differences, bear the scars of a culture that's founded on conquest, exploitation, and oppression. This tendency we have shown over time, to invest in the false myths of superiority or separation, seems to be at the root of our common challenges. With patterns so entrenched, so pervasive, and so overwhelming, how can we shift our course?

I began to see that we're all, in varying ways, responding to often unconscious influences and implicit biases from a legacy of disrespect and violence that manifests on all levels of society — from the personal, emotional, and physical, to the economic, political, and environmental.

Thankfully, we also know the power of community and connection, and we are gifted with a capacity for self-reflection and choice. Each time we opt to relate caringly, choosing to meet others on common ground instead of reinforcing separation with those whose views may differ, we begin to help heal and restore our social landscape. Each time we renew ourselves in nature, sensing with our full bodies, hearts, and intuitions the repair and guidance she so abundantly offers, we help the healing happen.

During the years since, Bioneers has evolved greatly, prompted in part by this understanding. We've sought to design for a whole-systems approach to how people learn. Since people process information in different ways — integrating audio, visual, and kinesthetic information with varying priorities — we've designed sessions that speak to those multiple ways of perceiving.

Appreciating that diversity includes speaking to introverts and extroverts, creative and analytical thinkers, people of all ages and ethnicities and disciplines and also of all classes, orientations, and abilities, we strive to be as inclusive and accessible as possible. We hope to meet people where they are, and reach peoples' hearts through their rational minds and sensing bodies, as well as their intuition and values.

We are also committed to not shying away from the difficult conversations, the challenging, complex issues, in order to deepen our own understanding and learning.

We hope to educate, inspire, and ignite engaged action, while identifying and illuminating the most promising solutions and strategies. By juxtaposing seemingly disparate issues and mingling them with arts and ceremony, we help reveal how all issues are part of one dynamic, interrelated living system, which embeds us within the context of the living world.

We all need each other to make the large-scale changes we face. Relationships of authentic cooperation, collaboration, and community will become absolutely critical in the years ahead, because we are facing immense challenges. Bridging our differences respectfully will determine whether or not we succeed at shifting human civilization from our current ecocidal trajectory.

In the past several years, I have realized that for me to be able to help create effective change *"out there"* in the world, I have to also work on seeing — and then changing — myself. There have been many ways in which I have internalized the unresolved wounds, blind spots, and biases of our U.S. culture, from gender bias to racial injustice. I am trying hard to reconcile them, to make peace within myself.

As I've searched for insights to help me in this quest, I've come to feel that, while racial divides still roil and rupture our societies and I can't imagine experiencing the discrimination and micro-aggressions so many minority people experience each day — the biases that privilege the masculine over the feminine create at least as great an unconscious barrier to equity and peace among people as faith, race, or cultural differences. In recent years, studies have shown gender to be the bias most deeply embedded in the human psyche, globally.

Like most women, I've experienced thousands of moments of feeling diminished, threatened, or intimidated because of my gender. Inwardly, I also see ways I've unconsciously acquired some learned beliefs about women and limited my own options and pathways as a result.

But I realize that gender and race are only two of the many ways we diminish each other and ourselves. Nearly all of us have experienced feeling slighted or disrespected somewhere, whether for our ethnicity, age, size, sexual preference, ability, class, or appearance. While I am inspired to see that much progress has occurred in some of these areas, we have far more work to do to heal the wounds that separate us.

I believe that investing in the leadership of women — and restoring the "feminine" to a place of equilibrium with the "masculine" throughout all of our lived experience as individuals, as well as in our institutions and culture — are essential to the global transformation that we, as a species, are being called to make, in order to shift our course to a life-affirming future on Earth.

Around the globe, we see clearly that wherever the rights, opportunities, and safety of women improve, benefits result for all areas of society. As women's leadership and gender equity increase, so too do economic prosperity, public health, education, peace, and the security of nations. As women's education and reproductive rights improve globally, they will also have significant effects in curbing population growth, drawing down carbon, and slowing climate change.

Since we've inherited some skewed stereotypes about what the masculine and feminine really mean, I suggest we seek to identify and reclaim healthy identities that can include and embrace a full array of our human capacities, regardless of what our physical gender identity might be.

We need the full generative capacity of the active principle, informed by the best listening and guidance of the receptive within us all, to succeed together at collectively midwifing a peaceful, regenerative, and just world, to be born out of this turbulence.

Since we all contain masculine and feminine within us, this is ultimately about restoring our human wholeness. About practicing listening and not-knowing, more often than asserting that we know the answers. About evolving from power over to power with and power to co-create change. It's about trusting that leadership is often better shared, and that win-win solutions frequently exist, if we seek them out patiently, practicing mutual respect, patience, and trust.

As Indigenous Peoples of the Amazon say, "the bird of humanity has been trying to fly for far too long with only one wing."

May we have the humility to listen for guidance from the land, from our ancestors, and from our bodies and hearts, as well as our minds, dreams, and intuition. May we have the wisdom to hear it, and act upon it, even if it comes from the least expected or most surprising places.

May we find the collective vision, courage, and will to decolonize our minds and hearts, reclaiming a balance of feminine & masculine, of receptive and active, of yin and yang in equal measure that flow through us each and all.

May our partnership with the land, our mother Earth, Gaia, and the sweet and salty waters that flow in her veins, the winds and clouds that caress and bathe her, and the fires that cleanse and restore her vitality, and our kinship with all the creatures large and small who share this sacred home become our devotional, long-term relationship practice.

May this lead us collectively toward a world that's re-infused with a sense of the sacred, where the future children of all species live and flourish in peace, and where restorative justice, health, and regeneration thrive.

Awomen. Amen. May it be so. Thank you.

PROMPTS FOR DEEPENING LEARNING
THROUGH REFLECTION, WRITING OR DISCUSSION

Healing at the Intersections: Environment and Social Justice Conjoin at Bioneers

THEMES

Bioneers has always embodied a whole systems approach to advance nature's designs and diversity, but our organization reached a deeper commitment to social justice when we realized that working on behalf of racial and social justice, women, democracy and the environment are all one and the same struggle.

PROMPTS

Bioneers made an evolutionary leap when we heard from renowned civil rights activist J.L. Chestnut that "The way our cultures have treated women, people of color, Indigenous Peoples, immigrants, and the earth are all octaves of the same legacy." I saw how our inherited biases are at the root of all our challenges.

- Do you think US mainstream culture has come to this understanding yet?
- Discuss in what ways you see such a shift, and in what ways not? What might be in the way?
- Can you give an example from your own experience of how environmental and social justice are related?

When did you first hear the phrase Environmental Justice and how do you understand it?

- What does the word intersectionality mean to you?
- In what ways has your understanding of these concepts shifted your own ideas, work or actions?

I like to end speeches with a prayer.

- Write or say your own prayer, expressing what your heart yearns for.
- Speak your deepest aspiration for people and planet out loud. Share with others.

ESCAPING THE TILTED ROOM

Has anyone among us not felt powerless, experienced being the dissenting or minority voice, or felt unfairly judged, devalued, or dismissed for being different?

We have all experienced a culture that elevates some while denigrating others. As a young woman right out of college, for some years I believed the feminist movement had accomplished its goals, and that I was stepping onto a level playing field. That same naiveté, mixed with idealism and some cultural blindness, also had me imagining that the Civil Rights Movement had largely ended racial bias and injustice in this country.

It wasn't until much later — after years of being the only woman in business settings, of negotiating biased gender dynamics personally, professionally, and politically, that I began to realize how much gender roles and related power dynamics were impacting my experience — and how painful and damaging those impacts were.

It was several years after that, when I began peeling back the layers of my own defensiveness and denial, that I began to learn how racialized our society still is, and to discover my own personal and cultural complicity in it. Gender and race are only two of the ways we rank and compete with each other — benefiting some, and harming others. In this society, we also create hierarchies based on age, sexual orientation, body shape, class, education, and abilities, to name just a few.

As I work to integrate and distill what I've been learning, an especially useful metaphor for me is the "Tilted Room." I found it in Melissa Harris-Perry's book *Sister Citizen*, about the stereotypes that Black women in America encounter as they work to establish a unique identity, and achieve agency and recognition. She describes a cognitive psychology experiment in which people were placed in a crooked chair within a crooked room, and asked to align themselves vertically. Researchers were surprised that — even in a room tilted as much as 35° — some people reported that they were perfectly straight, simply because they were in alignment with their surroundings. Only a few managed to find uprightness.

As Harris-Perry notes, "It can be hard to stand up straight in a crooked room." We're all products of a culture that's filled with tilted rooms, spaces designed to get us to relate in ways that defy the natural instincts of our bodies, hearts, and souls. Though the room may be tipped according to differing sets of biases, it's rarely level. Some benefit from a headwind, while many face persistent and systematized obstacles.

Our dysfunctional families, educational institutions, media, cities, food and health care, economic and political systems create and reinforce striated structures of race, class, gender, and other "isms" that keep us apart. Since these biases aren't conducive to symbiosis, and we all contain both victim and perpetrator within us, we become stuck in win/lose, dualistic, and polarizing dynamics. The systems that tilted rooms represent, and those biased perceptions and the policies and social structures they inform, keep us divided — preventing collaboration, coalition, and movement-building.

And, though it may seem otherwise, they damage the ones who benefit from the tilt as much as those who are disadvantaged by it. They hurt us all.

At a Cultivating Women's Leadership intensive, the women of color requested a time to caucus, where they could visit together apart from the White women. (I'll never forget this, as the sensory image is forever imprinted in my memory.) Across the lawn, the women of color and indigenous women gathered on a porch. Like birds with showy plumage, they were a feast of vibrant color. With long dresses, scarves, painted toenails, and hair done in ribbons, their visual expression was glorious and brilliant. Sound-wise too, they were expressive, as gales of laughter, a musicality in their voices and an occasional shout carried across the space between us.

Among the White women's group, everyone was wearing white, grey, and khaki. Their faces were glum, and their expressions sad, guilty, and depressed. They couldn't understand why such a division might be needed, and why it had been initiated. As they hesitantly voiced their chagrin at feeling the separation, I noted how much the dimming of our light, the quieting of our voices, as White women, might be a cost of our unearned privilege.

How do we escape the tilted room? It is no small feat. It requires practice to disengage from those prevalent, insidious beliefs within us that help keep it in place. It requires a willingness to learn, humility about what we don't see or know, and a choice to shift our perception and understanding.

It asks that we reorient ourselves toward reaching across these divisions of gender, race, and class — *and be willing to risk and to fail, for the sake of learning.* It means strengthening that intrinsic relational intelligence that comes from our body's wisdom, our heart's guidance, and our moral compass.

Being White, or male, or heterosexual, or middle class, or highly educated, or rich or successful makes it particularly difficult to recognize that a tilt exists. But if you're on the losing end of the tilt, it's hard to ever forget, or not feel, the injustice of it, every hour of the day. One friend, an accomplished leader of mixed ethnicity, told me she felt as if she is continually climbing uphill on her knees, with broken glass strewn across her path — while White folks have running shoes, a clear walkway, and the wind at their backs.

Hearing the truth of others' realities, and sensing how painful they've been, I have realized that I previously grappled with injustice principally through my rational analysis and intellect — and from a distance that my privilege afforded me. Now, trying to listen at the deepest level, while loving and respecting the beauty, dignity, and power I see in others' lived truths, has wrought a deeper change in me.

To overcome the tilted room, to heal ourselves from the habit of ranking, will require amplifying our listening to our hearts, intuitions, and bodies. Our minds as primary navigator tend to perpetuate patterns, and are treacherously good at inventing stories to rationalize behavior that seems 'normal,' because it's habituated. It's only by strengthening those ways of knowing and choosing to keep our hearts open, receptive to others' pain and feeling, that we can shift these insidious patterns and break free of the chronic tilt.

Many women across the nation and the world experienced it on the historic day of the January 2017 Women's March. It was transformative to see the kindness, creativity, and care that were exhibited that day, as well as to sense the joy of feeling aligned with others who are different, focusing on connection and commonality of purpose. No one was arrested. All were respectful. It gave us all a palpable sense of what's possible, together.

It also revealed the shadow side of women's leadership. During the weeks and months that followed, I read on social media rants by sub-groups who felt they'd been snubbed, disrespectfully treated, and were angered at the ignorance of many of the newcomers there. Generations of wounding revealed deep rifts among diverse women, where little empathy or understanding has been encouraged or taught. Frustration emerged from women of color, demanding rightfully that White women take responsibility for educating themselves. White women's feelings were hurt, and some of them turned away. Of course, the media featured and exaggerated these rifts.

As I practice getting better at appreciating these gifts (of feeling, intuition, and embodied awareness), I recognize and encourage them more, both in myself and others. This is helping to free me from tilted rooms, strengthening my resolve, and increasing my toolkit toward co-creating the beloved community that is my heart's deepest yearning.

Thankfully, we can cultivate relationship intelligence by choosing it.

One specific practice that I've discovered is that my body's reactions — when I think someone might have said something racially or otherwise offensive to another — are far more reliable than my mind. As my mother taught me, my body never lies. If I pay close attention, I notice that my stomach lurches when I hear something that could be perceived as harmful, though it likely was not intended to be. If I am paying adequate attention to notice this in myself, then I can say, *"My stomach just let me know that what you just said might have been hurtful or felt off to another in the room. Is that true?"* In that way, I can take responsibility for stopping the conversation, creating a pause so that if a harm was felt, it can be unpacked and learned from. By responding to my body's signals, I don't need to accuse anyone, or presuppose intent, but can simply notice a disturbance in the field.

Another story: I became friends with a young woman of mixed Lakota descent who participated in another CWL intensive. She was a young mother, a businesswoman, community organizer, and a cancer survivor who had created innovative opportunities to help women from her nation to come together for healing. I was deeply impressed by her courage and creativity, found her wise well beyond her years, and admired her greatly.

Months after the retreat, I learned she was going through a difficult time, though I knew nothing of the details. I called her to offer my support and express my concern on her behalf. She told me that she'd recently learned that her two nieces — aged 8 and 12 — had been raped. Sobbing uncontrollably, she told me their names, and about what loving, innocent, and tender young girls they'd been. She explained that the perpetrator lived within their family house, and that there were no counseling resources available to them. The girls were not willing to report the abuse, or leave their home. I listened to her express her pain, frustration, and grief for over an hour. When I hung up the phone, I felt shattered.

I had known about rates of rape and sexual abuse of women in Indian Country, but I had known about them from afar. I had read articles and seen news reports on the systemic challenges of jurisdiction on reservations, on the increased incidence of rape and sex trafficking in oil and gas drilling camps and on reservation lands, and had felt an affronted indignation at the failures of our systems to protect indigenous women and girls. Hearing this beloved friend wail her grief and frustration with the names and descriptions of her young kin brought the truth of that epidemic home to my heart, in a way I had not known before.

PROMPTS FOR DEEPENING LEARNING
THROUGH REFLECTION, WRITING OR DISCUSSION

Escaping the Tilted Room

THEMES
- Melissa Harris-Perry's metaphor "the tilted room" demonstrates how effectively unconscious biases distort our reality.
- Biases hurts those who hold them, as well as those on the receiving end.
- Deep listening and conscious practice are needed to become aware of bias and unlearn it, especially if you are on the benefitting side of the tilt.

PROMPTS
When did you first become aware of racial and/or gender ranking — of yourself or others being treated unfairly or as less? Share a memory.

Reflect on and name an internalized bias that limits your aspirations or behavior.
- Can you think of a bias you once held, and have changed?
- What allowed you to become aware of it? To shed it?

The 2017 Women's March, while a somewhat successful expression of solidarity and common values, also revealed the "shadow side" of women's leadership. Have you experienced this shadow side? Write or describe what you experienced.

To promote healing from bias and trauma, I believe it's essential that we listen to our hearts, intuition, and bodies and less to our rational minds.

- Do you notice ways your body or sensing registers harm, injustice, or unfairness?
- What do you do when you perceive that?
- Is it hard for you to witness another's pain and recognize your own complicity in it?
- Are you willing to learn, and to be uncomfortable, to strengthen your ability to be with and relate to difference, while discovering more about your own privilege or complicity?
- What do you sense holding you back?

TRAUMA, RUPTURE, REPAIR

One of the things that unites us deeply is that at some point, in order to become fully integrated as people, we all have to actually walk through the flames of the traumas that we and our ancestors may have experienced.

This is part of the shadow work that we need to address, the unconscious painful stuff we've often put aside or buried. We need to face into it in order to heal and integrate those wounds, so that we don't recycle them throughout our lives.

Trauma lives in our bodies in insidious ways that are hard to unearth because we have so many layers of conditioning and adaptation. Often, we try to banish or brush that trauma under the rug of our lived experience. It feels to me like I have to peel back layers and layers of an onion skin in order to reach my truest self.

I recall what Canadian author and physician Gabor Maté says about addressing trauma: that it's not really about the difficult event that happened, but rather about how each of us responds to it. To reclaim wholeness, there's often been a separation from self that must be addressed.

I hear a deep call to attend to some of the underlying wounds that we carry as individuals, as a society and through diverse cultural lineages today. I believe it's needed, and timely, so that we can move wholeheartedly toward co-creating the future we each want and need.

Over many years now of working with diverse women, I see

some similar intergenerational wounds that I believe all women carry as a result of the "burning times," or of various multicultural versions of it. Whether we might have been the observers, the partners, the children, or those who were tortured and burned, I believe those ancestral memories live within us all.

The science of epigenetics is showing that trauma can make an imprint that lasts through generations. And the "burning times" occurred over the span of seven generations in countries throughout Europe.

Whether our ancestors were from Africa, Europe, Asia, South or Central or from Native America, I believe that we each have our own versions of those lineage stories of gendered oppression, conquest, and persecution. We carry them in our bones or epigenetic memory.

There's a great deal of intergenerational trauma among many of our brothers and sisters who are people of color, as there has been among my Jewish ancestors, who were violently chased out of every land they ever called home.

But there's also tremendous resilience, courage and clarity about moving forward through times of challenge. Many know how to continue to dance and sing and do ritual. To care for ourselves in the face of especially in the face of violence, oppression, and opposition.

We who've benefited from the tilted room of White supremacy have a lot to learn from BIPOC peoples' fierce commitments to freedom, spirit, laughter, and expression. There's been a cost to our privilege, our unearned benefits, and I believe it's led us toward complacency, self-silencing, and resignation.

I feel increasingly called to leverage my privilege to stand in solidarity with Indigenous Peoples, the Movement for Black Lives, all BIPOC peoples, and all who are standing on behalf of justice and of the sacredness of life in its many forms.

In many ways, these United States, with all our myths of democracy, are built on a core of rot, deceit, and theft. The U.S. nation was built by slaves, upon land stolen from Native Peoples, and I acknowledge and feel the serial genocidal events that our government has rained down on Black, Latina, and Indigenous Peoples, through history.

I've had to accept what Ta-Nehisi Coates calls the "bloody heirloom" of this nation: the intentional and structurally reinforced myth of White supremacy.

There are some similarities across our cultures, but, of course, all our stories are very different.

I think we're living at a time when the experience of trauma is more widely acknowledged. It's important for us as women who want to bring our best selves to this moment, to look trauma squarely in the face, to see how we can become more effective agents of healing.

Now the question becomes: How can we begin to repair our relations with the Earth while rectifying the dysfunctional social systems we've inherited?

It's a question of relationship, because we live in a world where so many of our relationships have been ruptured.

Dawna Markova, a valued mentor, author, and educator, taught me that "Relationships are a function of rupture and repair." I invite you to consider this premise, whether you're thinking about your family or your loved one, your neighbors or your children. We all face conflicts; we all have fights and ruptures — that's just what happens in relationships with the inevitable process of negotiating between two different, lived realities. It's whether and how you choose to turn towards repair that confers strength and resilience to our relationships.

We have massive repair work ahead of us, and it needs to begin in the most intimate place first, with ourselves — and then with the Earth, as well as with our families, our communities, and our neighbors. In order to stand against the serial assaults we face, we must also stand together with those who may not look, act, or seem like us. However, as mystics and traditional cultures have always taught, they *are* us.

My friend Ilarion Merculieff, who's a traditional wisdom keeper from the Unangan people, reminds me that in his village, when greeting another person, it's customary to say, "Hello, my other self."

This commitment means sitting in discomfort sometimes, not knowing who's right, or whether or even how to repair, and not running away. That discomfort has often arisen for me in addressing issues, moments or comments about racial justice and White privilege.

I find that staying present while I'm uncertain and uncomfortable is a muscle I can strengthen through practice. It's also helpful in relationships with colleagues, family, or partners. If we commit to focusing our time and love to practicing this, we can evolve through a lot of messy growing pains and work together in a new and regenerative way.

An incident that pierced the shell of my privilege occurred during one of the Cultivating Women's Leadership workshops, which I co-facilitated with cofounder Toby Herzlich. We were in a rural retreat site in Northern New Mexico. Our time together included a collective dive into the pain of racialized wounding in very personal terms.

We heard about the Chinese grandmother whose bound feet hurt so much, she had to be carried. We heard about the great uncle who'd been lynched in the South. The Peruvian Indigenous grandmother who had been forced to leave her ancestral lands. And the woman of mixed ancestry who had grown up ashamed and targeted because she was the darkest of her siblings.

A White woman spoke of her slave-owner lineage, and acknowledged the shame and guilt she feels, alongside of her privilege.

We listened to each other's stories deeply, and held each other tenderly. We noted how darkness is widely demonized. We named positive associations for Black and darkness, to help reclaim their value.

We designed an embodied healing ritual. Each of us created a symbolic piece using artifacts from nature that spoke to us — often they were twigs, branches, flowers, and weeds. We crafted messages that captured the hurts and beliefs that we wanted to shed, and tied them to the piece with colored yarn.

Then, with help from the cleansing spirit of fire, and a drum to connect our heartbeats, one by one we burned the beautiful pieces of ceremonial art, naming the aspects within ourselves that we wanted to release to the flames. We basked in the sense of liberation and alliance we felt in witnessing each other's work.

On the last night of the workshop, Toby and I were awakened at 3 a.m. One of the women was having an asthma attack, and she had forgotten to bring her inhaler. We rushed to her room, uncertain what to do. We were in a country setting at high altitude, and hours away from any hospital or medical care.

I sensed the woman's panic, heard her gasping desperately for breath, trying to fill her lungs. I saw the terror in her eyes. My mind had no previous experience, and so was of no help at all, so I dropped into a place where I could receive my body's instructions.

With her permission, I held her head against my chest. I breathed slowly and deeply, hoping she might entrain her breath with mine. As I stroked her head, I began to sway, my body rocking hers in time with my breathing. To help comfort her, I began humming a wordless tune, like a lullaby.

I had come to love and admire this woman, and to care deeply about her leadership in the world. She was doing environmental justice work, and her asthma was likely due to the toxic pollution of the inner city she'd grown up in.

Every particle of my being was willing her to live, and I poured my love and desire for her wellness into her, hoping she would relax, yearning for her to recover and be able to breathe.

I don't have any illusion that I healed her. But thankfully, after what seemed like an endless time, her breathing steadied and slowed. As she calmed, I lay her head back down on the pillows. I sat beside her, stroking her forehead and shoulders. When she'd closed her eyes and was breathing regularly, I sank down to the floor beside her bed.

Tears were streaming down my cheeks. Wondering about the source of my sadness, I knew this was about more than relief. I knew that the shell of my separateness had cracked open.

I sensed that the barrier my privilege had created between my head and my heart had been pierced. I felt the pain and fear of this woman's asthma, acutely, and the profound injustice of her having to live with it and suffer from it.

I knew that it was caused by racial bias, redlining and corporate greed and malfeasance, and my heart ached even as my anger was ignited to change it. In that instant, I also knew my own complicity and accountability for it.

No matter how many years I'd known about the most toxic industries being sited in poor neighborhoods, and the suffering that results from the toxic inequities, corruption and corporate abuses of our current systems, no matter how long I'd known about the elevated rates of asthma and diabetes, of heart disease and cancer in those communities, I had known them from the distance my privilege had afforded me.

I had known them as statistics that had shocked and saddened me, but I had never before felt the direct impacts of that injustice the way I did so personally that night.

After holding her in my arms, rocking her and breathing with her, summoning every bit of love and will I knew how to muster, I had felt no difference between us. The mother bear within me had been wholeheartedly engaged, and my desire to stand with her fully, to see her live and thrive, had broken my heart wide open.

This experience changed me, as others have continued to do since. They not only widened the scope of what I feel in service to, they deepened my compassion and commitment toward justice. Justice became personal for me. As the author, educator, and activist Cornel West says, "Justice is what love looks like in public."

These encounters remind me to invest in my heart's experience when hearing another's pain, and to focus on feeling injustice, not just thinking about it. And they remind me to encourage others to practice deepening their own capacity for empathy. To practice developing both a thick and a thin skin, at once. To cultivate the ability to witness and feel the suffering of others, while also staying present, separate, and well-resourced in our capacity to respond to it.

Rather than feeling overwhelmed, incapacitated, or guilty when confronted with other's pain, I believe we must develop ways to be simultaneously compassionate, and aware of our own choices in responding to what we know will only change with our honest and resourced engagement.

PROMPTS FOR DEEPENING LEARNING
THROUGH REFLECTION, WRITING OR DISCUSSION

Trauma, Rupture, Repair

THEMES

- In a country built on White supremacy, its wealth a function of slavery, theft, and genocide, repairing and healing our ruptured relations with each other is essential to address our social problems.
- Discomfort and uncertainty are part of addressing racial and other types of wounding; staying present while uncomfortable is a practice.
- Repair happens in relationships when we commit to listening and negotiating between different lived realities, a process that confers strength and resilience.

PROMPTS

How have you personally addressed wounds from your past?

- Have you employed ritual?
- Have you shared your story with trusted friends?
- Have you used therapy or other methods? Would you consider therapy a form of ritual?

With her permission, I tell the story of holding a woman suffering an asthma attack as piercing the shell of my privilege.

- Has any experience pierced you in that way?
- How does it affect you to feel the pain of racial and other injustices?

We all have blind spots that come with privilege.
- How do you perceive your blind spots?
- Can you be kind to yourself, and hold yourself tenderly when you notice your mistakes?

When confronting the harms created by the systems we live in, how do we avoid overwhelm and guilt, but hold our own accountability, cultivating our capacity to stay present and respond?

What rituals or practices allow you to be present to the pain our movements are trying to rectify, but not burn out or get overwhelmed?

PATHWAYS FOR REPAIR AFTER RUPTURE:

Best Practices (Notes from the Journey)

On the deepest level, my core impulse has always been about healing relationships within ourselves, among each other, and with Mother Earth. I see them all as octaves of the same legacy of imbalance or cultural inheritance. In this time of polarization, conflict, and social turbulence, many pathways for repair are calling for attention and learning.

Experiences in my life have drawn me to respond to a particularly intractable problem: the tendency for well-intended diverse groups to rupture, even while they attempt to organize toward a common goal. I've seen how this fractures and decimates a group's capacity for coalition-building, or coordinated and aligned action, as I describe in the example that follows.

In my work co-creating connection among diverse women leaders, I've experienced many such ruptures that have happened around differences of race, class, and privilege. My *own* blind spots have been revealed to me, many times. A series of humbling "ahas" has kept me continually aware of my need to keep learning, to keep exploring others' lived realities — to increase my empathy, understanding, and resolve.

Rachel Bagby has been a close colleague and highly esteemed work partner of mine. She is an award-winning vocal artist and composer who graduated from Stanford Law School with a concentration in Social Change.

For over 30 years, Rachel has mentored girls and women leaders to unleash their voices and visions as instruments of transformation. She originated the poetic form Dekaaz, and is the bestselling author of *Daughterhoo*d, and *Divine Daughters: Liberating the Power and Passion of Women's Voices.* No wonder we work so well together.

We've delivered trainings designed to strengthen the voices and collaborative skills of women leaders within Organic Valley, the national dairy cooperative. We've also led three other gatherings that were designed to seed enduring relationships among diverse women leaders. The spectrum of differences we address in our work together is not only disparate in ethnicity, but also across many of the other ways we differ.

The first two trainings were quite successful. They affirmed the need to initiate long-term relationships that could lead to ongoing, nourishing alliances and mutual aid. The third gathering, in 2015 — almost from the very beginning — ruptured and splintered repeatedly over issues of cultural appropriation. Those painful rifts seemed intractable and unresolvable.

I continue to learn about cultural appropriation (or misappropriation). It describes when people from a dominant culture emulate, borrow, or integrate practices from other cultures. Sometimes, that is experienced as disrespectful and hurtful, particularly to those from Native cultures and their allies.

Now, this issue is complex, and nuanced. Some Indigenous People I know feel that the very best thing that could happen on Earth would be for all non-Native people to adopt indigenous worldviews and perspectives. It's also true that we are essentially social creatures. Cultures have evolved by learning and borrowing from each other throughout history.

I've come to understand, however, that cultural appropriation can be excruciatingly painful for some people of indigenous descent, especially due to the long and violent history of colonial rule.

The group that gathered in 2015 included Native and non-Native women, and I was naïve (I can see now, in retrospect) to imagine that the indigenous women would not view the work of the non-Native women as offensive because their work had grown out of long mentorships by indigenous teachers. But, in fact, the differences between them, and the unresolved wounding that occurred as a result, felt impossible to heal.

The title of the gathering we'd invited the women to was "Comadres," a name that I'd been careful to cite as being inspired by, and borrowed from Latina culture. Comadres refers to a sacred and lifelong relationship between women. As it turned out, our use of the name also ignited hurt and anger in some of the women, who saw it as an example of our having appropriated something sacred from another culture.

For four full days, anger, blame, and judgment continued to rupture and divide the circle. There was lots of facilitation skill among the participants, and we tried repeatedly to reset, regroup, and reorient the field, but it proved to be impossible.

Afterward, several who had come said they were grateful to have been there because of all that they'd learned, and everyone stayed through to the end. But I felt devastated. I searched my soul in the months that followed. I identified places where my own privilege, ignorance, and naiveté had blinded me. It led me to use language, and invite participants who I otherwise could have known might trigger each other.

I took responsibility for my part as best I knew how, extending apologies and making amends to everyone I could, in

varying and — I hope — meaningful ways. As I discussed the
experience at length with Rachel, we realized that this was not
an isolated incident. It represented a pattern that has plagued
progressive movement-building for decades.

I recalled the emergence of the environmental justice movement
in the early 90s. Low-income, indigenous and communities of
color began organizing at that time against the most toxic industries
continually being sited near their homes and schools, perpetuating
terrible health impacts. I remembered how large public foundations
brought leaders of many of those groups together, hoping to strengthen
their organizing through coalition-building, only to have the gatherings
repeatedly blow up.

I've come to understand that those ruptures were likely due to
two dysfunctional systems clashing: the foundations and the nonprofit
sector. The foundations may not have had the expertise, the savvy, or
the skillfulness to successfully convene such a gathering. Perhaps they
expected to see outcomes before taking the time to knit together solid
alliances and relationships.

The nonprofit leaders were likely exhausted — understandably
frustrated by the challenges they faced, and the daily pain of their
work. Sadly, they were likely also competing with each other for
scarce resources. Our social structures have habituated us more to
competition, unfortunately, than they have prepared us for cooperation.

I remembered again that all relationships go through rupture
and repair, and that the resilience and durability of any relationship
is determined by the nature and quality of repair after ruptures. So, I
turned my attention to that process.

Rachel and I decided to bring together a group of seasoned
professional facilitators and meet with them as a peer community

— women with deep experience in coalescing diverse groups to find common cause.

We conceived and named it a Community of Practice, a group that might reveal and cross-pollinate insights that could help develop greater skillfulness in the field. We wanted to explore the potential power of experienced people sharing their own learnings and challenges. We hoped that this group might surface "best practices" to help advance or accelerate our learning.

We carefully selected practitioners not only for their experience and knowledge base, but also for their levels of emotional maturity, self-awareness, and vision. The group came from all over the U.S. and Canada, and we chose to optimize diversity in every way — a design that is central to all our work with Bioneers' Everywoman's Leadership Program.

The women ranged in age from mid-thirties to seventies and were ethnically diverse. Four of the eleven were women of color, of mixed background. Each brought their experience working with people in diverse sectors and settings, spanning corporate clients, grassroots and frontline organizations, political (bipartisan) groups, and environmental and health-affected communities.

In addition to Rachel Bagby and myself, our group included the following esteemed participants:

- **Anita Sanchez**, PhD, who's an international best-selling author, leadership trainer, facilitator, and speaker;
- **Libby Roderick** is the director of the Difficult Dialogues Initiative. She teaches at the University of Alaska, Anchorage, and is a singer song-writer who records with Turtle Island Records;
- **Ana Sophia Demetrakopoulos**, a facilitator who focuses on community-based research and social innovation;

- **Teresa Younger**, lifelong activist, policymaker, and CEO and President of the Ms. Foundation;
- **Pele Rouge**, Earth Wisdom teacher & guide, and the co-founder of Timeless Earth Wisdom;
- **Sharon Shay Sloan**, a culture worker and social healer, who is also the executive steward of The Ojai Foundation;
- **Joan Blades**, is an activist, social organizer, and co-founder of Move On, Moms Rising, and Living Room Conversations;
- **Taij Kumarie Moteelall**, artist, activist, and social entrepreneur, and also the founder of Media Sutra and Standing in Our Power;
- **Jody Snyder**, a visionary and co-founder of Earth Matters, a Pachamama Alliance facilitator, and a convener of diverse groups seeking connection to the land and to each other.

The gathering was designed around practices that we'd developed through Bioneers' Cultivating Women's Leadership retreats. They encourage deep listening, leading from the heart, and tending to relationships before tasks. We spiraled in to learn about each other, slowly, employing rituals, as we've learned that ritual creates relationship.

Unlike most organizational settings — where planning, action and strategy take precedence — we spent the first few days together sharing stories about our lives and works, getting to know each other, eating and laughing, making art and playing games together.

Since we knew that these women were both skillful and wise, Rachel and I opened the gathering by inviting everyone to alter the program or initiate shifts whenever they felt that any might be needed. We welcomed them to share responsibility for guiding the program, encouraging their collaboration and shared leadership.

Our time together was imbued with a sense of very strong mutual respect, coupled with curiosity about one another as we co-created a Community of Practice.

We had open-space sessions, where anyone among the group could host a discussion on any topic they wanted to explore. Some shared specific practices, while others convened discussion circles to invite input on next steps in their work. The context we co-created was simultaneously flexible while offering the structure needed to encourage intimacy and relaxation. As a result, much spontaneous emergence occurred.

Everyone was welcome to bring their dreams, intuition, playfulness, and creativity to bear in our work together. This sense of spaciousness was quite intentional, as we'd learned that the feminine principle in us all *thrives* in spaciousness. In literal terms, this meant that at the front end of our six days together, we set aside unstructured time for conversations, walks in nature, experiential work, ritual, and play to emerge fluidly and organically.

So, when the time came to fulfill our "agenda" to elicit best practices, they flowed easily, generously, and swiftly from each participant. One woman taught an embodied somatic practice of shedding the physical effects of trauma through shaking. It was powerful and cathartic.

Afterward, we asked everyone to reflect upon their experience with groups, generally. To consider what had worked in setting up the conditions to repair hurt feelings or damaged relationships after a rupture had occurred. Each of us wrote lists in our journals, and then we shared them verbally with the group.

The question we posed, in order to discover what each practitioner knew, was this: "What do you know about creating conditions conducive to connecting meaningfully across differences that can often divide us?"

Some practices came in the form of agreements that were suggested, to solicit or share with a group at the beginning of a gathering. Others addressed the form and prerequisites for the meeting, and the ways of relating that were most conducive to repair, after ruptures occur.

The wisdom and common sense we gained from this wealth of experience still astonishes me and fills me with gratitude. I'm pleased to have been given their permission to share this abundance of ideas. For those who wish to read it, a full list of practices is available online in the Nature, Culture & the Sacred section.

Of course, each one of you facilitating a group will have your own unique style and purposes. Not all of the practices that follow will resonate for you equally, but my hope is that some might prove useful. I've found it's always wise to ask whomever you are working with for their best ideas. People often learn best what they are able to discover for themselves, rather than what they've taught by a facilitator.

As I've reviewed the abundance of insights that were offered, several themes have emerged clearly for me. They include:

Transparency in naming and valuing differences. This pertains to many aspects of this work, in that naming and appreciating the complexity, value, and kinds of diversity in the room gives everyone permission to show up in his, her, or their full uniqueness. This might include class, faith, ability, education, and sexual orientation as well as power and privilege, immigrant status, ethnicity, age, and political persuasion. Naming some of the differences — and if possible, creating time and space for participants to share stories about their backgrounds

— gives all those present permission to bring their own uniqueness fully into the conversation.

Name power dynamics and privilege differentials clearly and up front. Naming how privilege confers blinders, and reminding people that we all have inner victims and perpetrators as well as various kinds of privilege. It helps to keep people from polarizing. If possible, have a facilitator share a vulnerable example of their own learning, which helps make space for others to follow.

Have clear agreement on the intention, the purposes, and desired outcomes for the meeting. This correlates to the first theme, because it means making explicit the common goals that are shared by this diverse group and the purpose for coming together. It's important that everyone can agree to a goal of reaching some higher purpose together, perhaps common ground, or a sense of kinship. This also relates to the importance of choosing carefully and consciously who you'll invite to participate in a group.

Establish and agree to group norms and codes of ethics.
This describes the "how" we'll be together; which might include being brave, offering feedback generously and kindly, honesty, practicing self-awareness, deep listening, pausing for reflection before responding, and, importantly, what to do if ruptures or "ouches" occur.

Encourage embodied awareness, as our bodies rarely lie. Often, I've found, a heightened awareness of body sensations can help keep people in the room during an uncomfortable conversation. Physicality is a great equalizer, and it helps keep people grounded in their sensations and emotions, and out of conceptual, reactive, or habitual frameworks. Suggesting deep breaths, slowing down, and filling our bodies with dignity prior to unpacking an "ouch" can really help people to stay present in the room.

Representation matters. In facilitation or leadership, as well as in the composition of the room. Many people need to feel flanked by others who look somewhat like them in order to feel supported to be fully authentic, courageous, and present.

Prioritize relationship before tasks. Taking the time to establish whole-person relations among participants, in a deep way rather than only through superficial connections, can make or break a repair when all is said and done. Although many of us are products of a culture that's tended to devalue relationship, or relegate it to the realm of the "feminine," it's now essential that we cultivate skillfulness in community and collaboration. This has proven invaluable in many groups and situations, and I strongly advocate for the value of overcoming the impatience and cultural bias that tends to assign relationship-building far too low a status in establishing priorities for group work.

In addition to gleaning some best practices, we knit a community of practice together, and we learned a lot about how to do that. Reviewing all that was accomplished, I'm aware that we actually achieved more than we'd even intended.

Since we're all products of a culture that tends to separate and divide us, I believe that gathering communities of practice to knit practitioners in order to advance learning from and with each other is a potent and powerful act.

In these complex times, we're all asked to be more embodied in translating our values into behaviors, and not just expressing them as ideologies or lip service. Everything we can do to get better at this offers high value to each of our work, and to meeting the challenges that we collectively face.

The cross-pollination of ideas and experience can accelerate learning for others working to help coalesce groups across differences. It also addresses the isolation that many in leadership often feel.

It connects a network of colleagues who can then call upon each other for coaching, listening, or support, as needed. Each can receive the gift of experiencing group learning through reflection and sharing, which is in itself a shift in ways of doing things, a healthy evolution of revolutionary work.

Being able to refocus our internal and collective capacities on learning from and with each other, and away from the incessant focus on the "problems," was in itself a gift that opened new horizons for each of us.

And a community of practice can offer care for the caregivers — for those who so often are giving far more than they're receiving. It can co-create a safe space to rest, renew, and process challenging events or emotions.

As I reflect on the trajectory of my own learning, and the powerful pull toward purposeful action I feel on behalf of beloved community, I'm struck by one more big realization. Few White people, or people of privilege that I've heard speak on this, have mentioned how profoundly fulfilling and joyous it can be to fully engage in this work.

It's true that it's difficult, and often uncomfortable. I'll paraphrase Van Jones who said that if you embark on racial justice work, you just have to orient yourself, because it's like walking through a room

full of garden rakes. There's no way to cross that room without stepping
on rakes, and having the handles spring up and smack you in the face.

I've found that a terrifically useful metaphor. I've been amazed
at how much instinctual fear seems to arise in me whenever I stretch
my own learning edges about race and privilege. But what's also true,
which I've heard far less frequently, is how immensely worthwhile
the emotional bumps and bruises of engaging with racial justice have
been for me, as a White woman. I've never regretted them. I know I've
got lots more coming, as I'm sure to continue making mistakes in the
months and years ahead.

I've been amazed by the terror I've felt when speaking publicly
about cracking the shell of my own privilege. But I'm so grateful that I
pushed through my fear and did it anyway. I'm determined to keep taking
risks and learning on behalf of the beloved community that is the world I
want. There's no other work I see as more timely, needed and vital.

I hope many others are inspired to become devotional rake-
walkers, and add to their committed intents and purposes standing on
behalf of racial justice in a real, focused and determined way.

My hope and prayer are that these themes and practices may
help to repair or ameliorate the ruptures that will come. They'll come
inevitably, as we've been so thoroughly socialized and traumatized to
perpetuate them.

If they can, then the work of cultivating connective tissue
among our diverse constituencies in order to create a just, healthy,
and regenerative world for all can help inform our evolution towards
becoming beloved community. There are few things that I believe are
more urgently needed now and in the future, and there's nothing I
yearn for more.

PROMPTS FOR DEEPENING LEARNING
THROUGH REFLECTION, WRITING OR DISCUSSION

Pathways for Repair after Ruptures:
Best Practices

THEMES

From a gathering of diverse women leaders, some best practices and common principles emerged for inoculating against ruptures and dealing with repair:

- name power and privilege differences up front;
- seek mutual agreement on intention and desired outcomes;
- establish group norms;
- representation matters;
- encourage embodied awareness;
- prioritize relationship before task.

PROMPTS

I included a painful personal example of a rupture that occurred over an issue of cultural appropriation, because it taught me so much and it's emblematic of many other problems that arise when we try to work together.

- Have you had an experience of being among a group that came apart?
- How did it get resolved?
- What did you learn that may be beneficial to share?

What resonates for you among the best practices garnered from different women across a spectrum of age, class, nationality, sexual orientation, and issue area?

- What practices might you add to the list?
- How might they make a difference in your next meetings at work, in school or in your activism?
- If you anticipate there could be resistance, how might you diffuse it?

WOMEN FINDING VOICE

The Relationship Between
Inner and Outer Work

(A Conversation with Terry Tempest Williams)

T erry Tempest Williams may seem at first glance to be a paradoxical figure — part desert mystic and defender of wildlands and creatures who is comfortable alone deep in the wilderness; part scientist and scholar with a highly refined literary and artistic sensibility; and a woman strongly tied to her family's deep roots and Mormon religious heritage in Utah, and yet also a modern dissident and sophisticated, cosmopolitan citizen of the world. As such, she perfectly illustrates that amazing weaving of factors that makes for a transformative leader, in my view.

I am honored to also call Terry a beloved sister, friend, and teacher, and she's helped me understand a new relationship to paradox: she's taught me to eschew either/or solutions, to find ways to dance with and celebrate apparent contradiction, rather than being seduced by some effort to resolve it. In embracing all those parts of herself, she's blazed a pathway for each of us to celebrate our own inherent diversity.

She's most often thought of as one of America's greatest nature writers, and though her work defies comparison, she belongs in the illustrious company of John Muir, Aldo Leopold, Rachel Carson, Gary

Snyder, Barry Lopez, Annie Dillard, and Henry David Thoreau. She has won many of the most prestigious literary awards, but her writing explores and illuminates so much of the human condition that it transcends any categorization.

Her writing poetically and soulfully traverses the domains of love, family, activism, religion, art, nature, and the quest for healing and meaning. Witnessing how many passions and ways of being Terry weaves together into coherent narratives has given me greater permission to navigate multiple domains and systems at a time. Because of course, it's all one system.

She has long been recognized as one of our greatest defenders of wildlands and passionate advocates for peace, environmental and social justice, and freedom of speech. Her activism has taken many forms, from acts of civil disobedience on a nuclear test site to marching in the streets to testifying about women's health before Congress, to doing something only she could pull off: quoting Mormon scriptures to explain the wild desert's spiritual essence to a room full of stunned Republicans.

What is most inspiring to me about Terry is her essence, her being, her awakened presence, the penetrating authenticity and inquiry she brings to every encounter and conversation. This is a woman who is emotional, vulnerable, passionate, and ferociously engaged, but she is so deeply centered, so attuned, so refined, so devoid of any reactivity or malice, and radiates such intense dignity and purity of soul that her words have the potential to reach deeply into even hardened human hearts. From *Refuge* to *Leap*, and from *Finding Beauty in a Broken World* to *When Women Were Birds*, her books never fail to illuminate the invisible web that connects the world anew for me.

This podcast, hosted by Bioneers Everywoman's Leadership program, was a conversation between Terry and me that took place in July 2012. In it, we explored how women find voice, as well as the relationship between inner, reflective work and outer, activist work. Our conversation braids together so many threads and themes that have arisen throughout this book previously, pointing to essential aspects of leading from the feminine, including the practice of relationship intelligence, deep listening, and the power of emotions and grieving. I hope you'll find yourself resonant with it, and may even find some new wrinkles or clues that help illuminate your path forward.

Nina Simons: *Terry, I am thrilled to be able to talk with you about some of the ideas in your beautiful book* When Women Were Birds, *and to visit with you as someone who has been a really profound influence and role model and mentor for me in my life in finding my own voice.*

Terry Tempest Williams: Nina, I can say the same back to you. You continue to mentor me about what women's leadership from the heart looks like, sounds like, feels like. I will just honor you.

NS: Thanks for that. Hard to receive from someone I love and respect as I do you, but I hope it is getting easier as I practice. For me, what I have realized is that finding my voice has been directly connected to finding my own sense of purpose, or assignment, or that unique set of instructions that feel like they are mine to do. I was so moved by a quote in your book, Terry, where you wrote that your mother Diane said: "There are two important days in a women's life. The day she is born and the day she finds out why."

As I've witnessed the arc of your last fifteen years or so, it struck me that perhaps, like me, your sense of assignment keeps unfolding. It is not

like it lands fully blown in your lap and you suddenly know what you are
born to do. For me, it is more like crossing a river, where I step on a stepping
stone and I know that is the right place for me to step but I can't see the
next step until I am fully there. My instructions keep emerging over time. I
wonder whether you will be willing to share any reflections you might have
on your instructions and unique purpose.

TTW: That is so interesting that you shared those words, instruction and
purpose. And honestly Nina, I don't think about that. What I am aware
of is what I love, what I have lost, and what I have tried to reclaim. For
me it is very simple: it's a question of really being present in the moment.
If we are present in the moment, then we know what to do.

NS: Well, then let me offer you a reflection on one of the things that I feel
I have learned from you and keep learning from you: how to bring all the
parts of myself into full presence in the moment. When I reflect back over
your last several books, it seems that in each book you share something
about what guided you into that exploration of presence.
   In Finding Beauty in a Broken World, you talk about how you
asked the ocean for some words. What I notice about you, Terry, is that you
seem to be very good at listening for guidance from somewhere either deep
inside yourself or in the natural world or both. I wonder if you have any
idea how you learned to listen so well.

TTW: I remember after September 11th, you and I talked about this.
I was in Washington DC when the twin towers were struck, when the
Pentagon was hit. I witnessed people running across the White House
lawn, and I was with a group of photographers at the Copland Gallery
and we found ourselves stunned as I know everyone was. The next thing
I knew, we were in a cab in gridlock and the cab driver turned around

and asked, "Where would you like to go?" I realized there was no place to go. We were there.

That next year I made a conscious commitment to speak the truth as I saw it. I realized there are many forms of terrorism and environmental degradation. But during that year I realized my voice, my critique, had become as brittle and as hollow as those as I was opposing.

It was at that point that I went to the ocean. I addressed the ocean spirit, however we define that, and I said, "Give me one wild word, and I promise I will follow." So perhaps you are correct in using that word instruction, because the word that came back to me, the word that I heard in my own heart was "mosaic." It became a seven-year journey, following what mosaic is, how do we take those pieces that are broken and make something new, something whole.

With this book, *When Women Were Birds*, you know what I was listening to? I was listening to the very real fact of my uncertainty about my own mortality, realizing that I had turned 54, the same age my mother was when she died. I really was looking back and remembering what I had chosen to deny, that my mother left me all her journals before she died and all her journals were blank. And so, the book becomes a reflection and meditation, a deep listening, to what that emptiness might have meant.

NS: What inspires me in you is the way that you listen both for the ocean, for the spirit of the natural world, as well as for what's most alive and questioning and wondering and burning in yourself.

TTW: I think it is about survival, don't you? I mean, both of us are in very privileged positions but life is not easy. If we are interested in an evolution, a revolution of the spirit, then I think it demands that we ask

these hard questions and that we stay with them. That we don't avert
our gaze, that we sit with the uncertainty. Revelations do come, but not
without a cost, not without patience, and not without compassion for
ourselves and for those that we live closest with.

*NS: I agree, and I find for myself that the older I become and the more
aware I am of my own mortality, the more burning the questions become.
As I age, the more my desire to fully manifest the artwork of my life or the
assignment that my soul was given in its fullness burns in me. Because we
live in a time of so much transformation, and so much loss and so much
suffering, I feel called to bring my "all" in response to that. I also feel an
increasing need to not shrink away from what most frightens me. I think
you've modeled that for me.*

TTW: You know, I think of my grandfather when he said, every day
counts. I was just in Madison, Wisconsin, on the eve of the Scott
Walker election recall. There was such angst on both sides about what
would happen. Mat Rothschild, the editor of *The Progressive*, is a friend
of mine. We ended up that morning at dawn going out to Picnic Point
Nature Preserve and we watched birds. I cannot tell you the glory of the
moment when, as we were talking politics, wondering what was going
to happen, suddenly we heard this incredible prehistoric call. We both
smiled and a sand hill crane flew right over us, we could have touched
his or her legs. You know, you think, "Nine million years of perfection
just graced us," and it really does put things into perspective.

*NS: Yeah, it sure does. I am curious to lean toward the reconciliation
of paradox because just as you were saying, Terry, part what prompted
you to write When Women Were Birds was the legacy of your mother's*

journals and how her voice was reflected in the emptiness of words on
those pages. I find myself so drawn to the inquiry of how we unlock from
paradoxical duality.

For me, one of the most important capacities we can look to
develop is how we connect across difference. And you have modeled
that for me, Terry, in so many ways, from adopting a grown man from
Rwanda as your son, to studying prairie dogs up close and personal
for weeks. You model it by helping us understand their world by going
inside it and writing about what you learned. I am curious about any
thoughts you may have about how we connect across difference and the
value of it in this time.

TTW: Nina, I am struck by the words "reconcile" and "paradox,"
and I am not sure that I ever reconcile anything. I think I embrace
paradox. I grew up on the edge of Great Salt Lake, a body of water in
the American West that nobody can drink because it is salt water. So, I
think I am very comfortable with paradox.

I grew up in the Mormon church, which is very patriarchal,
and yet all the women around me were unbelievably powerful. You
know, paradox. It is true, Brooke and I are childless by choice and
suddenly, at 50 years old, I find myself adopting Willy into our family
and re-defining what family looks like. You know, I am not Willy's
mother and he is not my son and yet he has allowed me to be a mother.
To understand what it's like to have your complete heart, soul, mind
embodied by another person out of regard, and love, and care and
oftentimes, confusion.

I gravitate towards what I have loved. I think I am most
interested in what is other than myself. I know who I am, and I am
much more interested in who you are and what this world around us

feels like, looks like, tastes like; what it is like to touch. I think it is my curiosity that keeps moving me forward.

NS: Of course. As another woman who is childless by choice, you have helped me understand that whether or not we have biological children, we all, and I suspect regardless of our gender, we all can have the essence of parenting and mothering and loving another person so much that they become a part of our being.

TTW: I think that is right. I was having a conversation this morning with a dear friend of Brooke's over coffee. How do we expand? How do we amp up our frequency? I can speak this language with you.

I am very well aware of the desert. When we first moved to Castle Valley from Salt Lake City, Utah, five hours south, it took me several years to feel that my body was in frequency with the desert because the vibration in the desert is so high.

You know this from living in Santa Fe, Nina; very little is hidden. You are living in this very erosional landscape and it is asking of you to be bare-bone and exposed. I keep thinking with all the changes that are happening on the planet right now, with all that we are asked to take in, how do we keep expanding and allow ourselves greater porosity, so that we don't shut down, so that we don't become numb, so that we can continue to engage. That is the question that I am living with. At times, it feels like it is too much and yet as you say, I want to be of use. I want to be alive, awake, and alert to that which surrounds me.

NS: For me, that requires that I keep giving myself the permission to feel as deeply as I do, because I am mindful that we live in a culture where that permission is somewhat rare. And as a woman, I have often felt derided or ridiculed for being emotional. What I am learning is that actually love is the source of my strength, and my wisdom, and my power. And that in order to celebrate life — which I really think is part of why all human beings are here on the planet at this time — we have to allow ourselves to feel the loss and the pain of witnessing as what we love is diminished and threatened.

TTW: I so agree. Such power in what you are saying. What kind of human being we would be if we were not feeling this grief, if we weren't being emotional about the lives and the life before us.

I was thinking about abuse and I believe that we really are in an abusive relationship with the feminine, however we define it — whether it is emotion, truth-telling, anger, or understanding, or maybe silence — the feminine in all its diversity. I often find that we are minimized, trivialized, invalidated, we are discounted — that makes for craziness. So often, what I feel inside is not mirrored on the outside, and that makes me crazy.

And when we are talking about voice, we really do have to stand in the center of authenticity and realize, "No, this is what I am feeling. And, no, I will not allow you to minimize my thoughts or my actions. And, no, I will not allow you to discount me."

We cannot do it alone and yet we try to do it alone. That is why I think community is very important, and this is why I so appreciate what you have put together with your program. We cannot do it alone. I so appreciate what you have done with Everywoman's Leadership and Cultivating Women's Leadership because it shows that there is a community of women and this is what leadership from the heart looks like. It gives all of us the courage to follow our instincts and our intuition.

NS: I find myself feeling increasingly supported in the awareness that what the feminine offers us is the capacity to flex with changing conditions. To live with uncertainty. If there is a key to cultivating our whole humanity and our voice and our leadership, it has something to do with how we stay connected, and how we live with uncertainty. So, I wonder if you have any thoughts about that because you have lived with so much, Terry.

TTW: Nina, I think a lot about Wangari Maathai, who passed on too soon, on September 26, 2011. I think about the uncertainty that she lived. As an African woman, as a woman in Kenya, in a very patriarchal society, what was certain for her was that women were carrying the environmental crisis on their backs and that an environmental crisis is an economic crisis, is ultimately a crisis of social justice. That was certain to her. She saw it, she felt it, she witnessed it.

What was certain for her was that women could change the course of their lives and what was certain for her was the faith of a single seed. I love that and now, you know, how many millions of trees have been planted because of her love and her capacity to grieve for what we were doing to the planet?

Again, it is that paradox. What is certain, what do we know and what is uncertain and what we will never know? You know, none of us knows how long we are going to live. That is the first great uncertainty but we know that we're alive, that is a certain thing. You and I are speaking to each other. So again, it is a dance, this balance, this scale.

And I love how even the brush of a feather can tip that balance. So, I want to live with that feather.

NS: It is so beautiful because it is the power of the small and the particular to make big change...

TTW: Truly.

NS: What you are saying gets us back to the dance of paradox. I am reminded that nature's way of resolving paradox is a spiral. That when you pour cold milk into hot tea, the difference in their temperatures gets resolved by a spiral, whether you stir it or not. Just the liquid does that. When the seaweeds are dancing in the ocean current, they spiral in order to be resilient. It is a dance, not a marriage, or a reconciliation.

TTW: I love that. You know, there is a spiral all around us. Perhaps that is the nature of paradox. I went out with Willy and his friends to the spiral jetty out on the shores of Great Salt Lake and it struck me how profound that form and that metaphor is to progress, to evolution, to revolution.

NS: I also find myself wanting to appreciate what Wangari did, which was that she kept speaking even though she knew it meant incurring wrath and anger and violence to herself...

TTW: Even being separated from her children and hoping that they would understand and forgive her for what she was taking on. Again, that word "courage." As she often would say, it was not courage, it was just what needed to be done. Recently, I was talking with a student of mine about the definition of courage. She said, and I love this: to her, courage is sustained focus. For her courage is that. Don't you love that?

NS: It's beautiful. Because what we appreciate appreciates. I recently attended a memorial service for a dear friend and a remarkable activist who died too young, and I found myself so aware that like you, she brought celebration to the fight for justice. Always. I noticed as I was speaking at her memorial, how rare that is, because the fight can so often engender bitterness and anger and we can shut down because it is so hard. And the beauty and the power of staying connected to what you love, even as you are putting your body, your voice and your heart into helping to ignite change, is something I admire so much.

TTW: Yes. I just was at Dartmouth for the last three months. One of the most special days was being on the Dartmouth Green during the Powwow. Dartmouth was one of the first colleges in the country to honor Native People and Native American students. This was the 40th Powwow they have held on the Green. For two days I sat next to the singers and I just felt their drum beat going up my spine. In all the celebration of shell dancers, the jingle dancers, it was so thrilling, and yet, again the paradox, you don't know but you imagine the difficulties of the lives on the reservations.

Having worked in Navajo Country, I know this is America's hidden wound that we have never fully acknowledged, and yet, when I think about the deepest humor I have experienced, it's been from my Indian friends. And, when I think about the really dark humor with my own family, it's come out when we were facing the death of a loved one. Again, it's about survival, and we all have these evolutionary skills. I think rituals — singing, celebration, dancing — all these things help us move in that spiral of what it means to be human.

Often, we seem to be caught in a downward spiral, an entropy of work and scale. Lately, all I hear is: we need to work to scale or scale up, and I just keep thinking really, can we just scale down? I just do not understand that. I just find myself wanting to get quieter and quieter and smaller and smaller.

NS: [Laughter] Well, and your book invited me into a meditation in such a beautiful way because I want to be slower and stiller, and you know, it is the blur of fastness and pressure and too muchness and busy-ness, that causes me to miss the particularity and the beauty and sacredness and the humor that you are talking about.

TTW: And then we end up being tired, and angry and resentful, and we have all been there. More and more, I just want to be still. I also think about Robert Pinsky when he says, "Motion can be a place too." But my mother always talked about being the nest behind the waterfall. How do we find that core of stillness in our heart so that we can, again using your words, fully appreciate where we are here and now.

I think it is tied to voice and to paradox. When I was writing *When Women Were Birds*, I thought I was writing a book about voice, about how we as women speak to the truth of our times, to our own authentic nature. But what I have written, Nina, is a book of silences and stillness, and I think one begets the other. Again, it is that balance of space and time and scale.

NS: Well, I find myself aware that the need for silence is also a marker of the imbalance between the feminine and masculine in our culture and in all of us. I was just speaking to a friend the other night about the unfinished wounding in the conquest of this land. The huge destruction that has been wrought on Native Peoples all over the world and also the wounds of slavery, of sexism, racism, and ageism. How do we encourage and invite the healing that can come from naming and ritually pouring our love into addressing all those wounds? I see them as fractals of the same tear in our relational fabric.

TTW: Again, love is not the secret. Pain is. And why are we so fearful of that? Because I really believe if we embrace our pain, we can move beyond that. Again, I am scratching my head. Here we have a president that we have supported and admired, Barack Obama, and I will certainly be voting for him again. But with a community of people, we have been trying to embrace the Arctic to preserve this reservoir for our spirit, and yet it is Barack Obama and his administration that has opened up the Arctic for oil and gas drilling. They have opened the door to Shell.

Just last week in *The New York Times*, they were talking about how Shell has been very sensitive to the Native American people when in truth, I have an Alaska Native student who has been working with her father to stop drilling in the Arctic, to stop drilling in the Arctic Ocean. They are buying off Native Americans with trucks with boats and anything else you can imagine. So, what do we do? I keep thinking, do we lay our bodies down? Is it the time for direct action and yet how do we still proceed with calm and understanding? I don't know what the answers are. And that is the paradox where I find myself torn, by my anger and by my love, and sometimes I think they are the same thing. So, what do we fight for, and what do we accept?

NS: Yes, and how do we recognize that not only our pain deters us but our shame and complicity as well.

TTW: The only way I can reconcile the paradoxes of action and contemplation — and I'll use that word "reconcile" now — is in discernment. To me the power of discernment is most potently rendered in our own communities, on our home ground with our own people. That is where it is the toughest to speak truthfully because we cannot walk away from our friends and family.

NS: What you're naming so beautifully is the complementary wholeness that is created by combining contemplation with action, and that unless they are met in full measure, it is not the full humanness that I aspire to.

Terry, you've said that you "do not believe we can look for leadership beyond ourselves." Can you talk a little about what that means to you in both your personal and professional work, and how you maintain the connection between the two?

TTW: It is such a good question. I am going to pass it back to you, Nina.

NS: [Laughing] It is such a hard question and such a good question. What's clear to me is that the landscape that I can be the most responsible for is the one that lives within me. I need to keep challenging myself, I have to keep finding the spaces that scare me and the places that I have anger and actually lean into them so that I can find ways to bring myself into congruence.

I keep crafting myself inwardly as if there is a social sculpture in my own life that is me, and I am the only one that can make this artwork come out the way I hope and intend it. When I began to understand the extent of harm as a result of the invisibility of racial injustice to many people of privilege in this country, I began to realize that even though it terrified me to talk about it, I actually had to push myself towards that edge and find ways to challenge myself to step into it.

For me, weaving the boundary of personal and professional, the inner and the outer and the activist, feels like to me like it is the work of my life. And I observe you traversing that ground with quite a bit of grace. So, what do you think?

TTW: I have been very aware that my view of leadership is not the same as the traditional view of leadership: the kind with one powerful person at the top, who we follow. That is not the kind of leadership I am interested in. I'm interested in: What does leadership of the heart look like? What does leadership rising out of the community look like?

I think the Occupy movement has showed us an organic form of leadership where each voice has its own strengths and radiance. That takes time. We're used to top-down decisions, we're used to saying a leader is decisive and doesn't care what other people think. I am interested in a circle of leadership, in spiral leadership, in organic leadership that emerges out of community.

I'm also wondering, Nina, about how we can lead ourselves forward in courageous ways that sustain us and the people that we love. It takes self-reflection and accountability. If we want our country to change, we have to be asking how we change ourselves. The quote that you read from goes on to say that if I want my country to change, how do I change myself.

I was interested in a review of *When Women Were Birds* that appeared in Christian Review that the reviewer, male, said, "This woman must have written this book while looking in the mirror and mistook indulgence for literature." I mean, that is pretty harsh. It's interesting that if a man is self-reflecting, culturally we view that as wisdom, but if a woman is self-reflecting, then we view it as self-indulgence. So, I think that goes back to those traditional models of what we imagine leadership and wisdom to look like, the all-knowing or the all-questioning. And I would rather exist in the questions.

NS: Terry, I wonder how you navigate the challenge of balancing your service to the world with adequate self-care? I am so motivated by my love and I think because we as women have so much cultural conditioning that tells us to equate our value with what we can give, or how well we serve others, it is easy to give more than we can replenish.

I just find myself actually relying on the wisdom and love and reflection of friends and sisters who encourage me to take time off, who remind me of the value of stillness and self-care. I keep telling myself that we are in a marathon here, this is not a sprint. If I want to bring myself with this much passion, presence, and commitment, I have to take care of the instrument, myself. I need to find ways to ritualize and practice and strengthen my capacity to care for myself at the same time. What about you Terry?

TTW: I agree with you, Nina. We've all been there. I'm thinking a lot about source. What is the source of our joy, what is the source of our pain, what is the source of our strength? And each of us answers that differently, I'm sure. For me, my source is my solitude, my marriage, my community of sisters and friends. My ultimate source is in nature birds, plants, lying on the ground as barefoot and as exposed as I can be on the hot sand in the desert or walking in the forest barefoot, with that soft, yielding soil underfoot. Just water, ocean, shell. So again, it's discernment, it's assessment, it's all the things we have been talking about, each in our own way and in our own time, with the gifts that are ours.

PROMPTS FOR DEEPENING LEARNING
THROUGH REFLECTION, WRITING OR DISCUSSION

Women Finding Voice:
A Conversation with Terry Tempest Williams

THEMES

- The challenge of reconciling contemplation and action; dancing with apparent contradiction, and the value of discernment.
- What does leadership of the heart look like? Leadership of community? How do we sustain ourselves, balancing service and self-care?
- What is the source of our love, of our inspiration, our creativity?
- Observing and not caving to the systemic and archetypal silencing and continued judgment of the feminine.

PROMPTS

How do you respond to the form of this interview, which allows you to hear our unique voices? Does any particular exchange stand out for you?

I think of finding my voice as connected to finding my sense of purpose, whereas Terry relates her voice to being present, listening for guidance from the natural world, and informing her action. What is true for you? Are these distinct approaches connected?

Terry says that "We have to stand in the center of our authenticity and claim what we are feeling, with our truth and our anger and other emotions." What do you sense about the connections between your authentic voice and your emotions?

Terry points to a paradox we are all living in: we have to scale up solutions, the times are urgent, and yet we also need to slow down and be still and local to listen for guidance. How do you reconcile the two seemingly opposing needs?

- How do you relate to paradox?
- Can you give an example of paradox in your own life?
- Is your instinct to try to resolve, reconcile or embrace paradoxes when you encounter them?

The sources of Terry's joy and strength are: solitude, her marriage, friends and community, and nature. What are your sources of joy and strength, and how do they feed you?

NATURE, CULTURE & SPIRIT
Integration and Congruence
through Practical Magic

To heal the imbalances in the world, I believe we must first unearth and address those mirrored within ourselves. It's helped me to acknowledge, vulnerably and with humility, where the same patterns of ranking, polarization, and judgment that I see out in the world, live within myself.

As long as I can remember, congruence has been a benchmark for my own personal learning and growth. A life aim of mine is to bring the many disparate parts or aspects of myself into alignment; like braiding many strands into a coherent whole. I seek to be present with the same authenticity no matter where or with whom I show up. I hope that the council of Ninas that lives inside my psyche can get ever better at hearing each other, and at integrating their diverse voices toward coherence. One of our deepest human needs is to belong, so perhaps my quest for integration and congruence stems from a desire to have all parts of myself be accepted, present and accessible.

So much of what has previously defined womanhood has centered around our adaptability and responses to other peoples' needs, desires, and realities. My desire for liberation from that pattern prompts me to want to reach a sense of belonging fully to myself, and also to all that I love.

At the same time, in a complementary way, my sense of safety lies in belonging in relational community, being held by a web of relationships with people who I know fully hear, trust, and appreciate me, even with my blind spots and shortcomings.

This goal of inner integration asks me to identify, reconcile and nourish healthy versions of the feminine and masculine within me. An example: my 'masculine' conditioning taught me to work hard and long to accomplish much in short periods of time, without adequately attending to my body's needs for the rest, sensuality, creativity, and spaciousness that my feminine character requires. Seeking equilibrium has required me to take a long, hard look at the ways my insecurity causes me to perpetuate my overachieving behavioral habits in a quest for external validation. As I learn to value myself and my work more, I can better tend to my disparate needs.

I'm learning to replace that need for external validation with inner appreciation; practicing relational mindfulness, and creating disruptive opportunities to enjoy periods of play, creativity, self-care, and friendship time. Relational mindfulness is a version of meditation (and a book) that its creator, my colleague and mentor Deborah Eden Tull, calls "the subtlest form of self-love." It was her adaptation, after seven years as a Zen monk, to find integration with herself, and to cultivate practices for regenerative leadership. Practicing it helps me to stay centered under stressful circumstances, and connected with all my senses, emotions, and ways of knowing.

About ten years ago, I received a teaching from a Peruvian shaman named Oscar Miro-Quesada. It was within a yearlong training by Robert Gass, intended for people whose life calling was creating conditions for people to change, and he was a guest facilitator. He led a very long Solstice ceremony, lasting seven or eight hours, ending about 3 or 4 a.m. At the very end he said:

"If you remember only one thing from this time, remember this:
Consciousness creates matter,
Language creates reality,
Ritual creates relationship."

This teaching lodged in my heart and mind, and the more I considered it, the more useful I found it to be. I consider it as offering guidance for practicing practical magic.

Here are some examples of how it's become helpful to me, in my quest for integration and congruence.

CONSCIOUSNESS CREATES MATTER

As I was recovering from a hip replacement surgery, I experienced some ways that the invisible world influences the material one. Before the surgery, my caregiver and friend Linda suggested we do a ceremony to express gratitude and say goodbye to my old hip joint. It felt so good to do that, as it was an important part of me that's served me well for over sixty years.

Knowing that scientific studies have affirmed the effects of nonlocal healing — of people praying for those undergoing hardship or injury — I asked many friends to send me love and prayer and envision me wrapped in light during my surgery. As I fell into an anaesthetized trance, I felt their prayers holding me, palpably.

As my body repaired, I spent time each day visualizing the tissue, skin, and bones of my hip healing, and also poured love with intention and focus into my new hip. I encouraged my body to accept these new bionic parts, inwardly. My healing process progressed faster than anyone had predicted or believed possible.

When I spend a few minutes in the morning, before leaving bed, imagining how I hope my day will greet me, I am often well met by events and delighted by synchronicities. I'm also practicing visualizing and sending prayers as part of my sitting and walking meditations daily, as my lived experience keep validating that it has influence. The sacred I believe in and pray to is all around and within me, and throughout nature.

LANGUAGE CREATES REALITY

As I become more conscious of my choices of phrases and words, I can cultivate my congruence. The language we've inherited is filled with violence and gender bias. For example, instead of describing efficiency as "killing two birds with one stone," which perpetuates a kind of numbness toward violence, I've learned from my colleague Rachel Bagby to instead say "feeding two birds with one scone."

In women's groups, I notice how often we refer to each other as "guys," and it troubles me. I prefer to say "women" or "gaias" instead. People often refer to humanity as mankind, and as a feminist, I prefer to use the word humankind, as it includes everyone. We have a lot of creative renaming to do, to reshape our world.

After learning about climate change through Bioneers over the past 29 years, when I hear people frame it as a crisis about "saving the planet" I wince, knowing that their language is not accurate or true. Earth will survive, no matter what we do, though it may take millions or billions of years for it to recover. The climate crisis we face is about saving humankind. It's actually about how we do or don't create conditions for humanity (and many other species who are being lost due to our resistance to make change on the scale that's needed) to be able to exist or thrive on Earth.

For me, each of these language choices have become real and important, and I try to practice listening for where my language may be out of alignment with my heart's vision for co-creating the loving, equitable, and truthful world I yearn for.

RITUAL CREATES RELATIONSHIP

When I realized that I was perpetuating harm to myself each morning, by inwardly critiquing my body as I looked at myself in my bathroom mirror, I decided to experiment with the use of ritual to alter my pattern, and perhaps even create some new neural pathways. My purpose: to cultivate a kinder relationship to my body.

I invented a ritual to cease judging myself on a daily basis, and instead pour love into my physical being. I mix up body oil with moisturizer and essential oils whose scents please me, and when I step from the bath or shower, in lieu of self- judgment I anoint my body with the oils, as I thank every part of it for the ways it serves and supports me. I hold myself accountable for doing this every day.

One ritual we've used frequently in women's intensives works whether practiced for yourself or to help connect a group. We call it "Compost and Cauldron," and it's a way of naming and claiming what you are cultivating to strengthen in yourself and may be also sharing for the benefit of the group (that's the cauldron part, for what we're cooking, together) and what you may be consciously shedding, letting go of, or composting, to return it to the Earth to serve as nourishment for life.

Each in the circle speaks when and if they're inclined, and

speaking to the center says "I'm composting my _____ (eg: desire to please others ahead of tending to my own needs, fear of facing conflict, or whatever may be true for them), and I'm putting in the cauldron the courage I felt yesterday when…." The quality of truth being shared can be tender and deep, as people recognize the shared reality of challenges or issues we often face. It deepens relationship among a group, as well as within oneself.

After creating and practicing several kinds of rituals to alter patterns I've observed in myself, I've noticed that I reach a time about four weeks in where I question whether it's making any difference. When I accept that uncertainty, but remain firm in my commitment to keep practicing, I typically notice that somewhere between six and eight weeks, I can feel a difference in my behavior, and in my psyche.

Each of these practices is strengthening my belief in and capacity to engage with the invisible world. And, while the examples I've shared are personal and individual in nature, I believe the same principles apply to larger visions and intentions related to our ecological and social systems.

I am learning — in spite of society's conditioning to the contrary — to remember, respect, and listen for the guidance of the invisible world, the energetic realms, what I perceive as practical magic. Through practice and attention (and guided by my intention to get better at this) I'm improving my ability to listen, from all sorts of sources. Sometimes images or messages arrive in dreamtime, or just as I awaken, as an idea that pops in fully-formed. I'm not always sure whether it's coming from ancestors or guardians or intuition, but I'm learning to listen for it and respect it, regardless of its source.

I learned recently of a renowned scientist whose study of consciousness led him to believe more strongly in the power of the non-physical world. David Bohm, a physicist and colleague of Einstein's who studied with spiritual masters including Krishnamurti, suggested that reality is actually comprised of two realms of activity, which he called the explicate and the implicate order.

The explicate order, he said, is everything that we can perceive with our five senses, everything we can see, touch, hear, smell, or taste in the 'material' world.

The implicate order, on the other hand, is everything else, what's invisible and inaudible through our physical senses and therefore seems unprovable through the scientific method.

Most people, he noted, presume that the explicate — what's physically palpable to us — is the larger field by far, and has the greater influence on events in the world. However, his research revealed a very different perspective on reality.

The metaphor he used to describe the actual relationship was this: Imagine that the explicate order — all that we can perceive physically — is the foam that arises on the waves of the ocean. It comes and goes with the waves, winds and tides. The implicate order, he said, is the entirety of the sea itself. What's not perceivable to our senses regulates, in his metaphor, not only the waves, the tides and the foam, but the whole of Earth's weather system itself.

For me, Bohm's observation helps me counteract the negative voices in my head, the habituated biases that say, "Take time for setting intention, meditation, and visualization? There's far too much to be DONE." Coming as it does from a smart, White man, it helps to affirm my intuition and body's knowing that attending to the invisible world is vitally important to affecting social and ecological healing, and flips my inherited bias on its head.

INTEGRATION AND RECONCILING APPARENT CONTRADICTIONS

U.S. culture has had a propensity for separating people, ideas, or elements into categories and stressing their differences, often positioning them as opposing, as hierarchies or as binaries. One example is: activism and citizen engagement of all kinds, which often gets juxtaposed with and deemed superior to inner, reflective work like meditation or energy approaches that emphasize setting intention, visualization, prayer, or receptivity.

This false separation we've been habituated to, that ranks the value of activism as being superior to more inwardly-focused work, runs contrary to what I believe is needed for navigating this transformative time. If the conjoining of the two — engaging both the material, explicit world and the invisible, implicit one — might be so much more powerful than either one practiced separately, isn't that worth considering?

In lieu of the "divide and conquer" strategy that's been the norm for so long, we need to practice finding commonality across differing backgrounds, perspectives, and faiths. What if we focused on learning how to value our differences, rather than exploiting and aggravating them?

To influence a transition from a culture founded upon a win-lose, zero-sum, hierarchical paradigm to one based upon collaboration, mutual respect, equity, and love, we've got to reveal the false dichotomies that are embedded throughout our thinking and our language. The essence of our work involves shifting from a society based upon conflict, concentrating power, ranking and violence, to one based upon complementarity, shared authority, appreciating diversity, and peaceful collaboration. And from a Me culture to a We culture.

Many Native elders from varied cultures suggest that the time we are in — a time between worlds or octaves of realities — asks humanity to shift from a form of leadership that's led by analysis, intellect, and our minds, to a leadership that's guided by the heart's wisdom.

We are culturally-shaped and therefore implicitly biased, so that we navigate the world by ranking the guidance of head over heart, since centuries of Western culture has reinforced that perception. In recent years, however, science is revealing how much our hearts actually determine our physiological, psychological, and neural responses, determining our capacity to respond to life and to self-regulate.

Of course, neither of these examples — action and spirituality, or head and heart — can exist in their best form without the engagement and dance of the other. Sacred activism and wisdom-informed, heart-led action is what's actually called for. As Terry Tempest Williams and I reflected in the piece before this, these apparent paradoxes are actually meant to be embraced. Our challenge is to learn to have them dance together, to complement each other. Like the sun and moon, nature's design is based upon complementarity and reciprocity, and is not composed of binaries or opposites.

Just as nature resolves conflict or contradiction through spirals, so must we. In nature, as Janine Benyus (the founder of the emergent field of biomimicry) informs us, the places where different ecosystems meet are the spaces of greatest fertility and innovation. Where the river meets the ocean, and the grasslands meet the forest — it's at the conjoining of two worlds that new invention is most fruitful.

In a time when the very future of the human experiment on Earth is in jeopardy, doesn't it make sense for us to bring all the best of our human capacities into alignment, and into congruence, to ensure the greatest outcome? Why not learn to dance with the apparent paradoxes that appear to us, or to "call BS," as the youth from Parkland High School modeled so courageously, when we're presented with false separations that diminish our authority and undermine our collective power as change-makers?

As children of Mother Earth and the moon, and women whose cycles naturally align with the lunar phases, I believe we are all designed by nature to attune to her guidance, if only we will listen and heed her counsel. The future of humankind on Earth, and of many of our non-human kin, may depend upon it. Thankfully, it's also the most fulfilling, congruent, and joyful way to dance with life along the way.

I hope you'll join me in exploring this nexus, this dance of apparent contradictions. Together, may we co-create the community and connective tissue needed to help us travel the arduous path ahead. After all, as Clarissa Pinkola Estes notes: *"We were born for this."*

PROMPTS FOR DEEPENING LEARNING
THROUGH REFLECTION, WRITING OR DISCUSSION

Nature, Culture & Spirit:
Integration and Congruence through Practical Magic

THEMES

- A Peruvian shaman's teaching helps me create my own rituals for inner integration, cultivation, and self-care, as well as for strengthening communal bonds.

- Learning to integrate contradictions and embrace binaries, we can create inner balance, congruence, and magic.

PROMPTS

In this chapter, I share personal examples of my living into these three principles: Consciousness creates matter; Language creates reality; Ritual creates relationship.

- As you feel into these ideas, what comes up for you?

- Can you unpack these principles and translate them into your own understanding, finding examples of each from your own life?

Consciousness Creates Matter

- Have you experienced prayer or visualization or other spiritual practices create changes in your physical reality?

Language Creates Reality:

- Have you noticed yourself changing your own use of words and phrases to express your values more accurately?

Ritual Creates Relationship:
- Have you adopted or can you adopt rituals to manifest self-care and partnership with others?

We need to shift our culture's habit of ranking and binary realities based in separation towards a culture of complementarity, mutuality, and reciprocity. For example, there is a false notion that we cannot attend to our inner life or spiritual selves and be activists at the same time.
- Can you think of a contradiction or paradox in your life and imagine how you might dance with what may seem like contrary perspectives?

WHY I'M DEEPENING INTO INDIGENOUS ALLYSHIP

As the pandemic surged over the Earth, the multiple systems that supposedly held us unraveled, and the full scope of the uncertainties we face sank in, what held me were the webs of connection to the people and places whom I hold dear.

Sacred circles, now on screens in rectangular windows, knit me tenderly to close kin, elders, and cousins, and I felt closely tethered to my now deceased parents' families. These relationships have helped to stabilize me, as I imagine yours have, too.

To tend to my heart, I've tried to accept and express waves of emotion as they arise, and to pause inwardly to celebrate moments of progress, joy and breakthrough, like the embodied moments of overwhelming relief as the results of the 2020 presidential election emerged.

I've been awash with humility and gratitude for the women of color — the leaders, organizers, and their communities — whose skill, perseverance, leadership, and drive deserve credit for that outcome.

I've surrendered to my need to weep, regularly, as so much is being lost now, and my tears, sometimes without apparent or rational reason, have been a welcome release. They renew me.

I've felt elated to see the immense global protests after George Floyd's murder, and outraged by the bald-faced greed, criminality, and accelerated destruction of immigrants, wildlands, incarcerated peoples, birds, and waterways.

I've savored the space at home to nourish my personal partnership with Kenny. To enjoy the stillness of no travel, and the beauty of the land that holds us.

An overnight immersed me in nature, camping in the woods. It gifted me with some ceremonial time, and feeling cradled warm in a tent through a thunderstorm that echoed up and down the valley. I emerged so grateful for time away from technology, and feeling ten years younger.

To nourish my mind, I've deepened my learning about social healing, about systems of White supremacy that have become so normalized in our cultures, about historical cycles of disruptive change and pandemics.

I've oriented myself towards a longer time perspective, recognizing that the scope of change we face will require a marathon from us all.

At home, I've felt healing come from communing with the ancient, arid, and craggy arroyos filled with quartz and the scent of ponderosa pine needles. And from inhaling the wide skies of New Mexico. And from feeling grateful.

This year, what's emerged most strongly for me is a profound and deepening commitment to the health, sovereignty, worldviews, traditional ecological knowledge, healing, and ally-ship with Indigenous Peoples.

I've long appreciated that Native Peoples are incredibly strong, resilient, and innovative. They have survived and thrived despite historical genocide, theft of ancestral lands, forced relocation, and Indian residential schools, to present-day missing and murdered women, unequal access to health care, education, and voting rights.

From Bioneers' beginnings in 1990 in the Southwestern US, thanks to Kenny's vision, our organization has been informed and guided by the voices, experiences, and wisdom of Native Peoples.

In 1992, I heard Petuuche Gilbert, who was then a Governor at Acoma Pueblo, say in a panel of indigenous elders about the anniversary of Columbus arriving at this land: "500 years ago you came, and we welcomed you with open arms. If you came again today, we would do the same."

I was gobsmacked, as I felt the authenticity and truth of his words, though they seemed to contradict the history of violence I knew his people had endured. I began to understand then how much I might learn from Native Peoples about how to be a human being.

Over these thirty years, I'm grateful to have learned from many Native mentors, board members, and friends.

Living in the land of the Pueblo peoples, I've experienced tribal ceremonies, feast days, and the wealth of creative expression that emerges from the hearts, cultures, and hands of so many First Peoples.

I've also begun learning about the serial and ongoing efforts at genocide, culture and language demolition, and forced sterilization and relocation that our government has inflicted on Indigenous Peoples.

I've learned how systematically and globally extractive industries have targeted Native lands and reservations for mining and drilling. I've witnessed how destructive that's been to their waterways and their man-camps to Native women and girls. I've seen how corporations are damaging the peoples' health by toxifying their water and soil. Around the world, in their dying gasps, multinational companies are not only destroying ecosystems, but also pillaging sacred sites, cultural traditions, and attempting to uproot languages.

I've seen the sub-standard and inadequate health care, lack of fresh food, water, and jobs that plague many Native communities and create pre-existing conditions, all of which have rendered the COVID-19 virus even more deadly and destructive for them.

When the pandemic first hit, I was thankful to be a bridge
for generosity and caring for some whose suffering from extremes of
poverty, rural distance, poor health, and intergenerational trauma was
worsened by the virus.

Academics call it 'pro-social' behavior, acting to benefit another or
others. I call it heart-centered leadership, and practicing right relations.

When COVID-19 began, an opportunity emerged to provide
tangible support where it was greatly needed. A friend asked me where
to give resources to support Native Peoples (and especially elders)
through the pandemic.

I met with my colleagues Cara Romero and Alexis Bunten,
the gifted and committed leaders who co-direct Bioneers' Indigeneity
program, and we came up with a list of trusted allies and friends,
focusing on the places we knew best and that we knew were hardest hit.

Our list attracted caring donors who gifted us some funds to
distribute. Because of our abundant relationships, throughout Turtle
Island and even globally, we were able to send checks to directly support
families in rural areas to access food and water, and to help protect
elders and culture-bearers.

Alexis also attracted a grant from Google to gift computers,
tablets, and access to Internet to many of the Native youth she works
with, to aid in their home schooling. (Do you know that 40% of Native
kids in this country don't have access to technology or Wi-Fi for school
or connecting?)

At the same time, I've seen that within this country are hundreds
of sovereign nations that are immensely wealthy in cultural resources
and traditional knowledge. Some of their languages, traditions, and
knowledge systems are held precariously by a scant few esteemed
culture-bearers and elders.

I've explored the wisdom of Traditional Ecological Knowledge, or TEK, which are indigenous ways of being in right and sacred relationship to the elements of life — to fire, land, air, and water.

For example, witnessing the skills of dryland agriculture, and of adapting seeds to survive through droughts, I've understood how vital they will be for all of us in the years ahead as the climate crisis worsens and Earth becomes hotter and dryer.

I know that any quest to learn to live in a regenerative way ecologically has to begin by learning respectfully from what our Native relatives have known for millennia.

I'm acutely aware of the need to remain culturally humble about how much I don't know.

I'm mindful of the dangers of cultural appropriation, and I'm not aspiring to 'nativism' or any kind of White saviorism or copy-cat environmentalism. My intent is solely to share my heart's commitment in hopes that you may be sparked to join me in it.

Thankfully, all of my previous callings coexist well with this one. As I've worked with diverse women visionaries and changemakers over these many years, it's been the perseverance, truth-telling, and unshakable stands of women from many of our most marginalized communities that have often inspired me the most.

To many Native Peoples, nature is sacred and nothing is harvested without first receiving permission, and offering gratitude and reciprocity, or giving back.

Mother Earth is seen as female, and there's an understanding that what we're doing to the Earth, we're also doing to women, and vice versa.

When I looked for an example of a society where women are honored and treated with equality, I found it in the Haudenosaunee, or Iroquois Six Nations. Seeing how respectfully women were treated in their confederacy inspired the US women's suffrage movement, which was launched in Seneca Falls, New York, in the early 1900s.

As Oren Lyons, who is the Faithkeeper for the Iroquois Six Nations, tells it: the Haudenosaunee were instructed by the Peacemaker a thousand years ago that "since the Earth is female, the women will be in charge of the Earth, land, life, and water. The men would be responsible for fire and energy, and the balance. The combination of male and female necessary to bring forth life was seen as fundamental, so great care was taken to maintain that balance."

In their matrilineal culture, since the women are in charge of life, they raise the leaders and govern the families. The women select the chief, after observing the male children from a very early age to see which of them has the qualities needed to lead the people. And the women of their longhouse have the authority to rescind the chief's leadership, if he's not doing a good job. Imagine if this country worked like that?

Thankfully, this year, with leadership from Indigenous and Black women, young people and communities of color, perhaps we finally are beginning to head in that direction.

> *May we be bold, resolute, forthright, and strategic,*
> *Integrating the power of prayer, ceremony, and ritual,*
> *In demanding the systemic change and cultural repair*
> *Our future vision, the climate, and*
> *the health of the whole requires.*
>
> *May we advocate for the voiceless among us,*
> *For the finned, feathered, and furred,*
> *For the plant people and fruitful fungi*

And for the many — like the whales —
Whose voices we have yet to understand,
That their habitats and wildlands
May regenerate to shelter and renew them.

May we practice fierce compassion,
Cultural humility, forgiveness, and kindness.
May we sink our roots down, connecting locally,
Inwardly, and more deeply to strengthen ourselves.

May we shed the unconscious vestiges
of dying belief systems within ourselves
That rank, compare, and contrive to keep us small,
So that we may flourish in co-creating a new world together.

May we help to heal our relationships with ourselves,
with mother Earth, with each other,
and with all our living global communities and kin.

PROMPTS FOR DEEPENING LEARNING
THROUGH REFLECTION, WRITING OR DISCUSSION

Why I'm Deepening Into Indigenous Allyship

THEMES

- When the pandemic started, my heart led me to care for Indigenous Peoples, and the traditional knowledge and culture they carry.
- More and more I see how much we have to learn from the ways of First Peoples, and how wise we'd be to encourage and follow their leadership.
- We can reciprocate by humbly supporting them in material ways, listening to and being guided by their needs.
- The Haudenosaunee way of balancing the roles of masculine and feminine in power sharing and decision making is an inspiring model.

As I list some of the ways Native Peoples have been murdered, forced from their lands, oppressed, poisoned, stolen from, and betrayed, what arises in your heart, mind, body, or spirit?

How aware are you of Native Peoples' history and presence in the place where you live? Of their languages and practices? How much of their history were you taught in school? What do you perceive might be interesting or useful for you to learn about more deeply?

Are you surprised when I say that in spite of all the horror they've experienced, Indigenous Peoples have not only survived, but managed to retain many of their languages and cultures? Can you give an example of traditional ecological knowledge we might do well to learn about?

I am inspired by the example of how the Haudenosaunnee or Iroquois women of the long house select their leaders. Do you know of any other indigenous practices that you admire and think we should consider for the reinvention of our cultures?

FOR MY MOTHER:

Bridging the Worlds

We are living through 'tween times.

Times when we are navigating between worlds —
        bridging paradigms and generations.
Weaving among belief systems, truths revealed,
        and false stories.

In relation to Mother Earth, our ultimate bottom line,
Who is the context for *all* that we know,
        And so much that we do NOT,
we and all our relations are suspended between two poles.

Awakening to accelerated, destabilized climate conditions
        that threaten everything,
exacerbated throughout by corrupt and broken political systems,
        binary polarization and a global pandemic —

And an *abundance* of emergent, inclusive
        organizing and movements,
                innovations, and collaborations.

We are straddling the old world — the civilization that's dying —
and the one we're midwifing into flourishing co-creation.

It *can* feel awkward, unmoored, and scary,
          But also exciting and enlivening.

What's needed in order to bridge worlds?

My beloved mama who had so many names,
Rhea Selma Cantor Simons Goodman,
          died two years ago,
after several months of declining health and hospice.

While I helped her have the best end of life I could,
hers was my closest direct encounter with death to date.
After she died, I felt suspended between worlds myself.

She was an expressive, creative, and joyful spirit,
who loved swing dancing, singing, and tai ch'i chuan.
Perhaps like many mothers,
she was also deeply challenging in ways that grew me.

Over time, and with dedicated effort,
          I had learned to love her whole-heartedly.
She had also become one of my closest friends.

In the last dozen years of her life,
I saw her change, reshaping the texture of her life
by becoming more of who she aspired to be.

She showed me how we can remake ourselves at any age;
                              by choosing consciously and repeatedly,
          by practicing and holding ourselves accountable,
          we can become who we most yearn to be.

When I first recognized the immediacy
of her life-threatening illness,
my busy life distilled swiftly into single-focus,
                    becoming crystal clear.

Nothing was more important
than to offer my mother the most loving end of life possible.

For me, it was an opportunity to walk my talk,
              to put my devotional love into action.

When I showed up prepared for
              the deep, end-of-life reflections I'd imagined —
and found her intently determined to live another eight years,
I discovered I had to throw away my plans —
      and surrender to her own sovereignty, choices, and timing.

This was about serving *her* best transition,
              and not my own ego —
or my desire for resolution and my imagining
          of a graceful, conscious death.

I had to practice acceptance in each moment,
        staying present with whatever she chose,
in her own true time and readiness.

There was less and less she could control in her life,
        she who had savored her freedom
                and autonomy for so long.

Whether loving someone toward letting go of life,
        or living through a dying civilization,
I learned it's essential to honor
        each other's dignity and sovereignty,
                while we're losing so much else.

As her dying neared,
        time became distorted, disorienting and elastic.
I witnessed her pain increasing, her suffering grow
        and her physical capacities weakening.

Waiting for death to find her,
        for her to reach her own right moment to let go
felt interminably long, and then I felt guilty
        for wishing it might come sooner.

That impatience is so familiar, as it's haunted
        my experience of the snail's pace of change
                in the ecological, political, and cultural worlds.

As I sat at my mother's bedside,
      single focused on my love for her and
          on easing her passage,
my habit of perceiving my self-worth as
      being linked to work shriveled and fell away.

I sensed in a deeper way that we all have our own parts to play,
      in bridging worlds, in hospicing the old system
          and bringing forth the new.
I knew that I was exactly where I needed to be.

At her bedside, during her last week,
      I felt the 'reality' of this physical world meet
the invisible world, the energetic realms.

The place where hunches are born,
      where dreams come from, and
          where ancestors dwell and listen
              for our voices or our prayers.

I walked each day in a dream state,
      filled with simultaneous sorrow and aliveness,
          in a dance with patience and anticipation,
an eavesdropper listening in on multiple worlds.

I sensed the push-pull within her —
      her unfailing appetite for more dancing, more play,
          more juiciness, and more love embodied,

and the gentle, insistent tug of surrender…
of leaving her painful body behind.

I envisioned a welcoming team inviting her to come,
humming and coaxing her to join them, tempting her with
a dance of energies, color and light laced with love.

I had imagined that hospicing her through her illness
for months might prepare me for her death, but it didn't.

She died while I was out, washing her car to ready it for sale.
I comforted myself with knowing
that people often seem to go
when a loved one is absent.

Soon after, her tiny body lost its heat.
It became stiffer, as we washed her lovingly.

I applied a sacred oil I'd been given
to help release her spirit from her shell of a body.
I covered her with golden silk and flowers.

The chaplain we'd come to love,
who'd worked for the hospice center,
offered a Tibetan ritual to help her soul on its way.

We wrote her letters to say goodbye,
and burned them to send our messages up in smoke.

Nikko, her devoted chihuahua,

    wouldn't budge from his lion's pose under the table

in the next room where she lay.

Twenty-four months have now passed since her death.

    I still miss her presence, almost daily.

There's a hole in my heart

    where the reliability of her love used to live.

I connect with her now in odd moments and ways,

    like eating from the Southwestern vintage plate that she loved.

I thank her for the voice, boobs, style, and lust for living

    and learning that she gifted to me.

I remind myself she's still alive in me, now.

And savor it when her qualities show up

    in other people who enter my world.

Living through her death and the time beyond is teaching me

    to resolve a duality I've lived with all my life.

A binary inside me that had both a good mother and a bad one.

    A polarity I'd lived with for so long merged into one.

Remembering to look for healing within the wound,

    I see now how her need to always be at the center of things

Is teaching me now to more

    discerningly balance self and service.

I'm wider awake now to life's cycles

        to its fragility and to its resilience

in this toxic world we've created.

        Impermanence is more palpable for me now.

Death's nearness makes life shinier, more crystalline -

        full moons are brighter,

            foxes more breathtakingly formed,

turkey feathers a gift filled with wonder.

        Laughter, wildness, and freedom are more precious.

A friend knowledgeable about Mayan cosmology suggested

        I befriend the Death Mother, who lives in the South.

While the Life Mother in the North is

        nurturing, fertile, and generous,

the Death Mother rules boundaries,

        limits, and appropriate endings.

Throughout my devotion to Mother Life,

        (and reinforced by our biased culture),

I've focused mostly on the beginnings, the pollination,

        the wondrous, fertile, and hopeful regeneration

        of seasons, perennials, cycles, and systems.

Now, to better prepare myself for bridging worlds,

I'm attuning to the beauty of a snag that stays standing.

To how it becomes habitat for ravens, eagles, and woodpeckers,

        and the insects and mycelium

            who return it to become nourishment

for the next cycle of the soil's creation.

I've long believed that our collective focus
        on beginnings — while avoiding endings,
and on progress, at the expense of history, lineage, and tradition
is a relic of the patriarchal, colonial, and capitalist systems
        that so many of us were raised with.
Finding that same bias in myself is humbling.

To bring ourselves fully to this moment of pivotal change,
I believe we must face the true danger of this time -
        the climate emergency, and
                the realities of all that's dying.

For myself, I need to take in the whole context,
        to relate to the losses with my body, heart, mind, and spirit.
To find my own internal sense of balance,
to fully face its truth
        to be able to orient towards integration.

As James Baldwin famously wrote,
        "Not everything that is faced can be changed,
but nothing can be changed until it is faced."

Once, a few months after her passing,
        I prayed intently before bed asking for a dream, a sign
that her journey through the bardo was progressing.
        I wanted some evidence that she was ok.

Just before dawn, she appeared to me,
 in her unmistakable fashion, dressed to the nines.
She was lounging, leaning upon a marble kitchen counter,
 draped in olive colored velvet and silks.

She assured me in her purring tones
 that she was fine, truly ok — and then she was gone.

At other times, I sense her presence at dawn
 or in a dazzling sunset.
 Her eyes smile lovingly at me
 from a photo across the room.
My grief for losing her still arises often,
 remaining close to the surface.

I hear her voice within me,
as we sang that lullaby to each other before she died,
 the same one she sang to me as a baby,
 and it brings me to tears, every time.

Grief and mourning don't follow a timeline or schedule.

As I see it, our culture's avoidance of grief,
 and lack of our full feeling or expression
Is a root cause of the widespread
 violence, depression, and harm among us.

I am determined to change that pattern in myself,
       so I try to turn toward my sadness or loss when they arise.
Avoid swallowing or tucking them away,
      as I've been habituated to do.

Living through my mother's death up-close is changing me.

Life feels heightened to me, amplified,
      my senses alert to savor my body's wellness.
Moments that shimmer with dimensional connection.
      Times of laughing so hard that I can't stop.

I'm more disciplined and discerning
      at saying no to distractions,
         at prioritizing what matters most to me.
Knowing that my time is finite,
      integrating that reality in a deeper way,
         I sense each day's immense and irreplaceable value.

Invisible worlds are more real to me now,
      including the wisdom of plants, creatures, and stars.
Before, I asked and listened for them
      because I believed I should.
Now, I sense the exchange between us
      as palpable, energetic, and real,
         and as its own reward.

I remember to feel grateful more frequently now,

 thanking the thunder beings and rainclouds,

the people who dance and sing to call the rain,

 to honor the corn, the deer, the sun, the star people.

I am leaning fully into loving well,

 while learning all I can,

tending life in balance with cultivating the instrument of myself.

 Anything less feels arrogant — like sleepwalking or hubris.

When I pray now, I have greater trust that it matters,

 that it's somehow being heard or received.

Leading from my heart has stopped being aspirational for me.

 It's become second nature, a joyful default,

  feeling myself truly aligned with what I'm here to do.

My inner world and outer experience

 are more seamlessly connected,

  like a reciprocal loop. Or a mobius strip.

It's a feeling I wish for everyone alive today.

PROMPTS FOR DEEPENING LEARNING
THROUGH REFLECTION, WRITING OR DISCUSSION

For My Mother: Bridging the Worlds

THEMES

- Being with my mother as she was dying gave me profound lessons: the power of presence, patience, and love to face into the pain of our current losses of species, peoples, and cultures.
- Tending her forced me to slow down to accompany her process of dying.
- I felt how we are conditioned to prefer beginnings and productivity.
- As we perceive the beauty in endings and in death, we become more aware of the preciousness of our lives and relations and world.

PROMPTS

My mother's death was the first time I hospiced someone through the process of letting go of this life.

- What is your personal relationship with death?
- Have you witnessed or nursed someone you love through their dying?
- What did you find familiar? What is different?
- What have you learned from that person's process and from your own loss that you can name and share?
- Have you prepared for your own passing in any way?
  If not, why not?

Have you experienced the "in-between" state described in this poem, a "between worlds" state?

- What was happening at the time?
- What physical and emotional sensations accompanied this "in-between" or liminal state?
- Did the experience change you? If so, how?

Our culture barely acknowledges death or grief, but death's nearness makes life more precious. And grief is a function of love.

- What is your attitude towards grieving?
- Do you allow grief space and time in your life?
- Do you have a process or ritual?
- Do you grieve with others?
- What are your sources of courage and comfort?

NOURISHING AN
EMERGENT CULTURE

Over the past thirty months, since initially publishing this book, so much has happened to deepen my understanding of this culture we've inherited or had foisted upon us. It has sharpened my awareness of how urgent it is that we realize and womanifest a very different one.

As the pandemic shuttered the economy, high levels of anxiety were manipulated through cable news and social media, igniting a culture war that's being exploited and exacerbated. George Floyd's televised lynching by police triggered global demonstrations against the violent, widespread abuses of systemic racialized injustice. And while climate catastrophes accelerate, with globally disastrous impacts, extractive industries with politicians in their pockets are defeating efforts to slow or stop their destruction.

I've always felt that culture is a leverage point, a key to changing everything, and have chosen my work accordingly. During this time, I've been exploring how frames and stories relate — both within ourselves and collectively — to try to better understand this belief.

Culture is often insidious and hard to pin down. In the same way that water drawn from a lake or ocean carries the DNA of everything that's ever lived in it, culture carries the impressions of our past lineages, myths and archetypes, traumas and belief systems.

Culture can be defined as the stories that any group takes as given, or normalizes. And culture is always alive and evolving.

Unearthing those varied influences to make them visible to ourselves feels necessary to me, to contribute to cultural shifts for ourselves and for our collective future.

For example: as someone with the unearned privileges of appearing White, now I can see the White supremacy culture that's conditioned me to be silent, to not make waves when racial divides come up, or to feel ashamed of our nation's history. Being conscious of that conditioned response, I can decide that these times require me to compost that patterned behavior to stand strongly with allies on behalf of justice and transforming systemic racism, now.

Language also carries and spreads cultural memes. Things like "rugged individualism," "every man a millionaire," "chick flicks," "man up" or Earth as "resources to exploit."

The concepts, narratives, and images that comprise culture seep into our psyches in countless ways from early childhood on up, through education and policies, and all kinds of media, advertising and arts, as well as through our families' attitudes and the ways that history books describe (or omit) what happened in the past.

Culture becomes the basis through which a people express their values, which are only sometimes conscious and intentional. This makes it important to identify some of those ideas and memes that have brought us to this precipitous time.

In what follows, I offer a sampling of the constructs we've inherited and absorbed — but remember, we always have a choice. Now, with attention, practice, and perseverance, I am working to shed many of the cultural constructs that I find in me, to make room for the next evolution of our collective culture to emerge.

The Western colonial cultural legacy is riddled with false separations — within ourselves, among each other, and between us humans and the web of life. It presumes we are apart from nature, when actually we are nature.

A mechanistic worldview has oriented Western culture towards considering whole systems to be simply a 'sum of their parts.' This has led to commodifying nature, our bodies, and the whole Earth community, depriving societies of the mystery and complexity of the web of interactions that actually inform this world.

We're inundated with heroic superheroes and buddy movies — huge box office hits — that celebrate and normalize violence and revenge. They lean heavily on raw power and divide and conquer strategies.

Inflected with patriarchy, this culture turns us towards either/or binaries, and winner-take-all, scarcity, and win/lose paradigms. I monitor myself carefully to avoid falling into roles of victim or perpetrator, especially when I feel coerced or steamrollered by a guy who's used to getting his way. The toxic gendered identities that we've inherited — combined with a tendency to rank, blame, and judge ourselves and each other — have led to epidemics of abuse and rage, shame and pain.

We've allowed ourselves to be seduced into believing that having more money, buying more things, achieving fame or working harder will make us happier. At the same time, our implicit gendered biases have devalued other, more authentic pathways toward joy: relegating emotions, intimacy, and relationships to the historically less-valued realm of 'the feminine.'

The culture many of us have grown up with has spread values of patriarchy, White nationalism, colonialism and capitalism globally, exporting ideas that separate us from our empathy, connectedness, and full humanity.

Perhaps, as cultural historian Richard Tarnas suggests, we are having a near-death experience as a species. It is a transformative moment. Those times tend to focus the mind, to clarify what's important, to cause people to soberly consider and change the values that inform and guide cultures.

The mythologist Michael Meade has called this era an initiation, as many cultures have seen encounters with mortality as part of rituals designed to affect maturation, intended for coming of age or for entering new stages and seasons of life.

The cultural values I'm trying to strengthen create nourishment for conscious learning, and for deepening reciprocal regenerative relationships with all of life.

So far, around the world, it is often the women and female-identifying leaders, BIPOC and Indigenous Peoples, and young people who are making the strongest stands, raising their voices loudest and risking their bodies to stand as protectors of water, life and the places they call home. But given how high the stakes are, I hope that everyone who cares deeply enough will engage.

Perhaps the impacts of climate catastrophe, fascism, sexism and White nationalism had to become this blatant, urgent, and extreme — atop a global pandemic — to elicit the immune response needed to stir us into action. This frightening time has strengthened my endurance and oriented me toward a longer view, shaking me out of my comfort zones and complacency into active work on changing our collective culture.

Since culture is both culprit and solution, transforming culture is clearly called for. But we don't need to start from scratch. There are stories, ideas, and values we can respectfully study from history and traditional cultures that offer guidance on how to be a good human being. These will always evolve into new forms. We can co-create culture from the best integration of tradition, innovation, and our collective yearning for a future that works for all.

To understand more about how stories shape our lives, I turn to Iindigenous mentors.

Pat McCabe, or Woman Stands Shining, shared a traditional protocol around story (from both the Diné and Lakota Peoples). She learned that among neighboring Indigenous Tribal Nations, while each one has its own creation story, they are all equally respected and all are held as being true. Oren Lyons, who is Faithkeeper for the Haudenosaunee or Iroquois Six Nations, says that if he wants to understand a people's culture, he asks to hear their creation stories.

An author and educator from the Potawatomi Nation, Robin Wall Kimmerer, notes a core difference between Western culture's creation story and that of the Anishinaabe peoples, which has been passed down through centuries of oral tradition.

In the Anishinaabe story, Sky Woman falls through a hole in the sky, and encounters a sequence of creatures who come to her aid: geese who float her on their wings, and then turtle, who supports her in the water by carrying her on his back. Then, the animals take turns diving to get mud from the ocean floor to help her have land to live on. Only muskrat can dive deep enough to succeed, but he sacrifices his life in the process. With the mud muskrat brings on turtle's back, Sky Woman dances her gratitude, and the mud grows to create Turtle Island. It's a story of reciprocal kinship, of respect and caring and mutual aid. It's a story of Mother Earth being a place of interconnection and harmony.

The creation story that has informed much of Western culture is that of Adam and Eve, and the Garden of Eden. It's a story of original sin, of judgment, power over and shame; a story that condemns the seeking of knowledge. It's a story of banishment from the Garden, which is described as a place that's separate from, and better than, Earth. It's a tale of separation, conflict, hierarchy and punishment.

The two stories couldn't be more different, and the values they express are deeply and insidiously embedded in our cultures. In one, humanity's home is infused with respect, and cultivated by kindness, mutuality, and care. It also includes courageous sacrifice for the well-being of another. In the other, the people are shamefully banished from a place of abundance and beauty to live out life on Earth in disgrace, enduring toil, pain, and hardship until they die.

Stories don't have to be large-scale, public, or mythic to be transformative. Some of the most potent cultural stories are deeply personal and intimate. Jerry Tello, a servant leader, author and educator from Los Angeles' Latino community, tells stories from his childhood about his grandmother. He describes how each night, she'd come into his room and wake him up, placing her hands on his forehead to bless him before she went to bed.

After sharing his experience in vivid detail, he invited us each to close our eyes and imagine our own grandmother placing her hands upon our forehead to give us her blessings. I wept as I felt the gift of that connection. He reminded us that our ancestors' spirits, medicine, and blessings are with us all the time. His stories offer cultural medicine for reclaiming our sacredness, healing manhood, and intergenerational connection.

In traditional cultures, stories are passed on and enacted through rituals and ceremonies that embody the ideas and connections people believed kept them healthy and in right relationship.

I am inspired by my own Jewish culture's deep valuing of independent thinking, of questioning, and of learning. I love the Hebrew phrase *tikkun olam*, which means "world repair." It guides each of us to leave the world more whole, healthier, and more just than when we were born into it. I am grateful to know that my people were once slaves who freed ourselves, and that the annual ceremony of Passover is meant to awaken the journey from oppression to freedom within each of us.

Stories are the cornerstones of culture. Their messages are not only communicated in narrative forms, but are also conveyed in poetry, music, visual and performing arts. Stories (and the values they carry into culture) can also be transmitted through design, architecture, and the laws and policies that our societies produce. While written or spoken narratives are received through our sense-making abilities and our minds, they also affect our emotions, our intuitions, and our physical nervous systems. Sometimes we receive them in dreams or visions.

But like culture, stories are not static. Like rivers or clouds, they are fluid and always changing. Stories evolve as each new carrier of a story or vision imparts their own original imprint to it. Artists and storytellers are often the first to imagine a future that's possible, or has been repressed or hidden, and so they become initial co-creators that help to seed emergent forms of culture.

Onandaga Turtle Clan Faithkeeper Oren Lyons has shared with us that Native elders from around the world had come to a four-word conclusion about what was needed for life to continue. Those four words are: "Value change for survival."

For me, this means both that we need to change our values, and value change itself, to survive. Given how vehemently we tend to resist change, that's a tall order. As Greta Thunberg points out, "We must change almost everything in our current societies. I want you to act as if our house is on fire. Because it is."

As women and female-identifying people, we may have some affinity or gift for facing into change. Perhaps it has something to do with nature evolving us to experience childbirth. I recently heard Bill McKibben speculate on why so many global climate leaders are female, and he said, "Perhaps they're better at facing difficult realities." An ancient Wiccan chant to invoke the power of the sacred feminine says, "She changes everything she touches, and everything she touches changes."

I'm finding it helpful to challenge and reframe my old ideas of what security means.

For my own sense of safety or support, I rely upon a web of loving relationships that holds me. People with whom I can be utterly honest and un-edited, and whose vision, discernment, and counsel I trust. Friends I know I can turn to, if needed, in hard times. This helps me to strengthen a core value of moving from a me-culture to a we-culture.

In sensitive situations with people who are polarized around issues ranging from racism or White supremacy to politics or health, I'm trying to avoid being rigidly identified with a position. Instead, I attempt to dance with apparent contradictions and paradoxes. To ask questions, remain respectful and curious, and listen deeply, in order to explore whether a third path becomes possible.

I'm scanning myself closely, especially in multicultural interactions, for patterns of White supremacy. Some of those for me include: a habit of perfectionism, a drive to over-perform at work, talking more than I listen, a sense of entitlement in any form, and an assumption that I need to act, when listening with full presence is often what's needed most.

I am also cultivating what Professor Kamilah Majied calls "discomfort resilience." I try to remember that when someone from another culture corrects me or offers me insight about a way that I may have been ignorant or inadvertently offended, I don't have to feel hurt, defensive, or explain. I need only to receive their feedback, and to consider it a contribution toward my learning.

To transform values and culture among work colleagues, institutions, groups, and governance, my experience with Bioneers and women's leadership retreats have offered some insight. They have shown me the power of participating in an embodied experience of the cultural values most vital to the future we yearn to co-create. In both of those contexts, I have seen over and over how transformative the physical and emotional experience of authenticity and mutual respect can be, while embracing differences within a field of common vision. Once you have experienced in your body what Buckminster Fuller called "the preferred state," there's no turning back.

The culture I'm voting for includes prioritizing relational intelligence and appreciating emotions as one of nature's ways of communicating with us. If we could liberate and express our healthy anger, despair and grief, collectively, that alone might ignite enough civil resistance to change everything.

The culture I'm living into creates connective tissue across different octaves of life experience, weaving the personal and the transpersonal together. As I learn about and sense the cascading loss of species occurring rapidly throughout the natural world, I remember what I learned with my mother prior to her death. Although my mind wanted to skip ahead and start grieving her loss while she was still alive, I had to practice being present, relating to her with full care and attention as she was. When I did that, I could celebrate being with her and the love between us, instead of using that precious time to mourn a loss that was yet to come. In a related way, I now practice savoring luminous lavender juniper berries beneath a tree, or tall blooming hollyhocks attracting hummingbirds, even while I also allow space to feel the losses.

Ultimately, I believe that people are more deeply motivated to change because of love and attraction than fear. We won't transform culture by believing we're right, being armed with enough facts, or making a better case. We'll win over hearts and minds by making it more appealing to play in our sandbox. We'll do it by loving the present enough to be as deeply passionate about the future we're co-creating.

On the most basic level, we need to liberate our imaginations from the false barriers that limit them. To encourage ourselves to dream, draw, write, and co-create an emergent culture that guides us towards a healthy, just, and healing world. Trusting that each of us has a perspective or a facet that is essential to contribute.

To do that, we need to reclaim our inner authority, our sovereign will, and our power. We need to value the particular stories that come through us, those that are ours to tell. To show up to support, each in our own ways, the people and places we love and those who are in greatest need. To support feminist, BIPOC, and youth-led climate justice work around the globe.

And then to share our loves, our stories, and our actions, in any creative form, trusting that vulnerability is a superpower. After all, they say that people will remember what you make them feel, not what you make them think.

I believe from deep in my bones on outward into the stars and ethers that this is our time. Motivated by love, and a devotional dedication to a liberatory, just, and free future, I can feel the feminine uprising, fueled by perseverance and determination, moving with grace and flexibility, and sourced by the power of what we cherish most. I sense Mother Life reflecting that truth through many women and female-identifying people of all colors, alongside BIPOC leaders, men, youth, and elders who are standing for right relations, and standing for the land, water, and all of life. Together, we are standing for the children of all species, and for a future we're womanifesting, each in our own way.

When preparing fermented foods, given the right conditions, it only takes a small amount of sourdough, yoghurt, or sauerkraut culture to ferment a much larger batch.

I close with these words from matriarch Casey Camp Horinek, a tribal council leader and climate justice and Rights of Nature activist of the Ponca Nation.

"What do you vote for personally? Do you vote for a change in the way that we relate to the world around us? Or do we continue to be the brainwashed people who are forced into a certain form of education, a certain form of dressing, and on and on? Or do we break free from that and see what has worked and what needs to work next?

And then we take it to that level, and we warrior up. Quit waiting for someone else to show you a way. Go internalize. Sit inside yourself. Meditate, as they say. And find what your spirit needs you to do.

It is time to protect. It is time to go forth, take to the streets if you have to, take city halls if you have to, create the policies within your community that will engender that seventh generation philosophy that we all have been taught, no matter what the words are that we use, and set a place at the table that is going to be there for your great-great-great, for the simple things that we enjoy — air, food, water, earth and the sacredness of all."

PROMPTS FOR DEEPENING LEARNING
THROUGH REFLECTION, WRITING OR DISCUSSION

Nourishing An Emergent Culture

THEMES
- What is culture made of, and where does it come from?
- Many inherited cultural stories are not based in values that will lead us to a thriving future.
- To heal division and polarization, we need to develop empathy and cultivate "discomfort resilience."

How would you define culture?

Reflect and name some cultural patterns, stories, and myths you have inherited that you want to share.
- Pick one and discuss how you might shift that in yourself.
- How might changing that affect the larger culture?
- Can you name any harmful cultural stories and myths can you name that are accepted as reality? Make your own list.

Some say we are in a "near death" experience as a culture.
- Do you think this is true?
- If so, what does this call upon us to do? And to become?
- What does value change for survival mean to you?

Have you had an experience of being in a community bound in common values and love? If so, what have you noticed about your body and mind, emotions and spirit?

How does the phrase "this is our time" or "we were born for this" land in you?

- What do you think it means?
- What emotions or judgments come up?
- What if it's true?

FROM DISCIPLINE TO DISCIPLESHIP:
Cultivating Love, Collaboration, & Imagination

In conclusion, I feel called to share with you some of the ideas, practices, and perspectives that are helping me find my way through the anxiety, grief, and anger of this era of massive change. It's a time that one of my beloved mentors, Joanna Macy, named The Great Turning.

To remember and retrieve my own agency, my sense of sovereignty and connection to the sacred, I'm peeling away layers of unconscious biases inherited from a constellation of deadly systems whose violence is being amplified by the current pandemic: Patriarchy, Colonialism, Racism, and Capitalism.

As a species, we're facing nothing less than a near-death experience. Thankfully, throughout history, people have often shown a capacity to rapidly change values and to precipitate large-scale change during periods of intense collective crises.

Cultivating our hearts' capacity to love is the most powerful, enduring, and regenerative of all the resources we have available to help us survive this tumultuous time and contribute to co-creating the future that our hearts yearn for.

I'm learning that disciplining my heart is central to increasing that ability.

The word discipline used to trigger an immediate reaction in me of rebellion, resistance, and defiance. I assumed that it implied some external authority that I needed to resist, in order to protect or defend my own agency.

But that changed when the idea of discipline was reframed as disciple-ship, the taking on of an intentional apprenticeship. It involves humbling myself to learn to do something more consciously and purposefully than I had before — in this case, to understand my heart's immense capacity for love.

For me to become a more effective and magnetic lover of life, in the midst of the tumult of our time, I need to be rigorous with myself, remembering or relearning how to value myself for my uniqueness and intrinsic value, discarding old habits of comparison and self-judgment that limit my expression.

To hold myself accountable, I must give up my complacency, my learned illusions of helplessness, and my rationalizations.

To love and care for yourself is not a self-indulgent act. It's essential for each of us to embody the world we want to co-create, and to become more able to contribute meaningfully to it. By loving ourselves, we deepen our capacity to love others, and as we do so, we can become far more effective allies and advocates for changing the systems that oppress and destroy so many of those we love. Cornel West says, "Justice is what love looks like in public."

I know I need to apply discipline (or discipleship) in how I relate to those I don't agree with, or people who are decidedly different from me. This is not easy to do, but it is also *so* necessary.

Those of us who want to help make positive change in the world must grapple with the vast imbalance of the power differentials we face. Our class, gender, and racial inequities are so systemic and so ingrained that no matter how hard I try, I continue to discover my own blind spots and embedded patterns of White supremacy, internalized misogyny, and privilege. We must be willing to undertake this excavation work, no matter how uncomfortable it is.

In the biblical tale of David and Goliath, a small shepherd boy conquers a giant by slinging a rock at his exposed forehead. According to Malcolm Gladwell's interpretation of this story, we tend to think of David's victory as a miracle, as proof that sometimes, the weak can conquer the strong.

Instead, Gladwell proposes that David's win may have less to do with luck than with perspective on the things we *assume* to be disadvantages. A giant weighed down with too much history or money may actually be at a disadvantage, while innovation and creativity confer advantage. Having lived through prior traumatic events can confer strength.

Gladwell also notes that while underdog tactics can be highly successful, many don't adopt them because they require harder work, greater adaptability and a willingness to think outside the box.

But with so much at stake in every domain of our lives, it's time to exercise discipline as discipleship. It's time to act to protect, defend, or reform systems on behalf of what we love, even if we feel scared; even though we know it's hard.

The path ahead promises to be challenging and uncertain. It requires higher levels of centering, practice, accountability, and responsibility.

For me, it means shedding old simplistic and idealistic notions that I held, often unconsciously — that change was possible without confrontation, that leadership was possible without sacrifice, and that I didn't have to adopt a warrior stance to be an activist. As I've sought to leverage my privilege to become a better ally for indigenous and other people of color, it's required humility, dedication, and perseverance. And it's definitely a work in progress.

For the future my heart yearns for, we'll need lots of us expanding our skills to create connective tissue among our communities, our movements, and our issues. To succeed, we surely need each other — many of us — all working together.

Over a thousand years ago, the Iroquois Five Nations or Haudenosaunee had been in violent cycles of destruction, with endless conflict and revenge killings for many years. The Peacemaker was born among them, and he brought them into unity by the clarity of his vision, and by sharing the Great Law of Peace.

As Onondaga Faithkeeper Oren Lyons tells it, the law's basic elements are three-fold:

- The first is peace. They all laid down their arms and agreed to fight no more.
- The second is the power of the great minds united, the amplified intelligence of the collective.
- And the third was symbolized as one bowl, one spoon. That means to honor Life's limits, and to share, with gratitude and equity, among the people.

Much later, some of the governance principles of the Haudenosaunee Six Nations Confederacy informed the creation of the US Constitution and Bill of Rights. Their model of gender equity inspired the US women's suffrage movement of the early 1900s.

I choose to believe in the power of the people rising up in collaborative movements. The peoples' voices together speaking in many tongues: *Enough! Basta! Arréte! No more Blah Blah! It's time for Change!*

This vision asks us to embody the power, strength, and interconnectedness of all the issues we face.

Sadly, many people have an easier time imagining the end of the world than the end of capitalism. As *The Guardian* columnist George Monbiot recently noted, "Then let's begin by imagining something that's easier to comprehend: the end of concentrated wealth. Our survival depends on it."

May we fling open the doors and windows of our minds to let some fresh air in and be willing to risk that change.

Pat McCabe, also known as Woman Stands Shining, a colleague and friend from the Diné Nation, offered a challenge: she suggested we need to find ways to *love the future.*

When I heard her words, I realized how often I've held the future in a dim light. I recognized how hard it's become to hold a future vision that my heart can fully embrace.

In the late 1980's, well before apartheid ended in South Africa, journalist Catherine Ingram interviewed the Rev. Desmond Tutu. She noticed that he kept saying, "*When* we end apartheid." At that time, she thought "Yeah right, dream on."

Afterward, she reflected: "I didn't want to rain on his parade or anything, but in my heart of hearts, I thought, *not in your lifetime.* And lo and behold, a year and a half later, it was over. It was really a profound lesson about what can happen when the will of people aligns."

Sometimes, it's hard to see massive changes while they are emergent. But we must be able to imagine them, watch for them, name them, continue working towards their happening, invest our hearts in their outcomes, make art that calls them in, speak and dance and pray them into being.

Now, learning to love our future is becoming part of my practice, not in a naïve way or one that denies the truth or complexity of what is, but as part of my discipleship towards cultivating congruence.

In many ways, our greatest challenge may be to unleash our imaginations. To be able to visualize and feel in an embodied, empathic and sensory way the future we want, the futures our hearts desire, the futures we yearn for and imagine are possible. Then we must share our visions.

In a recent interview about climate change, Michael Pollan, a writer who's tackled issues as complex and varied as our industrialized food systems, psychedelics, and consciousness, said he believes we still have a real chance as a species to shift our course. "Nothing is inevitable; everything's evitable," he said; "We're very fatalistic. People assume things are *the way they have to be* and they're not."

As meaning-making creatures, we are innovative and hard-wired for story. But these gifts are multivalent: they can be both a blessing and a curse, and everything in between. What this means is that it all comes back to agency: to our ability to choose, moment by moment, what path to take, how to interpret what happens, and how to respond to it. We have the power to help shape our lives, both individually and communally.

To be able to lovingly and whole-heartedly, with acceptance and courage, engage ourselves in this period of intense change, we must be in discipleship to growing ourselves and loving life, while stretching to become enduring connective tissue with each other.

I hope that in the future, this era may become known as "The Time of the Great Web Forming" or "The Time of Rivers Coalescing."

As Patti Smith sang to a crowd of 30,000 global activists assembled at COP26 in Glasgow, Scotland, to address climate change:

> *People have the power*
> *The power to dream, to rule*
> *To wrestle the Earth from fools.*
> *Listen, I believe everything we dream*
> *Can come to pass through our union.*

May it be so.

PROMPTS FOR DEEPENING LEARNING
THROUGH REFLECTION, WRITING OR DISCUSSION

From Discipline To Discipleship: Cultivating Love, Collaboration, & Imagination

THEMES

- It's important to peel back the layers to see and shed unconscious biases that live deep within our psyches.
- Ongoing self-cultivation is necessary, through practice and discipline or discipleship, strengthening our hearts and skillfulness to connect across differences.
- Values and worldviews are changing, within ourselves and collectively; it's important to nourish the liberation of our imaginations.

PROMPTS

In scanning yourself for learned patterns from systems of patriarchy, capitalism, White supremacy, or colonialism, what can you see that you'd like to shed?

How might the idea of disciple-ship alter your own relationship to discipline?

How does the long history of social movements, and the endurance that's required to 'bend the arc of the moral universe toward justice,' relate to how you feel about your own leadership?

Have your values changed in response to the pandemic, climate emergency, racial injustice, and emergent authoritarianism? If so, how?

What are the skills and capacities we need to strengthen in order to contribute to the vision of a movement of movements, connecting across the many differences that currently factionalize efforts toward progressive change?

How might you love the future, and what might that future look like or feel like? What do your inner voices of judgment say, as you reach for a vision of a future you can whole-heartedly love?

Given your own preferred ways of processing information (visual, auditory, and kinesthetic), what might help you to free up your imagination?

- What experiences have opened your mind or heart to envision new realities?

PROMPTS FOR DEEPENING LEARNING
THROUGH REFLECTION, WRITING OR DISCUSSION

Embodied or Group Practices for Part III

RITUAL

Create a ritual or ceremony to honor and thank the source or sources of the bounty in your life: Have it emerge from your own heart, in words, song, rhythm, movement, prayer, art-making, gift-giving. Engage others to participate with you.

DECISION-MAKING THE OKANAGAN WAY

When a decision needs to be made in a group at work or in a volunteer or other organization, you can try this experiment.

In examining the decision, have one person speak for Tradition (what has worked before), one for Vision (what is a preferred future), one for Relationship (the impacts of a decision on the people), and one for Action (how the decision will be implemented). Then allow all members of the group to speak to what has been learned and how the decision might change based on valuing all of these factors equally.

COPING WITH DISCOMFORT

How afraid are you of another's pain and your own complicity in it? To help cultivate the muscle to witness and feel the suffering of others and of ourselves while staying present and well-resourced:

- Turn within. Adopt an attitude of kindness and curiosity.
- Notice your particular ways of being triggered, or the kinds of issues that trigger you. What do you notice in your body? What

emotions arise? What thoughts or memories may be connected to the feeling?

- Stay present and breathe. Witness whether the feelings change, and if so, how.

EXPLORING PRIVILEGE

A process of exploring our privilege:

- Sit with someone with whom you share a kind of privilege in common:
- Describe a specific experience of awakening to your privilege. Notice and share the feelings that emerge. Shame? Anger? Guilt? Sorrow?
- Also note whether positive feelings were part of the experience, such as relief, feeling special, smarter or better than.
- After each of you shares, discuss what you might learn.
- End by appreciating each other for honesty and caring to do the work.

BEST PRACTICES

From a gathering of wise mentors, we delved into best practices for bringing together groups across differences, and certain common principles emerged:

- name power and privilege difference up front;
- forge agreement on intention and desired outcomes;
- establish group norms;
- representation matters;
- encourage embodied awareness;
- prioritizing relationship before task.

Discuss each of these principles with any work team or group you are active in. Decide together which you may adopt and define a process by which you can witness the results.

RITUAL CREATES RELATIONSHIP

Is there a ritual you can create to help heal or strengthen your relationship with yourself? Create your own personal ritual and be accountable to practice it daily for four to six weeks. Notice any shifts in your attitude towards yourself.

RITUAL: COMPOST/CAULDRON

Engage in a ritual that creates group connection and cohesion.

In a circle, reflect on and name what you want to shed, and what you want to cultivate in yourself. Designate an object or space in the middle as the compost bin, and another as the cauldron.

Now go around the circle with each person naming something they are ready to let go of in themselves and placing it in the compost, as well as something they appreciate in themselves and wish to grow, which they put in the cauldron.

Notice any commonalities among those in the circle, and how the field among you may feel after this exercise.

ALLYSHIP, INDIGENOUS AND OTHER

Do you know the names of the Indigenous Peoples who lived and cared for the place where you now make your home?

Can you or your group think of a way to respectfully support a nearby Native community, or one connected to an issue or cause you care about?

DEATH

How much do you navigate the awareness of death in your life? Reflect on a personal example of death denial or death appreciation that you've experienced. Write a poem or create a piece of visual art, song, or dance to honor death.

CREATE A GRIEF ALTAR

Use earth elements, photos, flowers, candles, whatever appeals. Then design a short grieving ceremony. Invite at least one other person to share the ceremony at your altar with you.

SHIFTING CULTURE

Culture is in part a function of our language and values, as expressed in the stories we tell about ourselves and each other. Negative and apocalyptic stories abound but there are not as many of a beautiful positive future. What we cannot imagine, we cannot create or move towards, so we need to liberate our imaginations to envision "the more beautiful world our hearts know is possible," to quote Charles Eisenstein.

Imagine and express a story of a positive future, individually or as a group. In a group, one person could begin the story, and have it evolve as it passes around the circle, with a guideline that the story you weave embodies a future you want to love into being.

ACKNOWLEDGMENTS

So many hands, hearts, skills, creativity, courage and relational intelligence have helped to inform my life, learning and this book.

My deepest heartfelt thanks to Kenny Ausubel, my beloved life partner and extraordinarily talented co-creator, as the ways we continue to grow each other astonish me and lift my wings. And to Anne Ausubel, my mother-in-law of 101+ years: who knew I could be adopted by another mother at my age, and be this lucky to find such a dazzlingly unique, wise, loving and witty one to boot?

I will always be grateful to my editor, writing partner and friend, Anneke Campbell, whose soul purposes are so aligned with my own, and whose skill and discipline helped make this book and all my work flourish.

My heartfelt thanks to Sharon Zetter, whose insight, cultural sensitivities, organizational prowess, and aesthetic discernment as a book designer have all made such huge contributions.

I'm deeply grateful to activist, mentor, dear friend and artist Mayumi Oda, whose glorious image graces this cover and so embodies the leadership I'm listening to evolve towards. And my heartfelt thanks to Lorraine Weiss, my beloved soul sister, friend, and soprano saxophonist wise woman, whose collaboration with musician friends Laura Inserra on hang drum and Kevin Smith on mallet harp and djembe graces the audiobook version.

My heartfelt appreciation to Jennifer Browdy and Green Fire Press, as her patience, guidance, deep caring, commitment to our shared vision and loving support have added so much to the beauty and evolution of this work.

Thanks to Stephanie Welch, J.P. Harpignies and the entire team at Bioneers, whose enduring support and contributions have directly helped to make this book and all my writing better. My loving thanks to Cara Romero and Alexis Bunten, whose generosity as mutual mentors models a quality of allyship I continue to learn so much from. And a deep bow of gratitude to Bioneers' extended community of kin, whose care, support, and consistent love have kept me afloat.

I am grateful to the ancestors upon whose shoulders I stand, to those who endured slavery, oppression, and genocide, which informs my quest for equity now. I am grateful to my family. To my mother, Rhea Goodman, whose questing life continues to accelerate my learning, even after her death. To my brother Tony Simons, who is helping to shift business culture towards greater alignment, relational intelligence and integrity. And to my father, Barnett Simons, whose consistent love and creative panache gifted me with such a strong and resilient foundation.

I bow in heartfelt thanks to so many beloved mentors and friends whose innovative paths have liberated and revealed options for my own. Some have influenced me in person, and others through your artworks, including especially: Terry Tempest Williams, Jeannette Armstrong and Marlowe Sam, Toby Herzlich, Rachel Bagby, Sarah Crowell, Akaya Windwood, Deborah Eden Tull, Marion Weber, Ohki Simine Forest, V, Joanna Macy, Alice Walker, Karla McClaren, Pat McCabe, Starhawk, Sarah Drew, Susan Griffin, Jean Shinoda Bolen, Ana Sophia Demetrikopolus, Deena Metzger, Sandra Ingerman, Winona LaDuke, Leny Strobel, Jodie Evans, Amisha Ghadiali, Anita Sanchez, Rha Goddess, Osprey Orielle Lake, Naomi Katz, Clare DuBois and Gloria Steinem. And gratitude beyond measure to Azita

Ardakani, for offering me the opportunity to deepen into my own assignment and trust my knowing.

A virtual hug to my web of beloved sisters and friends who hold me with reliably strong, challenging and enduring love, who buoy me when I get low and offer ballast when I need centering: Zuleikha, Lana Holmes, Sharon Smith, Lorraine Weiss, Amanda Coslor, Hilary Giovale, Sarah Cavanaugh, Polly Howells, Joan Porter, DeeAnn Downing, Ginny McGinn, Kristin Rothballer, Pat McCabe, Jess Rimington, Kate and Jeff Haas, Jody Snyder and Noel Littlejohns, Lyla June Johnston, Kappy Wells, Pele Rouge, Maggie Kaplan, Laura Loescher, Linda Stonestreet, Marion Weber, Barbara Whitestone and Melissa Engestrand.

And a very special tender and fierce honoring and thanks to Rachel Bagby, who has partnered with me through many years of our convenings and learning, through some very bumpy times, always with her strong voice of truth, clarity and compassion.

Lastly, a deep bow of gratitude to all of you who have participated in my wild and sometimes choppy evolutionary learning journey: the extraordinary UnReasonable Women for the Earth, the magnificent alumna of Cultivating Women's Leadership, those who have trusted Rachel Bagby and myself in gatherings including CoMadres, Wisdom Council and Community of Practice, and Women Bridging Worlds. And to those who've done workshops with me and Deborah Eden Tull. Thank you all for the gifts of your time, and your investments of trust, vulnerability and your presence.

May all of our leadership be liberated to dance with nature's brilliance, to shed beliefs and biases that hinder our progress, to help humanity to take full wing, and to transform our culture to one that's creatively enlivening and healing. And may it all be sourced from the sacredness of our love.

photo by Genevieve Russell

NINA SIMONS is co-founder of Bioneers, and a social entrepreneur passionate about reimagining leadership, restoring balance to the feminine and masculine, and helping to heal relations with ourselves, each other, and the Earth. She is co-editor of *Moonrise: The Power of Women Leading from the Heart,* and a contributor to *Ecological and Social Healing: Multicultural Women's Voices.* She co-facilitates transformative intensives and retreats and loves co-evolving in beloved community. Nina has been honored to receive a Robert Rodale award and in 2017, the Goi Peace Award. For more about her work, and to learn where she may be speaking or teaching, visit Ninasimons.com or Bioneers.org.

ANNEKE CAMPBELL has worked as a midwife, nurse, yoga teacher, English professor, death educator, writer in many genres, community organizer, and activist. She co-authored (with Thomas Linzey) *We The People: Stories from the Community Rights Movement in the U.S.* and co-edited (with Nina Simons) *Moonrise: The Power of Women Leading from the Heart.* She wrote and co-produced, with her husband Jeremy Kagan, a 10-part series of films on civil rights for the ACLU and the dramatic feature film *Shot.*

SELECTED BIBLIOGRAPHY

For access to the full resources (people, organizations, and media) referenced in Nature, Culture & the Sacred, *visit: Bioneers.org/NCS.*

Alexander, Michelle. *The New Jim Crow: Mass Incarceration in the Age of Colorblindness.* The New Press, 2012.

Amini, Fari, et al. *A General Theory of Love.* Vintage, 2001.

Ausubel, Kenny. *When Healing Becomes a Crime: The Amazing Story of the Hoxsey Cancer Clinics and the Return of Alternative Therapies.* Healing Arts Press, 2000.

—. *Dreaming the Future: Reimagining Civilization in the Age of Nature,* Chelsea Green, 2012

Bagby, Rachel. *Divine Daughters: Liberating the Power and Passion of Women's Voices.* Harper San Francisco, 1999.

—. *Daughterhood: Sounding Hidden Truths, Ignite Your Freedom.* Amazon Digital Services LLC, 2016.

Benyus, Janine. *Biomimicry: Innovation Inspired by Nature.* Harper Perennial, 2002.

Bohm, David. *Wholeness and the Implicate Order (Volume 135).* Routledge, 2002.

Browdy, Jennifer. *Purposeful Memoir as a Quest for a Thriving Future.* Green Fire Press, 2021.

Campbell, Anneke and Nina Simons, editors. *Moonrise: The Power of Women Leading from the Heart.* Inner Traditions International, 2010.

Capra, Fritjof and Pier Luigi Luisi. *The Web of Life: A New Scientific Understanding of Living Systems.* Anchor, 1997.

—. *The Systems View of Life: A Unifying Vision.* Cambridge University Press, 2016.

Caprioli, Mary, et al. *Sex and World Peace.* Columbia University Press, 2014.

Coates, Ta-Nehisi Coates. *Between the World and Me.* Spiegel & Grau, 2015.

Cullors, Patrisse Khan. *When They Call You A Terrorist.* MacMillan, 2018.

D'Antonio, Michael and John Gerzema. *The Athena Doctrine: How Women (and the Men Who Think Like Them) Will Rule the Future.* Jossey Bass, 1994.

Drew, Sarah. *Gaia Codex.* Metamuse Media, 2014.

Dunbar-Ortiz, Roxanne. *An Indigenous Peoples' History of the United States.* Beacon Press, 2014.

Einstein, Albert. *Einstein on Politics: His Private Thoughts and Public Stands on Nationalism, Zionism, War, Peace, and the Bomb.* Edited by David E. Rowe and Robert Schulmann, Princeton University Press, 2013.

Ehrenreich, Barbara and English, Deirdre. *For Her Own Good.* Knopf, 2013

— *Midwives, Witches and Nurses.* Feminist Press, 2010

Eisler, Riane. *The Chalice and The Blade.* HarperOne, 2011.

Ensler, Eve. *The Good Body.* Villard, 2005.

—. *The Vagina Monologues.* Villard, 2007.

—. *In the Body of the World: A Memoir of Cancer and Connection.* Picador, 2014.

Estes, Clarissa Pinkola. *Women Who Run with the Wolves: Myths and Stories of the Wild Woman Archetype.* Ballantine Books, 1996.

Forest, Ohky Simine. *Dreaming The Council Ways: True Native Teachings from the Red Lodge.* Red Wheel/Weiser, 2000.

Garcia, Alixa and Penniman, Naima. *Climbing Poetree.* Whit Press, 2014.

Gibson, Ruby. *My Body, My Breath,* iUniverse, 2008

Haines, Staci. *The Politics of Trauma: Somatics, Healing and Social Justice*. Penguin Random House, 2019

Harjo, Joy. *How We Became Human*. Norton, 2003.

Harris-Perry, Melissa V. *Sister Citizen: Shame, Stereotypes, and Black Women in America*. Yale University Press, 2013.

Hawken, Paul. *Drawdown: The Most Comprehensive Plan Ever Proposed to Reverse Global Warming*. Penguin Books, 2017.

Hill, Julia Butterfly. *The Legacy of Luna: The Story of a Tree, a Woman and the Struggle to Save the Redwoods*. HarperOne, 2001.

Hill, Julia Butterfly & Jessica Hurley. *One Makes the Difference: Inspiring Actions that Change our World*. HarperOne, 2002.

Hudson, Valerie, Balliff Spanville, Bonnie, Caprioli, Mary and Emmet, Chad. *Sex and World Peace*. Columbia University Press, 2014.

Johnson, Ayana Elizabeth and Wilkinson, Katherine, editors. *All We Can Save*. Penguin Random House, 2021.

Kaur, Valarie, *See No Stranger: A Memoir and Manifesto of Revolutionary Love*. One World, 2021

Kimmerer, Robin. *Braiding Sweetgrass*. Milkweed Editions, 2010.

King, Thomas. *The Inconvenient Indian*. Doubleday, 2012.

LeGuin, Ursula K. *Dancing at the Edge of the World: Thoughts on Words, Women, Places*. Harper & Row, 1989.

Macy, Joanna and Brown, Molly. *Coming Back to Life: The Updated Guide to The Work that Reconnects*. New Society Publishers, 2014.

Markova, Dawna. *Collaborative Intelligence: Thinking with People Who Think Differently*. Spiegel & Grau, 2015.

—. *Reconcilable Differences: Connecting in a Disconnected World*. Spiegel & Grau, 2017.

Maté, Gabor. *In the Realm of Hungry Ghosts: Close Encounters with Addiction*. North Atlantic Books, 2010.

—. *When the Body Says No: Understanding the Stress-Disease Connection*. Wiley, 2011.

Maturana, Humberto. *The Circularity of Life: An Essential Shift for Sustainability*. Jane Cull, 2013.

Menakem, Resma. *My Grandmother's Hands*. Central Recovery Press, 2017

Merton, Thomas. *Conjectures of a Guilty Bystander*. Image, 1968.

Mohawk, John. *Utopian Legacies*. Clear Light Publishing, 1999.

Neiman, Susan. *Learning From the Germans*. Farrar, Straus and Giroux, 2019.

Nelson, Melissa. *Original Instructions*. Bear & Company 2008.

Pert, Candace B. *Molecules of Emotion: The Science Behind Mind-Body Medicine*. Simon & Schuster, 1999.

Poo, Ai-jen. *The Age of Dignity: Preparing for the Elder Boom in a Changing America*. The New Press, 2016.

Proust, Marcel. *In Search of Lost Time*. Modern Library, 2003.

Reed, Donna. *The Burning Times*. National Film Board of Canada, 1990.

Rifkin, Jeremy. *The Empathic Civilization: The Race to Global Consciousness in a World in Crisis*. Polity Press, 2010.

Shinoda Bolen, Jean. *The Millionth Circle: How to Change Ourselves and The World: The Essential Guide to Women's Circles*. Conari Press, 1999.

Starhawk. *Dreaming The Dark*. Beacon Press, 1982.

Strobel, Leny Mendoza. *A Book of Her Own: Words and Images to Honor the Babaylan*. Tiboli Publishing, 2005.

Tull, Deborah Eden. *Relational Mindfulness: A Handbook for Deepening Our Connections with Ourselves, Each Other, and the Planet*. Wisdom Publications, 2018.

Twist, Lynne. *The Soul of Money*. W. W. Norton & Company, 2017.

Whelan, Linda Tarr. *Women Lead the Way: Your Guide to Stepping Up to Leadership and Changing the World*. Berrett-Koehler Publishers, 2011.

Wicks, Judy. *Good Morning, Beautiful Business: The Unexpected Journey of an Activist Entrepreneur and Local-Economy Pioneer*. Chelsea Green Publishing, 2013.

Wilkerson, Isabelle. *Caste*. Random House, 2020

Williams, Terry Tempest. *Refuge: An Unnatural History of Family and Place*. Vintage, 1992.

—. *Leap*. Vintage, 2001.

—. *Finding Beauty in a Broken World*. Vintage, 2009.

—. *When Women Were Birds: Fifty-four Variations on Voice*. Picador, 2013.

Wilson, Edward O. *Biophilia*. Harvard University Press, 1984.

Yeh, Lily. *Awakening Creativity: Dandelion School Blossoms*. New Village Press, 2011.

ABOUT BIONEERS

As the world hurtles from urgency to emergency, we can move from breakdown to breakthrough. We can shift our course to reimagine how to live on Earth in ways that honor the web of life, each other, and future generations.

Bioneers highlights and helps realize the profound transformation already taking hold around the globe: the dawn of a human civilization that partners with the wisdom of nature's design, and practices values of justice, diversity, democracy, and peaceful co-existence. Around the world in diverse fields of endeavor, social and scientific innovators have been developing and demonstrating far better technological, economic, social, and political models inspired by the wisdom of the natural world and traditional peoples. Human creativity focused on problem-solving is eclipsing the mythology of despair.

Since 1990, Bioneers has acted as a seed head for the game-changing social and scientific vision, knowledge, and practices advancing this great transformation, with First Peoples and indigenous knowledge systems as central to our work. As a community of leadership, Bioneers is helping disrupt our current failed institutions by offering people better choices. We show a compelling vision, practical models, and "the how," through our annual national conference, award-winning media, local Bioneers conferences and initiatives, and leadership training programs. Learn more at www.bioneers.org

ABOUT GREEN FIRE PRESS

Green Fire Press is an independent publishing company dedicated to supporting authors in producing and distributing high-quality books in fiction or non-fiction, poetry or prose.

Find out more at **Greenfirepress.com**.

Other Green Fire Press titles you may also enjoy:

A Short Course In Happiness After Loss, by Maria Sirois, PsyD.

A lyrical gem of a book, combining positive psychology with the wisdom necessary to thrive when facing life's harshest moments, rising through pain into a steady, resilient and open heart.

Dance of the Deities: Searching for Our Once and Future Egalitarian Society, by Patricia McBroom

Patricia McBroom compiles evidence of the ancient Nature goddesses, while calling for contemporary women to replace comic book images of feminine beauty with authentic Earth-based images of female power and authority.

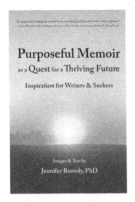

Purposeful Memoir as a Quest for a Thriving Future: Inspiration for Writers & Seekers, by Jennifer Browdy, PhD.

A book like no other! Award-winning author Jennifer Browdy, PhD, creates a magical tapestry of inspiration and exploration, weaving her own story together with the inspiring voices and visions of more than 15 of the writer-activists she calls "worldwrights" — writers who write to right the world, including such beloved mentors as Joy Harjo, Audre Lorde, Jane Goodall, Terry Tempest Williams and many more.

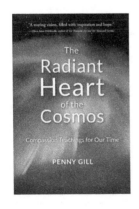

The Radiant Heart of the Cosmos: Compassion Teachings for Our Time, by Penny Gill

"Penny Gill — a gifted writer, an irresistible teacher and a humane mystic — shows how openness to, and compassion for, one's own suffering develops the universal compassion that heals oneself, our fellow beings, and our world."

—Donal O'Shea, President Emeritus of New College of Florida

CPSIA information can be obtained
at www.ICGtesting.com
Printed in the USA
LVHW101152290922
729562LV00001B/64